The Mass

ancient liturgies and patristic texts

To understand the Mass as it was celebrated by the first generations of Christians, we must situate it in the Paschal
Vigil during which the new converts
received Baptism, and then participated in their first Mass. In offering the
Mass they offered themselves. Every
week henceforth, on Sundays, the day
of the Resurrection, perhaps even every
day, they are going to celebrate this
same Paschal mystery in the Eucharist.

The present volume contains:

1) The actual texts of the Mass as it
was celebrated during the first four
centuries: the Euchologium of Serapion, the Apostolic Constitutions, the
Anaphora of St. Basil, and the Anaphora of St. John Chrysostom.

2) Commentary of the Fathers on the
chief Eucharistic texts from Exodus
to 1 Corinthians.

3) Occasional writings, especially Sermons, in which the pastors of the 4th
century expound the mystery of the
Eucharist. For them the Mass is truly
the sacrament of faith, because it is
situated at the heart of the Christian
mystery. It is the eucharistic act of a
redeemed world.

1 ALBA Patristic Library

The Mass

ancient liturgies and patristic texts

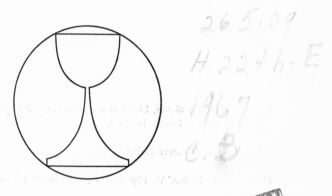

Editor: André Hamman, O.F.M.

English Editorial Supervisor: Thomas Halton

DIVISION OF THE SOCIETY OF ST. PAUL   alba house STATEN ISLAND, N.Y. 10314

Original title: La Messe, liturgies anciennes et textes patristique; published by Bernard Grasset Éditeur, Paris.

Translated by Thomas Halton

Nihil obstat: Daniel V. Flynn, J.C.D. — Censor Librorum

Imprimatur: ✠ Terence J. Cooke, V.G., D.D.
New York, N. Y. — March 24, 1967

Library of Congress Catalog Card Number: 67 - 15202

Designed, printed and bound in the U.S.A. by the Pauline Fathers and Brothers of the Society of St. Paul at Staten Island, New York as a part of their communications apostolate.

Vatican II, in its *Decree on the Training of Priests* (16), insists that the study of the Bible ought to be the soul of all theology. The great themes of Divine Revelation should be explored by daily reading of the Scriptures and thorough exegesis. Dogmatic theology should be so arranged that these biblical themes are first of all presented. Then students should be systematically introduced to what the Fathers of the Eastern and Western Church have contributed to the faithful transmission and development of the individual truths of revelation.

The present series provides a set of the most important patristic texts on the main truths of revelation. A brief introduction and linking commentary help to situate these texts within the history of their development in early Christianity. The most extensive recent work of this nature on the Eucharist is that of Jesus Solano, S.J., *Textos Eucarísticos Primitivos,* 2 vols., (Madrid, 1954). Closer to the spirit and manner of the present French series (edited by the distinguished patrologist, A. Hamman), is the recent German series, *Texte der Kirchenväter*: *Eine Auswahl nach Themen geordnet,* edd., A. Heilmann, H. Kraft *et al.* (Munich, 1963 -), of which volume 4 (1964), 275-313 is devoted to the Eucharist. This English translation of Père Hamman's work will introduce English readers to a representative cross-section of the ancient liturgies and patristic homilies, letters etc., connected with the Lord's Supper.

It will be seen from a study of these primitive documents that many of the recent changes in our own liturgical life, far from being innovations, have a long history: the restored Litany prayer, for example, the use of the shortened form "The Body of Christ" at Communion, the emphasis on the integration of the homily into the Liturgy of the Word, and the idea of priestly concelebration.

As Leo the Great said, "the partaking of the Body and Blood of Christ does nothing other than transform us into that which we consume" (PL 38. 389). The process of transformation must surely be helped by a prayerful study of the earliest documents which provide living witness to belief in this central reality of the Christian life. How central it is has been well expressed in Vatican II's *Decree on the Ministry and Life of Priests*: "The other sacraments, as well as every ministry of the Church and every work of the apostolate, are linked with the holy Eucharist and are directed toward it. For the most blessed Eucharist contains the Church's entire spiritual wealth, that is Christ Himself, our Passover and living bread."

PREFACE TO FRENCH EDITION

The Mass, if it is to be understood as it was celebrated in the early days of Christianity, must be located in the Paschal Vigil celebrated by the newly-converted. For them it was the first Mass of their lives. The Lenten preparation drew to an end. The catechumens now know the history of the people of God, the truths of the Faith, the Lord's Prayer. In the course of the final Vigil, which serves to introduce them to the Paschal mystery of their baptism and communion, they hear now the readings of the great stages of salvation, creation and redemption. This history is to become their own.

When they ascend from the baptismal font they have become the people of God. Dressed in white they enter the church to celebrate the eucharistic sacrifice, the sacrament of the death and resurrection of Christ. They offer it—they offer themselves— *laetus obtuli universa;* in their joy and enlightenment they offer everything. This is their first celebration of the Pasch of God.

Every week on the Lord's Day, the day of the resurrection, perhaps even every day, they are going to celebrate the same Paschal mystery in the Eucharist. Their whole life has been transformed. Everything has become a eucharistic act, a paschal celebration which will never end. The light of this night, clearer than the day, will never be quenched in their hearts, will never be extinguished in their eyes, until that day—perhaps near—when they will drink the wine new in the kingdom.

We must enter into this experience to understand and place in context the eucharistic texts of the early Christian centuries. The Liturgy of the Mass, on which the Fathers comment, is in this way clearly focused. This unforgettable, unique experience, renewed in each celebration, explains the emotion of John Chrysostom, and the joy of Augustine, when they receive the newly-baptized. This is their history; this is the history and the mystery of the Church.

ABBREVIATIONS

ANF = *Ante Nicene Fathers*
FC = *Fathers of the Church series* (Catholic University of America Press, Washington D.C.)
LFC = *Library of the Fathers of the Church*
NPNF = *Nicene and Post-Nicene Fathers of the Church*
PG = Migne, *Patrologia Graeca*
PL = Migne, *Patrologia Latina*
PLS = Migne, *Patrologia Latina Supplementum* (Hamman)
RAC = *Reallexikon für Antike und Christentum*
SC = *Sources Chrétiennes*

Contents

Preface to English Edition 5
Preface to French Edition 7
Introduction

1. Historical survey 15
   Origins 15
   A Second Century Mass 17
   The Mass according to the *Apostolic Tradition* . . 19
   The Celebration in the Fourth Century 20
   The Liturgy of the Eucharist 22
   Diversification of Liturgies 23
2. The Teaching of the Fathers on the Eucharist
   Biblical Catechesis 24
   Liturgical Catechesis 26
   Doctrinal Catechesis 28
   Note on the Composition of the Work 31

I. Liturgical Texts

The Apostolic Tradition 35
The Euchologium of Serapion 37
The Apostolic Constitutions 48
The Byzantine Liturgies:
   The Anaphora of St. Basil 70
   The Anaphora of St. John Chrysostom 74

II. Commentary on Biblical Texts

1. The Passover Narrative 83
   Ps. - Chrysostom, *On the Pasch* 84
2. The Institution of the Eucharist 88
   St. Ephraem, Mimré 4, *On the Passion* 89
   St. John Chrysostom, Homily 82 on Matthew .   .   . 93
3. The Bread of Life
   St. John Chrysostom, Homily 46 on John .   .   . 107
   St. Augustine, Tractate 27 on John 115
   St. Cyril of Alexandria, Commentary on Jn. 6, 48-64 . 125
4. The Eucharist at Corinth
   St. John Chrysostom, Homily 24 on I Cor. .   .   . 154

III. The Teaching of the Fathers on the Mass

St. Irenaeus, *From Jewish to Christian Sacrifice* .   .   . 171
Inscriptions of Abercius and Pectorius 183
Cyprian of Carthage, Letter 63 186
Hilary of Poitiers, From Eucharist to Trinity .   .   . 198
Basil of Caesarea, Letter 93 201
Augustine of Hippo, Sermon 227 204
                    Sermon 272 206
                    Sermon 329 208
                    Sermon on the Sacrament
                    of the altar 211

Sermon Denys 6 213
Sermon Mai 129 216
Sermon on Easter Day . . . 218
Peter Chrysologus Sermon 95 221
Sermon 108 225
Sermon 109 228
Ps. - Faustus of Riez, Homily on the Body and
Blood of Christ 233
Caesarius of Arles, Sermon 227 240
Bibliography 245
Comparative Table 248
Chronological Table 250

Index 251

Introduction

1. HISTORICAL SURVEY

For as often as you shall eat this bread and drink the cup, you proclaim the death of the Lord until he comes (I *Cor.* 11, 26). These words tell us of the mystery of the Mass; the focus of all Christian life: a remembrance of the works of God, the presence of the resurrected Christ, the expectation of his return.

Origins

Christ instituted the sacrament of the Eucharist in the form of a supper on Holy Thursday. He has bequeathed it to his Church until the end of time as a sign and proof that the messianic community will reassemble around him. The Acts of the Apostles and the Epistles of St. Paul already describe the primitive community *steadfast in the teaching of the Apostles and in the communion of the breaking of the bread and in prayers* (*Acts* 2, 42).

"Prayers and the breaking of bread" constitute the liturgy of the earliest Mass. The Eucharist remains linked to a fraternal repast. It utilizes the Jewish ritual of religious unions: Israel assembled by the word of God responded by a prayer of adoration, thanksgiving, and supplication. In its turn the apostolic community, assembled around the Savior invisibly present, is not content with receiving broken bread which prolongs the action of the risen Savior at Emmaus; it responds by prayers inherited from the synagogue in which it celebrates in the Eucharist the work of salvation realized by Christ. There is joy in the heart of all, because faith allows them to discover the risen Christ in the midst of those whom he unites, and hope tells them that one day, perhaps soon, he will return.

The connection between the celebration and the supper did not continue for long. It still existed at Corinth in the time of St. Paul; there the faithful brought provisions to the supper but did not always share them in common, to the great scandal of the

Apostle. The prayers of the *Didache* give evidence of a real meal connected with the celebration of the Eucharist.

This love-feast or *agapé* rapidly became an independent institution in the West. When the feast was abandoned the primitive expressions "breaking of bread" and "the Lord's Supper" disappear and are replaced by the term "eucharist" which we find in Ignatius of Antioch (✝ c. 107) and Justin Martyr (✝ 165/166).

The term "eucharist" means "thanksgiving" and takes its name from the prayer of Consecration pronounced by the president of the liturgical assembly. The liturgical texts (of which we will provide the most ancient types) enable us to grasp the dynamic nature of this thanksgiving since the prayer of consecration effects the conversion of bread and wine into the body and blood of Christ, while at the same time celebrating the mystery of salvation accomplished by Christ which the Church has a mission to carry out to the end.

For the Christians of the first centuries the liturgical assembly is central, uniting as it does all the baptized of town and country; it constituted the very life of the community. We have a very moving testimony in the Acts of the Martyrs of Abitina, near Carthage, in North Africa. Fifty Christians had been arrested at the very end of the celebration of the Eucharist, the pagans, doubtless, being more certain of recognizing them on such an occasion. The question posed to them, the decisive one, was: Had they participated in the worship? And why? They could have saved their lives by denying. But to deny the Christian Supper was to deny the Faith.

Under torture the reader Emeritus explains participation in the liturgy in this way: without the Mass we cannot live. Felix replies to the same question thus: "As well can a Christian live without the Mass as can the Mass be celebrated without Christians." And he replies to the judge's address: "Do you not know, Satan, that the Christians make the Mass and the Mass makes the Christians and that one cannot exist without the other."

The Christians do not just assist at Mass; they celebrate it with their bishop and priests. They take an active part. They enter into dialogue with the celebrant. They participate in an action common to priests and faithful. The faithful bring gifts as their contribution. They raise their hands in unison. The kiss of peace, from celebrant to assembly, unites a fraternity joined in community love. All join in chorus in the parts said aloud, the

refrain of the psalms, the responses to the invitation of the celebrant. And when the latter has ended the eucharistic prayer which
consecrates the offerings all respond in a solemn "Amen" of
assent. All the Christians, even the absent ones, thanks to the
deacons, receive the Eucharist in communion.

A Second century Mass

Justin Martyr (c. 150) is the first to furnish us with a complete description of the celebration of the Eucharist. He speaks
of it twice—first in regard to the newly-baptized and secondly
in regard to Sunday.

The first text is as follows:

"As for us, when we have baptized the one who believes and
joined him to us, we conduct him in turn to that place where
those who are called 'the brethren' are assembled.

Then we pray fervently together for ourselves and for the baptized, and for all the others everywhere in order to obtain through
knowledge of the truth the grace to do good and to keep the
commandments so as to attain our eternal salvation. We give one
another the kiss of peace and conclude the prayers.

Then bread and a chalice of water and wine are brought to
the president of the assembly of the brethren. He takes them,
gives praise and glory to the Father of the universe in the name
of the Son and of the Holy Spirit; he makes a lengthy thanksgiving
for the blessings which God has deigned to give us. When he has
concluded the prayers and the thanksgiving, all the people exclaim:
Amen. 'Amen' is a Hebrew word which means 'so be it.'

When the president has given thanks and all the people have
responded, those whom we call deacons distribute to each of
those present a particle of bread and of the eucharistic wine
mixed with water, and they also bring them to those who are
absent" (I *Apol.* 65, 1-5).

Justin specifies that the bread has been consecrated by the
prayer formed from the words of Christ (I *Apol.* 66, 2).

A second description of the Eucharist complementing the first
is found a little later in the *Apology* with regard to the Sunday
liturgy: (see J. O. Cobham, "Sunday and Eucharist," *Studia
Liturgica* 2 [1963] 8-28).

"On the day called Sunday all who live in the cities or country
assemble in one place. The Acts of the Apostles are read, or the

writings of the prophets, as long as time permits. When the reading
has ended the president instructs by word and exhorts us to imitate
these good teachings.   Then we all rise together and pray, and,
as we have said already, when our prayer is ended, bread and
wine and water are brought in.   The president also offers prayers
and thanksgivings according to his ability and all the people respond
by exclaiming 'Amen.'   Then the Eucharist is distributed to each
and a portion is sent to those absent through the deacons."

Both descriptions in Justin distinguish two parts in the meeting:
the Liturgy of the Word and the Liturgy of the Eucharist.   The
first consists in a reading from the Prophets and Apostles, followed
by a homily.   Then come the common prayers in which the
catechumens also participate. These conclude with the kiss of peace.
The *oblata* are then brought forward.   Next the president pronounces the great prayer which consecrates the offerings. We must
analyze this prayer in which all the assistants join and conclude
with a triumphant "Amen."   It consists of a Preface, a eucharistic
prayer, and an Anamnesis or Commemoration.

The Preface is addressed "to the Father of the universe through
the Son and the Holy Spirit" (I *Apol.* 65, 2-3).   God is glorified,
"having created the world for man and all that it contains" (*Dial.*
41); "for the life which he has given us, the care which he takes
to keep us in health, for the variety of things and the changes
of the seasons" (I *Apol.* 13, 2).

The Eucharist: The order of creation is a figure of the order
of salvation, just as the eighth day of the resurrection corresponds
to the first day of creation which it perfects.   Here the praise
is turned in the eucharistic prayer to the Word of God, Jesus
Christ, "who has taken flesh and blood for our salvation" (*ibid.*
66, 1), for the passion he endured, for the men whose soul
is purified of all evil, for us who have been freed from sin, for
the definitive destruction of principalities and powers by him who
is still suffering by his own will, "the great high-priest crucified"
(*Dial.* 116).   The work of salvation is here described as the
purification from sin and the victory over the forces of Hell. Elsewhere the promise of eternal salvation is underlined (I *Apol.* 65,
1). We will find all these elements in the Roman liturgy described
in the *Apostolic Tradition* of Saint Hippolytus.

The final Amen which closes the eucharistic anaphora expresses for the faithful the realization of the promises.   It is
shouted in acclamation by the whole congregation.   Justin mentions

it twice. It signifies that the prayer of the celebrant is not a monologue but the prayer of the whole assembly. All present join their prayer to that of the president and proclaim their faith in the risen Christ present at the eucharistic offering.

The Mass According to the
Apostolic Tradition (3rd cent.)

The Apostolic Tradition of Hippolytus of Rome († 235) enables us to trace the path of development covered in a century. It provides us with the only surviving liturgical text before the diversification of rites. In an age when improvisation still maintained its freedom (cf. R. P. C. Hanson, "The liberty of the Bishop to improvise prayer in the Eucharist," *Vigiliae Christianae* 15 [1961] 173-76), the text of Hippolytus offers a sort of blueprint which can assist the more laborious efforts at improvisation of various celebrants. It is a venerable text, still in use today in the Mass among the Ethiopians.

In connection with episcopal consecration Hippolytus furnishes a thanksgiving formula for the celebration of the Eucharist, a fact which explains why he does not treat of the Liturgy of the Word eventually replaced by baptism, as in the case of Justin, or by episcopal consecration.

This is the liturgical prayer *par excellence,* one which both give thanks and consecrates. The eucharistic action of Christ and of the Church constitutes and effects the liturgical action. Hippolytus furnishes us with a text of a single piece, a single flow, which develops without break or interruption of any *Sanctus* though it is attested for this era by Tertullian and Origen. The composition is centered on Christ and develops the mystery of the redemption. We find point by point the teaching of Justin: the Institution narrative, the eucharistic commemoration, the reenaction of the death and resurrection of Christ. The only exception is that the invocation of the Holy Spirit finds no parallel in Justin.

The *Apostolic Tradition* provides other precisions: the faithful offer different gifts e.g. oil, cheese, olives. Milk and honey are presented to the newly baptized, symbols of the Promised Land which they reach through the Eucharist. Milk and honey express the sweetness of Christ and of his word, which succeeds the bitterness of the Captivity, and this brings us back to the theme of the Exodus and presents Christianity as a return to Paradise.

The Christians in receiving the Eucharist answer "Amen" to express their assent to the mystery in which they participate. Then they return to their everyday life to put into practice the works of faith, presented as a service of God.

The Celebration in the Fourth Century

It is relatively easy to reconstruct in its main outlines the Mass as it was celebrated in the time of Basil the Great, John Chrysostom and Augustine. The preaching of the Fathers makes many allusions to it and often gives an extended commentary on the rites themselves. The *Euchologium of Serapion* and the *Apostolic Constitutions* provide us with texts (for texts cf. pp. 37-48). The liturgies, though diversified, all maintain common characteristics.

The celebration is divided in two parts. The first, which can be called the Liturgy of the Word, or the Liturgy of the Catechumens, is made up of biblical readings, instructions, and prayers. The second, which is the Eucharist proper, comprises the eucharistic prayer which consecrates the *oblata*. There is no question of a juxtaposition of two rites but of two elements of the same rite which are found already united in the Jewish rite which inspired them. The Liturgy of the Word like the liturgy of the bread expresses the same epiphany of the word of God in the course of history. In Christ the word of God and the response of man become one. On both sides the mystery of salvation, proclaimed in the assembly, arouses a response which is given to him and which constitutes the prayer of the people of God.

As early as the fourth century, the celebration begins with a processional entry. The celebrant mounts his throne and salutes the congregation. The readings which open the celebration are three in number in the East, according to John Chrysostom and the *Apostolic Constitutions*: a prophecy taken from the Old Testament, an excerpt from Acts or one of the Epistles, followed by the Gospel. Between the readings the psalms were chanted, where the people took up the refrain linked with prayers as the *Euchologium of Serapion* testifies. The readings are followed by a homily. This consists of a commentary on the Scripture just read whose text had been chosen with a view to the sermon. The preacher applied the text to daily life.

The homily—that is the name of the commentary, borrowed from the synagogue—was already practiced by Jesus himself, as the Gospels testify. By the fourth century Origen preached every day; Augustine likewise, and sometimes even twice a day. The homily always ended with a doxology. Some two hundred of Origen's sermons survive, Scriptural commentaries, especially on the Old Testament.

In the fourth century the bishop is the rightful celebrant of the Liturgy of the Eucharist, but the Liturgy of the Word could be performed by priests. We have surviving a number of the sermons of St. John Chrysostom from the period when he was a priest at Antioch, given in the course of Lent at liturgical celebrations. This preaching preserves a familiar, catechetical character. Often improvised, it is preserved for us thanks to stenographers, official or private, who collected them.

This improvisation sometimes turned to dialogue. John Chrysostom has barely made an allusion to a parable. The congregation shouts, "That is Dives and Lazarus." "Yes," the preacher answers, "I see that you are intelligent and have already grasped what I wanted to say. But let me tell you all the same."

The homily is a commentary on Scripture or on the meaning of the liturgical celebration. Augustine has given us a commentary on the Fourth Gospel, John Chrysostom on Gospels and Epistles. We borrow their commentaries on the biblical texts concerned with the Eucharist. The instruction of the newly baptized afforded an opportunity for many a homily on the Mass. Those of St. Augustine are among the most beautiful.

The sermons published here for the most part were actually delivered. They have sometimes been reviewed by the author, sometimes circulated without his knowledge. Fathers like John Chrysostom or Augustine who were acclaimed as public orators even before their baptism were unable to shed completely the oratorical art in their preaching. Augustine makes us smile when he rails against the abuses of a florid style which he has been unable to avoid himself.

Within the whole ambit of patristic preaching, the East is more prolix—Gregory of Nazianzus preaches for a whole hour as does Chrysostom,—more given to the use of imagery, and more theological. It does not disdain to use rhetorical devices borrowed from pagan masters. Western preaching is generally shorter, simpler, more direct, and more practical.

After the sermon the non-baptized, those interested in the faith, or catechumens, and penitents were invited to kneel. The deacon recited over them a litany prayer to which those assisting answered: *Kyrie Eleison, Lord have mercy*. The celebrant then blessed them and they were dismissed.

The Liturgy of the Eucharist

The Mass properly so called—the Mass of the Faithful—begins. The structure is clearly marked by the Institution narratives of the Gospels: Jesus i) takes bread, ii) pronounces a blessing (eucharist); iii) breaks it and iv) distributes it. This fourfold system is found in all the liturgies.

This second part begins with a prayer already mentioned by Justin, which will be called the Prayer of the Faithful. The Deacon enumerates the main intentions of the Church for which the people pray in silence. The Roman liturgy has preserved this usage on Good Friday. Then the faithful exchange the kiss of peace at the moment of bringing the offerings.

The offertory can take two different forms: either the bread and wine, prepared beforehand, were carried in procession as was done in the East and in Gaul, or the faithful came forward to offer the bread carried by themselves as was done at Rome.

Over the offerings the celebrant pronounces in the form of a thanksgiving the prayer of consecration, of trinitarian structure, which the Eastern church called the *anaphora*. It opens with an invocation of the celebrant that the community around him should raise up their hearts: *Sursum corda*. The *anaphora* which begins with *it is truly right* celebrates God the Father for creation, for the marvels of the history of salvation * which have been realized by the coming of Christ. It recalls the institution of the sacrament and finishes with an invocation of the Holy Spirit that the plan of salvation may be achieved through the sanctification of the faithful. Very soon this prayer is interrupted by the chant of the *Sanctus* or *Trishagion* received from Jewish tradition.

To the great prayer the people respond with the customary *Amen* of approval, shouted by the crowd, Jerome tells us, amid

---

* This part, which develops economy of salvation, borrowed from the religious repasts of brotherhoods, is well exemplified in the **Apostolic Constitutions**. See further, pp. 58-62.

thunderous applause.   There follows a prayer of intercession for the living and the dead (which the Latin church finally integrated in the Canon of the Mass), then the *Our Father* and the breaking of the bread.   The celebrant holds aloft the consecrated species, saying: *Holy things for the holy.*

The celebrant receives communion, then, in turn, the priests, deacons, and the faithful.   In distributing the consecrated bread the bishop says: "The body of Christ."   The deacon presents the chalice.   The faithful answer, "Amen."   During the distribution an appropriate psalm is chanted.   At Jerusalem it was the psalm, *I will bless the Lord at all times* and the people chanted in refrain the verse, *Taste and see how good the Lord is.*   The celebrant ended with a prayer of thanksgiving, a sample of which is provided by Serapion.   Then the bishop gave the final blessing.

Diversification of Liturgies

The *Apostolic Tradition* (c. 220 *or* 250) testifies to a liturgy still common to East and West but it is not the same a century later.   The essential elements remain the same, but the rites and prayers undergo an intricate development in which they are transformed and enriched.

The East in the fourth century has two types of liturgy, the Syrian centered at Antioch (*Apostolic Constitutions*), and the Alexandrian centered at Alexandria (*Euchologium of Serapion*). The two great Eastern metropolitan sees with their jurisdiction and influence carried on their respective liturgies with only minor differences of detail.   All the subsequent diversity in Eastern liturgies derives from these two primitive families.

Likewise the Syrian liturgy, of which the *Apostolic Constitutions* provide an example although it had no official status, gives birth to the so-called Liturgy of St. James.   St. Basil revised this latter and recast the *anaphora* whose text is found below (see the text, pp. 70-74); it is still in use today.   A notably shorter version, called that of St. John Chrysostom, appeared at the end of the fourth century throughout the Byzantine world.   From it we reproduce the consecration prayer or *anaphora* (see the text, pp. 74-77). These texts give us an idea of the liturgy celebrated and commented on by John Chrysostom or Basil the Great.

From the West, on the other hand, no text survives.   In Italy and at Rome we must wait until the sixth century to find a Mass text. The Gelasian Mass is as far from Justin as from the Eastern liturgies. Profound changes had taken place, how, we do not know, in the Roman canon, but thereafter it remained unchanged. In essentials, however, today's Mass, as is shown in the Table at the end of the book (see p. 248), remains the same as that of the Fathers.

2. THE TEACHING OF THE FATHERS ON THE EUCHARIST

We find no systematic treatise on the Mass in the Fathers like those encountered later in the Middle Ages. The Eucharist is a reality more lived than discussed. All the texts published here are topical documents, expositions that relate to a theological abuse or development. This is so in the writings of Cyprian or Irenaeus, in Scriptural commentaries where there is question of the Eucharist, in post-baptismal homilies which initiated the newly baptized to the mystery of the Eucharist which they had recently received. What this exposition loses in theological structure it gains in spontaneity and existential value. Allusions to the Eucharist are frequent and are especially common in John Chrysostom and Augustine; for them it is the mystery given by faith, lived in daily life, linked to the life of every day. "It is your mystery that you have received," says Augustine.

The catechesis of the Fathers on the Christian Supper continually applies itself to the Scripture texts, the Liturgy of the Word preparing for that of the Eucharist, while that on the liturgical rites and prayers helps toward an understanding of the mystery.

Biblical Catechesis

Christian antiquity explains the Mass first of all from Scripture. The Fathers speak freely of the two-fold eating of the Word, under the species of the Gospel and under the species of the eucharistic bread. The pastors in the first place comment on the Institution narrative, on the discourse in St. John's Gospel on the living bread, and on the episode of the abuse at Corinth (1 *Cor.* 11,

17-34), and the allusions to the Eucharist scattered in the Acts and the Epistles.

As in baptism, catechesis on the Eucharist has recourse to the typology of the Old Testament. This allegorical interpretation goes beyond the letter to the spirit and is rooted in the New Testament. Already in the Fourth Gospel a parallel is established between the Eucharist and the manna in the desert. This typology is traditional in the teaching of the Church as early as the second century. The letter of Cyprian or that of Faustus helps us to gauge the place which it occupies in the ancient catechesis.

The principal types are provided by the Pentateuch: Melchisedech, *priest of the most-high God* appears as the figure of Christ, king and priest. His offering of bread and wine for the patristic tradition announces the sacrifice of the Eucharist (*Gen.* 14, 18). The psalm-text: *The Lord said* and the Epistle to the Hebrews enable Christ to be seen as the image of Melchisedech, the one who is *constituted priest by God for all nations.* The manna in the desert which belongs to the same group announces as early as the Fourth Gospel the living bread come down from Heaven (*Exod.* 16). Ambrose connects with the manna episode the one where Moses causes water to gush from the rock. Cyprian sees in it an image of baptism in his controversy with the Aquarians. Methodius of Olympus, like Ambrose, associates the three figures— the side of Adam, the rock from which the fountain issues, and the wound of Christ on the Cross which symbolize the sacraments of Christian initiation, baptism and the Eucharist.

Another figure, equally frequent in the Fathers, is that of the loaves of proposition (*Exod.* 25, 30). "The Old Law ordained that bread be offered, a symbol of the body and blood of Christ, and that a lamb be immolated, a symbol of the perfect Lamb," writes Cyril of Jerusalem. The paschal lamb is above all a figure of the passion. The Paschal Homilies of pseudo-Chrysostom establish the parallel between the Pasch and the Eucharist.

To this common stock can be added the blessing of Juda where it is said: *He will wash his garments in wine* (*Gen.* 49, 11). Justin and Irenaeus apply this to the passion, Cyprian to the Eucharist. The last-named relates the inebriation of Noah to the Eucharist. He discovers "the sweetness of the Savior" theme, which often recurs in the Fathers, synonymous with spiritual inebriation.

The Psalms in turn provide figures of the Eucharist. They constitute the prayer of the people of God, the prayer of the liturgy, both of head and members. Augustine returns repeatedly to this in his commentaries. The psalms enjoy a central role in the celebration of the Eucharist. The verse: *And wine delights the hearts of men* accompanies the newly baptized from the font to the altar; Psalm 34 and especially the verse *Taste and see how good God is* is chanted during the distribution of Communion; the Psalm *God is my shepherd* belongs in the procession of the newly baptized on Holy Saturday. It is in itself a eucharistic catechesis and its title is continually commented on by the Fathers. The Psalms and the Book of Proverbs enable the Fathers to establish a parallel between sacramental union and mystical union, between sacrament and Christian perfection. The Eucharist is both the sacrament and the principle of mystical union. The consecrated wine produces spiritual intoxication and ecstasy which anticipate the joys of heaven.

All these traits of the Old Testament applied to the Eucharist are strongly marked on the catechesis of Christian antiquity. We find them in the frescoes of the catacombs and the visions of the martyrs. The paintings of early Christianity bear witness to the teaching received in the first initiation to the mysteries of the faith. Perpetua sees Christ in the garb of a shepherd keeping step with the sheep.

This biblical typology shows that the salvation announced to the nations and brought by Chrsit is offered to us in "the sacrament of redemption."

Liturgical Catechesis

The rites in turn enable us to uncover the riches of the Eucharist. They form the principal object of the mystagogical catechesis of Cyril of Jerusalem and Theodore of Mopsuestia. This is not the place to enter into a detailed account of these explanations (cf. A. Hamman, ed., *L'Initiation chrétienne,* Ictys, Paris, vol. 7, pp. 48-60; 143-191). It must suffice to trace the main outlines.

We have already explained the meaning of the Mass of the Catechumens or the Liturgy of the Word. The Mass of the Faithful begins with the preparation of the offerings, the washing of the hands, and the kiss of peace. These last two rites express the purification and union necessary for offering sacrifice, according to Cyril of Jerusalem and Theodore of Mopsuestia.

The great *anaphora* or offertory prayer is said in the plural because the celebrant is the "common tongue of the Church," when "he offers the oblation and immolates the sacrifice of the community." The prayer of consecration is one of praise and adoration in which the *Trishagion,* or threefold *Sanctus* ("Holy, Holy, Holy") expresses the mystery of the Trinity. This contemplation disposes us to consider the divine gift with reverence and awe. This consideration which recurs frequently in John Chrysostom and Theodore creates a sacred atmosphere proper to the celebration of the mysteries.

The bishop continues, developing the economy of salvation realized by Christ. Then he invokes the Holy Spirit on the gifts and on the faithful "so that, just as by their new birth they have become perfect in one body, so now they may be solidified in one body by communion with the body of our Savior and may advance to unity in concord, peace, and dedication to goodness."

Then follow the breaking of the bread and the *Our Father,* which is recited by the congregation and arouses dispositions of pardon and unity for "receiving the communion of the sacred mysteries." Augustine, in his commentaries on the *Our Father,* constantly stresses the lesson of pardon and unity furnished by the Eucharist.

The priest says " Holy things for the holy." And the people respond, "Only one is holy, only one is Lord, Jesus Christ." Cyril of Jerusalem adds, "We also are holy, not by nature but by participation, by fasting and by prayer." Theodore of Mopsuestia explains at length the meaning of communion. He deduces the meaning of unity and develops the necessary conditions for participation in the liturgy: submission to God, absence from evil, mercy to one's neighbor, and concern for everything heavenly. John Chrysostom loves to describe the social dimensions of the Mass. He is especially concerned to confess to the world, as Tertullian expressed it, the same *Trishagion,* the God thrice holy, chanted and celebrated in the eucharistic liturgy. Figures and rites enable the Fathers to mark off the essential lines of the mystery of the Eucharist which it remains for us to fill in.

The Eucharist already enabled Justin to establish the con-
tinuity between creation and salvation (cf. texts pp. 17-18). The
Father of the universe is the Father of the Son of God, the Word
made flesh. We find outlined in Justin a theology of the eighth
day commemorating the resurrection which coincides with the
first day of the Jewish week, the anniversary of creation. The
resurrection of Christ, celebrated in the Sunday Eucharist, appears
at the same time as a new creation and the fulfillment of the
first creation. That is what the Byzantine mosaics express in
depicting the resurrected Christ rescuing Adam and Eve from
hell in a universal restoration.

The same teaching is more powerfully orchestrated by Irenaeus of Lyons (cf. text pp. 171-183). In reply to Gnostic objections he situates the Eucharist at the center of his vision of the world
and of history. Just as Christ has assumed human nature in its
integrity and totality—the first fruits of the entire human race—
so the offering of bread and wine are the elements of the sacrifice
of the new covenant through which the Church offers to God the
new oblation throughout the world.

The Eucharist constitutes in effect the first fruits of creation
in the sense that they are taken from the elements of the created
world. Christ, first born in the order of creation, is also firstborn
among the dead and therefore the first fruits of the new order and
the new covenant. The latter is also symbolized by the consecrated bread and wine, the first fruits of paradise where the
future kingdom is already established.

We find here, in an elaborated form, a conception already
encountered in the primitive Church, the correspondence between
the order of creation and the order of redemption with a progression
from one to the other. Christ is the keystone of the entire divine
economy. Irenaeus compares him to a grain sown in the ground,
an image of his death, which ended in the resurrection when the
grain sprang up to a new life and prepared the harvest of the
universal Church. Christ is the last link in the chain of being
and completes the history of all the sacrifices of the world which
are figured by the bread and wine of the earth. The Eucharist
anticipates the whole history of salvation from the beginning to
the end of the world. It is harvest in anticipation which communicates to it its interior dynamism, its movement toward per-

fection. The spirit of Christ thus restores the dispersion to unity and offers to God the first fruits of the nations in rendering communion with God possible to all. Augustine returns to the theme in the *City of God.*

In the fourth century the Fathers develop the Eucharist as "the sacrament of redemption" which renders present and efficacious the sacrifice of the cross. "We offer him," exclaims Chrysostom, "even in making commemoration (*anamnesis*) of his death. This is one, not manifold. It is offered only once, as he entered but once into the holy of holies. It is the one sacrifice which we offer, not one today and another tomorrow. One Christ everywhere, everywhere entire, one body only. As there is only one body there is but one sacrifice. Our High-priest has offered one sacrifice. This is the same sacrifice which we still offer."

The Fathers never dissociate death from resurrection, as the epistle of Cyprian already testifies (see, p. 186): there is question of the same mystery which conducts Christ and his body to glory. Augustine goes even further. The symbolism of the Mass not merely expresses the sacrifice of the Cross—of the Head—but also of the Mystical Body. On the altar it is the mystical body, head and members, which offers and is offered. "This is the Christian sacrifice: to be all in one body in Jesus Christ. This is the mystery which the Church celebrates in the sacrament of the altar, where it learns to offer itself in the oblation which it makes to God" (*City of God,* 10, 6).

On these foundations the Fathers erect a spirituality of the Eucharist which directs the Christian life. They devote some vigorous expositions to the subject of incorporation in Christ and the unity of the Church. Hilary of Poitiers is the first to develop an intimate, substantial union established between Christ and his communicants. He compares it to the assimilation which happens to nourishment in asserting that a symbiosis is effected between two living beings (see pp. 198-201).

To describe the fusion, the Fathers use in turn the similes of spirit and body, host and guest, head and members, husband and wife in reference to the birth of Eve from Adam's side: *flesh of his flesh,* or to ideal marriage: *two in one flesh.* Theodore writes: "In eating the members of the spouse and in drinking his nuptial blood they become united to him."

The Eucharist, then, is the sacrament of our becoming divine. Hilary of Poitiers and Cyril of Alexandria have both developed the theme. "As Christ has taken the flesh of our body and is truly man born of Mary, we receive in communion the flesh of his body, and we become one, the Father being in him and he in us" (see, p. 198). The Eucharist thus becomes a prolongation of Christmas.

Augustine develops the ecclesial aspect of the Eucharist as the sacrament of the mystical body: "It is your sacrament which is placed for you on the Lord's table; it is your sacrament which you receive. To the words: *The body of Christ,* which you are, you reply, *Amen* and your response is like a signature" (see, p. 207). He draws a concrete lesson for a life of charity, union, and peace in the fusion of hearts (see, pp. 219-220).

Anxious to connect liturgy and life, charity received and charity practiced, John Chrysostom reveals the prolongation of the Eucharist in the life of the Christian. "For you the Father has not spared his own son, his only born son; yet you, you disregard this son when he dies of hunger. And yet God has given his own son to us and you have not given him even a crumb of bread, he who has been immolated and delivered up for you." He compares almsgiving to the sacrifice of the Mass. "The altar is found everywhere, at all street corners, in all places."

It would not be difficult to multiply citations which unite cult and charity, Eucharist and life. Cyprian chides a noble lady who has not brought her offering to Mass: "Your eyes do not see the necessitous and the poor because they are clouded in dense night. You are rich and fortunate, you imagine that you celebrate the Lord's Supper, without taking part in the offering. You come to Mass with nothing to offer, suppressing the part of the sacrifice which belongs to the poor" (cf. *De opere et eleemosyna,* 15).

Finally, Christian antiquity unites the Eucharist and martyrdom, especially from the time of the persecutions. The marytr appears as "a sort of permanent witness rendered to the actuality of the mystery and, more precisely, to the manner in which this actuality of the death and life in Christ ought to be realized in us" (L. Bouyer, *La vie de la liturgie* [Paris 1956] p. 272).

These varied extensions of the mystery of the Eucharist into the various phases of Christian life bring us back to our point of departure: the mystery of Christ. His Eucharist is the oblation of the world, taken up and saved, the eucharistic act which assembles the new people until the hour of his second coming. It harmonizes the Christian life with the history of the world, with its joys and sufferings, its struggles and snares. The faithful discover the existential meaning of their faith, deriving lasting assurance of the certainty of victory despite the force of the struggle, with faith and hope prevailing over trials and death.

For them the Mass is truly the mystery of faith, because it situates them at the heart of the Christian mystery. It presents to them the invisible presence of the risen Christ in the world, like the ferment of which the Gospel speaks, which invisibly ferments the whole mass, called to participate in the eucharistic act of a new world.

NOTE ON THE COMPOSITION OF THE WORK

In the absence of a systematic exposition of the Mass, it is not possible to reduce the teaching of the Fathers to categories to which they do not lend themselves without extrapolation, and without making excisions and artificial regroupings. We have preferred to group the texts of this collection under three headings which make up the three parts of the present work:

1. Liturgical Texts

What were the rites and prayers to which the Fathers refer in their catechesis? Here we present the formulas of the third and fourth centuries, even though they have only an illustrative value in an age when the part left to improvisation was still very considerable. Most of the texts are still in use in the East at the present time. Here is the list:

The Liturgy of the Eucharist in the *Apostolic Tradition*.
The Prayers of the Mass in the *Euchologium of Serapion*.
The *Anaphora* of the *Apostolic Constitutions*.
The *Anaphoras* of Sts. Basil and John Chrysostom.

2. Commentaries on Biblical Texts

The teaching of the Fathers on the Eucharist refers to the Bible, principally to the texts from the Gospels and Epistles. These commentaries, preached to the congregations of Antioch or Hippo, enable us to meditate on the following major eucharistic texts:

The Passover Narrative (*Exodus* 12, 1-12, 14).
The Institution of the Eucharist (*Matt.* 26, 26-29).
The Bread of Life (*John* 6, 48-64).
The Celebrations of the Eucharist at Corinth (I *Cor.* 11, 23-34).

3. The Eucharist in the Fathers

In this final section we assemble all the relevant texts of the patristic tradition from the second to the sixth centuries. These texts and testimonies are widely different in origin and type. They take the form of excursus, as is the case with Irenaeus or Hilary; or of inscriptions, in which Abercius and Pectorius profess their faith in the Eucharist; or of letters, in which Cyprian speaks of the manner of the celebration of the Lord's Supper, and Basil writes of frequent communion; or finally of sermons, in which Augustine explains the Mass to the newly-baptized, and the late Latin Fathers, Peter Chrysologus, Faustus of Riez and his imitator, Caesarius of Arles, preach "the mystery of the altar."

* * *

A number of the texts which make up the present volume have not previously been translated into English. This is especially the case with pseudo-Faustus of Riez and Caesarius of Arles, and the recently edited sermons of St. Augustine.

* * *

Acknowledgment is made to *The Fathers of the Church* series, Catholic University of America Press, Washington, D.C., and to Regnery, Chicago, for permission to reproduce their translations.

PART ONE

Liturgical Texts[1]

1. THE APOSTOLIC TRADITION
2. THE EUCHOLOGIUM OF SERAPION
3. THE APOSTOLIC CONSTITUTIONS
4. THE DERIVATIVES FROM THE SYRIAN TYPE:
   THE BYZANTINE LITURGIES
   THE ANAPHORA OF ST. BASIL
   THE ANAPHORA OF ST. JOHN CHRYSOSTOM

THE APOSTOLIC TRADITION

The most ancient formula of consecration of the eucharistic offerings is provided for us by Hippolytus, probably of Egyptian origin, and adopted by the Roman clergy. The intention of the author seems to have been to give a model of a prayer of unquestionable orthodoxy to celebrants for whom the task of improvisation was excessively laborious.

The prayer of consecration addressed to God did not elaborate on the benefits of creation or on the stages of salvation but concentrated, as in baptism, on the mysteries of Christ, especially on His death and resurrection—the Paschal mystery realized in the Mass. It ended with an invocation of the Holy Spirit whom the Eastern liturgy held dear and through whom unity and sanctity in the Church are achieved.

We can discover four divisions—the preface, the Institution narrative, the *Anamnesis,* and the *Epiclesis* or invocation.

---

1. The translations of The Euchologium of Serapion and The Byzantine Liturgies are from A. Hamman ed., **Early Christian Prayers,** tr. W. Mitchell (Regnery, Chicago 1961). They are reproduced here with the kind permission of the publishers.

Giving thanks with all the priests, the bishop says:[2]
  The Lord be with you.
And all shall respond:
  And with your spirit.
  Lift up your hearts.
  We lift them up unto the Lord.
  Let us give thanks to the Lord.
  It is meet and right.

Preface

And then the bishop shall proceed immediately:
  We give you thanks, O God, through your beloved Servant
Jesus Christ, whom at the end of time you sent to us a Savior and
Redeemer and the messenger of your counsel. He is your Word,
inseparable from you; through whom you made all things and
in whom you are well pleased. You sent him from heaven into
the womb of the Vrgin, and he, dwelling within her, took flesh,
and was manifested as your Son, being born of [the] Holy Spirit
and the Virgin. He, fulfilling your will, and winning for himself
a holy people, stretched out his hands when he came to suffer,
that by his death he might set free them who believed in you.

Institution Narrative

When he was betrayed to his death freely accepted, that he
might bring to nought death, and break the bonds of the devil,
and tread hell under foot, and give light to the righteous, and set
up a covenant, and manifest his resurrection, he took bread and
giving thanks said: *Take, eat: this is my body, which is broken
for you.* And likewise also the cup, saying: *This is my blood,
which is shed for you. As often as ye do this, do it in memory
of me.*

Anamnesis

Calling to memory, therefore, his death and resurrection, we
offer to you the bread and the chalice, giving thanks to you, be-

---

2. This implies concelebration at Rome — i.e., a single celebration by
bishop and priests together.

cause you have counted us worthy to stand before you and to minister to you.

Epiclesis

And we pray that you would send your Holy Spirit upon the offerings of your holy Church; that, gathering them into one, you would grant to all your saints who partake to be filled with the Holy Spirit, that their faith may be confirmed in truth, that we may praise and glorify you. Through your Servant, Jesus Christ, through whom be to you glory and honor, with [the] Holy Spirit in the holy Church, both now and always and world without end. Amen.

THE EUCHOLOGIUM OF SERAPION [3]

Serapion, bishop of Thmuis in Lower Egypt (mid. 4th cent.), friend of Antony and Athanasius, is better known to us from his contemporaries than from his own works. The *Euchologium* or Prayerbook consists of numerous prayers,—several of which carry his name and all of which seem to be his work. They were discovered as recently as 1894 in a Mt. Athos manuscript.

This contains thirty prayers with reference to the Eucharist, baptism, ordination, blessing of the oils and funerals. Eighteen of these prayers are connected with the Mass. There is no certain rule to determine their exact order. Their probable sequence was as follows:

The first prayer before the readings.

The prayer after the homily.

Intercession for the catechumens, the people, the sick, (each ended by a blessing), the harvest, the Church, the bishop, the community, and finally, the prayer on kneeling. All these prayers of the Mass of the Catechumens are rich in doctrinal content. They end in a doxology addressed to the Father, through the Son, in the Holy Spirit.

The admirable Prayer of Oblation opens with an expression of praise for the grandeur and mystery of God which is revealed in his Son. This is followed by the Institution narrative, the

---

3. Its authenticity has recently been questioned: B. Botte, "L'eucologe de Sérapion, est-il authentique?" **Oriens christ.** 48 (1964) 50-56.

Anamnesis, the Invocation of the Word (and not of the Spirit), that he may effect the change in the *oblata*—this doubtless the of the Living and the Dead and a prayer for those who have provided the offerings.

The *Euchologium* ends with the Prayer at the breaking of the Host, the Post-Communion Prayer, and a Blessing which brings the celebration to a close. [4]

Here are the eighteen prayers of the Mass restored to their natural order by the editor, Father Hamman.

The First Prayer on Sunday

We ask for your help, Father of Christ, Lord of all that is, Creator of all the created, Maker of all that is made; we stretch out our clean hands to you and lay bare our minds, Lord, before you.

Have mercy, we pray you; spare us, be kind to us, improve us; fill us with virtue, faith and knowledge.

Look at us, Lord; we bring our weaknesses for you to see. Be kind and merciful to all of us here gathered together; have pity on this people of yours and show them your favor, make them equitable, temperate and pure; send out angelic powers to make this your people—all that compose it—holy and noble.

Send the Holy Spirit into our minds, I beg you, and grant that we may learn to understand the holy scriptures he inspired. May we interpret them correctly and fittingly, for the benefit of all the faithful here present.

Through your only Son, Jesus Christ, in the Holy Spirit. Through him may glory and power be yours, now and forever and ever. Amen.

Prayer after the Homily

God our Savior, God of the whole universe, Lord and Creator of all that exists, Father of that only Son whom you begot as a true and living Image of yourself and sent out to help the human

---

4. See P. Rodopoulos, "Doctrinal Teaching in the Sacramentary of Serapion of Thmuis," **Greek Orthodox Theol. Review** 9 (1963-64) 201-214.

race, by his means calling men to you and winning them over: we pray you for the people here assembled.

Send them the Holy Spirit, and may the Lord Jesus visit them, speak in the minds of them all and prepare their hearts for faith; may he draw all souls to you, O God of mercies.

Take possession, too, of the people in this town that are yours; make a real flock of them, through your only Son, Jesus Christ, in the Holy Spirit. Through him may glory and power be yours, now and forever and ever. Amen.

Prayer for the Catechumens [5]

Helper and Lord of all men, Deliverer of them that find release, Protector of the redeemed, Hope of those who come under your strong hand: you have made an end of sin; through your only Son you undid what Satan had done, frustrated his tricks and freed the prisoners he kept in chains.

We thank you for calling the catechumens to you through your only Son and giving them knowledge of you. We beg you, therefore, make their knowledge firm, that so *they may come to know you, the only true God, and your envoy, Jesus Christ.* May they persevere with undivided attention in learning what you have to teach them, and go on until they are fit for the bath that will bring them new birth, fit for your holy mysteries; through your only Son, Jesus Christ, in the Holy Spirit. Through him may glory and power be yours, now and forever and ever. Amen.

Blessing of the Catechumens [6]

We stretch out our hands, Lord, and beg that your own hand, your holy, lifegiving hand, may be stretched in blessing over this congregation.

They have bowed their heads before you, uncreated Father, through your only Son.

---

5. This prayer and the previous one suppose the presence of people not yet baptized.

6. This blessing, which was doubtless pronounced at the moment of dismissal of the catechumens, ends the first part of the liturgy, which corresponds to our present Mass as far as the Creed.

Bless this people with the blessing of knowledge [7] and devotion, the blessing that flows from your mysteries, through your only Son, Jesus Christ. Through him may glory and power be yours, now and forever and ever. Amen.

Prayer for the People [8]

We acknowledge your excellence, O God, Lover of men; we cast our weaknesses before you and ask that strength may be given us. Forgive us the sins we did in the past, pardon our former faults and make new men of us. Grant that we may really and truly be your servants. We consecrate ourselves to you; accept us, God of truth, accept this people. Make them truly yours, make them all live blamelessly, without reproach. May they gain equality with the inhabitants of heaven and be counted as angels, may they all become elect and holy.

We ask your help for those who have faith, for those who know our Lord Jesus Christ; may they increase in faith and knowledge and learning.

We pray you for this congregation: be gracious to every member of it; make yourself known to them, show them your splendor. May they all learn to know you, the uncreated Father, and your only Son, Jesus Christ.

We pray you for all in authority: may they have peace in their time and give tranquillity to the Catholic Church.

We pray you, merciful God, for slave and free, men and women, old and young, rich and poor. Show them all how good you are, extend your kindness to all of them, have pity on them and grant them the grace of setting their course towards you.

We ask your help for travellers: send them the angel of peace [9] for their companion, to protect them from all that may do them harm, wherever it may come from; and so let them reach their journey's end with great cheerfulness.

---

7. The word "knowledge" which frequently occurs in Serapion, reminds us that these prayers come from the land of Clement and Origen. The knowledge meant is a specially intimate knowledge of God.

8. A litany which must have been in use from very ancient times. See Clement of Rome's prayer and the **Apostolic Constitutions**, 8: 12.

9. The angel of peace is mentioned in the **Apostolic Constitutions** 8: 36 and 38.

We ask your help for the afflicted, for prisoners and for the needy. Give relief to all of them, free the prisoners from their chains, free the needy from want; comfort them all, O Comforter and Consoler.

We pray you for the sick: give them health, let them recover from their illnesses; make them perfectly sound in body and in soul.

For you are the Savior and Benefactor, the Lord and King of all men; to you, therefore, we pray for them all, through your only Son, Jesus Christ. Through him may glory and power be yours, in the Holy Spirit, now and forever and ever. Amen.

Blessing of the Laity

May the hand that holds life and purity, the hand of the only Son, the hand that sweeps away what is evil and stays and supports what is holy, be over the heads of this congregation.

May they receive the blessing of the Spirit, heaven's blessing, the blessing of the prophets and apostles. May their bodies be blessed with chastity and purity and their souls have the grace to seek and know the mysteries and take part in them.

May they all alike have blessing through your only Son, [10] Jesus Christ. Through him may glory and power be yours, in the Holy Spirit, now and forever and ever. Amen.

Prayer for the Sick

To you we pray, Lord, to you who watch over us, you the Author of the body and Creator of the soul, the Maker of man, the Governor, Guide and Savior of the whole human race, you who love men enough to give them reconciliation and calm. Be kind to us; help and heal the sick, cure their diseases, raise up the downcast; glorify your holy name, through your only Son, Jesus Christ. Through him may glory and power be yours, in the Holy Spirit, now and forever and ever. Amen.

---

10. Note the strongly theological basis of this prayer, which asks the Father that his Son may give the blessing.

Blessing of the Sick

Merciful Lord God, stretch out your hand and grant the sick
the grace of healing, fit them for health, free them from the illness
that now besets them. May they be healed in the name of your
only Son; may his holy name be their remedy, may it make
them sound and whole; for through him glory and power are
yours, in the Holy Spirit, and yours they will be forever and
ever. Amen.

Prayer for a Good Harvest

Creator of heaven and earth, you have studded the sky with
stars and made it bright with lights, enriched the earth with fruits
to satisfy men's needs, given to the race that took shape under
your hands the clear light and the shining stars to enjoy, the
earth's produce to feed on. We pray you, send us rain, abundant,
plentiful, fertilizing; and make the earth yield fruit and to spare;
for we know how you love men, we know what your kindness is.

Do not forget those who call upon you; see that your holy
Church, which alone is catholic, receives honor; hear our petitions
and prayers and bless the whole earth, through your only Son,
Jesus Christ. Through him may glory and power be yours, in
the Holy Spirit, now and forever and ever. Amen.

Prayer for the Church

O Lord, God through all the ages, God of all reasoning minds,
God of the pure-hearted and of those whose prayer is sincere
and pure, visible and known in heaven to the pure spirits, living
and worshipped on earth in the Catholic Church, praised by the
holy angels and the pure of heart, your truth praised and glorified
by the heavens themselves, which you made a living choir for the
purpose: give life and purity to this your Church, give it heavenly
powers and pure angels to help it, that the praise it offers you
may be pure.[11]

We ask your help for all the members of this Church. Grant

---

11. The words "pure" and "purity" occur no fewer than seven times
in this paragraph. The prominence given to the idea obviously reflects
a preoccupation in the mind of the author.

them all reconciliation, give them forgiveness and remission of their sins; grant them the grace never to sin again; be as a rampart to them and make temptation powerless against them.

Have pity on the men, the women and the children of the Church. Show yourself to them all. And may the knowledge of you be written in their hearts, through your only Son, Jesus Christ. Through him may glory and power be yours, in the Holy Spirit, now and forever and ever. Amen.

Prayer for the Bishop and the Christian Community

To you we pray, Savior, Lord, God of all flesh and Lord of every spirit, blessed yourself and Giver of all blessings: make our bishop holy, preserve him from all temptation, give him wisdom and knowledge, lead him to know you.

We ask your help also for the priests who work with him: give them holiness, wisdom and knowledge, see that their teaching is sound and make them dispense your holy doctrine rightly and irreproachably.

Sanctify the deacons, too. May they be pure in body and in soul, and with a clean conscience do you their service and watch over the holy body and the holy blood.

We ask your help for the subdeacons, lectors and interpreters: [12] give strength to all the ministers of the Church; grant them pity, compassion and spiritual progress.

We pray you for those leading the eremetical life and for those who live as virgins: may they finish their course without reproach and their lives without incident; may they spend all their days in purity and holiness.

Have pity, too, on all who are married, men and women and their children as well: grant them the blessings of progress and amendment, whereby they may receive life and election, through your only Son, Jesus Christ.

Through him may glory and power be yours, in the Holy Spirit, now and forever and ever. Amen.

---

12. The reference is to those who translated the text for the benefit of the people who did not understand the language in which it was written. St. Epiphanius speaks explicitly of them in his **Explanation of the Faith,** 20 and 21. See also the **Pilgrimage of Etheria,** 47; ed. H. Pétré, 260-2, Méliton de Sardes, *Sur la Pâque,* ed. O. Perler, [SC 123, Paris 1966], 131-133.

Prayer on Kneeling

Father of the Only Begotten, kind, compassionate, merciful: you love mankind, you love souls, you are generous to all who turn to you. Accept, then, this prayer and give us knowledge, faith, devotion and holiness.

Curb every wayward stirring of passion and of sense in this your people, uproot all their sins, cleanse them all and pardon their offences.

We kneel to you, uncreated Father, through your only Son. Make us fair-minded and always ready to be of service. Grant that we may seek you and love you; give us the grace to study and ponder your holy utterances; hold out your hand to us, Lord, and set us on our feet. Yes, merciful God, pull us to our feet, make us look upwards, open our eyes, give us courage. May we have no need to blush or be ashamed, no cause to reproach ourselves. Revoke the sentence that stands against us, write our names in the book of life, put us with your holy prophets and apostles, through your only Son, Jesus Christ. Through him may glory and power be yours, in the Holy Spirit, now and forever and ever. Amen.

BISHOP SERAPION'S PRAYER OF OBLATION

Preface

It is right and proper that we should give you praise and hymns and glory, uncreated Father of Jesus Christ, who is your only Son.

We praise you, God uncreated, unsearchable, ineffable, beyond the grasp of any created being.

We praise you because you are known by the Only Son, proclaimed and explained by him to created beings and known in turn by them. We praise you because you know the Son and reveal to the saints the glories that are his. We praise you because you are known by the Word you begot and are seen by the saints and understood by them after a fashion.

We praise you, Father, invisible, Giver of immortality. You are the source of life and light, the source of all grace and truth; you love men and love the poor, seek reconciliation with all men and draw them all to you by sending your dear Son to visit them.

We beg you, make us really alive. Give us the spirit of light, that we may know you, the supremely true, and your envoy, Jesus Christ. Give us the Holy Spirit and enable us to discourse at large upon your ineffable mysteries.

May the Lord Jesus and the Holy Spirit speak in us and praise you through us, for you are high above all princedoms, powers, virtues and dominations, above everything that can be named, both in this world and in the world to come.

Angels, archangels, thrones, dominations, princedoms and powers stand in their tens of thousands, their countless myriads, about you. The six-winged seraphim, the two most eminent, are by your side. Hiding their faces with two of their wings, hiding their feet with two more, with the other two flying, they cry out in praise of your holiness. Accept our acclamation when we too say with them:

Holy, holy, holy is the Lord of hosts. Heaven and earth are full of your glory. Heaven is full, earth is full of your wonderful glory.

Institution of the Eucharist

Lord of the virtues, fill [13] this sacrifice with the virtue of your participation. For we offer you this living sacrifice, this bloodless oblation. We offer you this bread, which is like [14] the body of your only Son.

This bread is like the holy body because on the night when Jesus Christ was betrayed, he took bread and broke it and gave it to his disciples, saying:

Take some and eat it: this is my body, broken for you, to remit your sins.

Anamnesis

For that reason we too offer you bread as we represent his

---

13. In the Alexandrian type of rite, the prayer is knit together by the idea of fulness, which is introduced by the Sanctus.

14. This expression, which is also found in St. Ambrose, **De Sacramentis**, 5, is not a denial of the real presence of Christ; it means that the symbolism suggested by the bread is there after the consecration of the host as well as before.

death, and we beg you through this sacrifice to show us your favor and be friendly to us, God of truth.

As the elements of this bread, once scattered over the mountains, were gathered together and made one, so may it be with your holy Church. Build it up from every nation, country, town and village, from every house, and make of it one, living, Catholic Church.[15]

We offer, too, the cup, which is like the blood of the Lord Jesus, because when he took the cup after supper, he said to his disciples:

Take it and drink some of it: this is the new testament; it is my blood, shed for you, to remit your sins.

For that reason we too offer you the cup as we represent the manner of his dying.

Epiclesis

O God of truth, may your holy Word [16] come down on this bread, that the bread may become the body of the Word; may he descend on this cup, that the cup may become the body of the Truth. Grant that to all who communicate, the means of life [17] they receive may bring the healing of every sickness and the strength for every kind of progress and virtue; may it not lead, God of truth, to their confusion, condemnation and disgrace.

We call upon you, you the Uncreated, through your Son, in the Holy Spirit. May this people have your pity and become fit for greater things. May angels be sent to be with your people and defeat the Evil One and strengthen the Church. We pray you, too, for all who are asleep and whose names we call to mind.

Here the names are mentioned.

Make all these souls holy: you know them all. Sanctify all the souls that are sleeping in the Lord, include them in the number

---

15. Serapion modifies the quotation from the **Didache** 9:4. He is thinking not of the final gathering together and the second coming of Christ but of the return of those who have fallen away through Arianism.

16. Here for once the epiclesis is addressed not to the Holy Spirit but to the Word. "It thus seems highly doubtful," says Dom Capelle, "whether the epiclesis of the Logos [Word] is a legacy from the past."

17. Cf. Ignatius, **Letter to the Ephesians**, 20:2.

of your holy powers and give them a place to live in your kingdom.

Accept, too, this people's thanksgiving and bless those who have provided the offerings and oblations. Grant health, soundness and a cheerful heart to all this congregation and let them make all manner of progress, both in soul and in body, through your only Son, Jesus Christ, in the Holy Spirit. So it was with him, so it is, so it will be, forever and ever, through all the endless successions of aeons. Amen.

Prayer at the Breaking of the Host

Make us fit to receive this communion, God of truth: give us chastity in our bodies and prudence and knowledge in our minds; give us wisdom, God of mercies, with our share of the body and blood.

For glory and power are yours, through the Only Begotten, in the Holy Spirit, and yours they will be forever and ever. Amen.

Prayer after the Communion of the People

We thank you, Lord, for calling the fallen to you, choosing for your disciples men who had sinned and overlooking the sentence against us, which your kindness revoked, our conversion cancelled and the knowledge you gave of yourself annulled.

We thank you for giving us a share of your body and blood.

Bless us, bless this people, and grant that our lot may be with the body and blood, through your only Son. Through him may glory and power be yours, now and for ever. Amen.

Blessing of the People after the Breaking of the Host

I stretch out my hand over this people and beg that your hand, with its gift of truth, may be stretched out to bless them, God of mercies, kind God, through these mysteries. May the hand that holds prudence and power, the hand that corrects and purifies, the hand that confers holiness, bless all the members of this congregation and give them the conditions they need for their progress and amendment; through your only Son, Jesus Christ, in the Holy Spirit, now and forever and ever. Amen.

THE APOSTOLIC CONSTITUTIONS

The Apostolic Constitutions are a compilation of canons and liturgical material in eight books, composed by an unknown author in Syria about the year 380.

Book Eight is the most valuable because it provides us with the text of the so-called "Clementine" liturgy. A literary fiction of the time attributed it to Clement of Rome which gave it a Judeo-Christian flavor. The dependence on the *Apostolic Tradition* of Hippolytus is obvious.

The text gives us the order and prayers of the Mass of the Catechumens, such as is easy to find in the works of St. John Chrysostom and Theodore of Mopsuestia:

> Reading from Old and New Testaments. Homily. Prayer for the Catechumens, the possessed, the candidates for baptism, the penitents. Dismissal. Litany prayer for the faithful. Kiss of Peace. Washing of the hands.
> Offering of the *oblata*.
> Prayer of oblation: Preface, Sanctus, institution, anamnesis, epiclesis to the Spirit, and memento.
> Communion.
> Thanksgiving and Dismissal.

The *anaphora* is especially remarkable. Its composition is clearly trinitarian. It follows the scheme of the Jewish prayer of religious repast, later found in the *anaphoras* of Sts. Basil and John Chrysostom: Adoration of God, development of the works of the Father in creation and redemption along the stages in the history of salvation. This development finds its object and achievement in the mystery of Christ and of his cross, his death and resurrection.

The *anamnesis* which follows is a eucharistic thanksgiving, and the Eucharist is an *anamnesis;* the Church offers and possesses in the Eucharist the testament left at the Last Supper. The *anamnesis* goes from the passion on to the glorification and Second Coming. It underlines the expectation of the Second Coming. The change of the offerings into the body and blood of Christ is asked from the Spirit. The prayer ends with the litany of the chief intentions of the Church in which the Spirit works our sanctification.

MASS OF THE CATECHUMENS

And after the reading of the Law and the Prophets, and our Epistles, and Acts, and the Gospels, let him that is ordained salute the Church, saying, *The grace of our Lord Jesus Christ, the love of God and the Father, and the fellowship of the Holy Spirit, be with you all.* And let them all answer,
And with your Spirit.

And after these words let him speak to the people the words of exhortation; and when he has ended his sermon and instruction, I, Andrew, [18] the brother of Peter, speak:

All standing up, let the deacon ascend upon some high seat, and proclaim:

Let none of the hearers, let none of the unbelievers stay; and when there is silence let him say: —

Prayer for the Catechumens

You catechumens, pray.

And let all the faithful pray for them in their mind, saying: *Lord, have mercy.*

And let the deacon pray for them, saying:

Let us all pray fervently unto God for the catechumens, that he that is good, he that is the lover of mankind, will mercifully hear their prayers and their supplications, and so accept their petitions as to assist them and give them those desires of their hearts which are for their advantage, and reveal to them the Gospel of his Christ; give them illumination and understanding, instruct them in the knowledge of God.

May he teach them his commands and his ordinances, implant in them his pure and saving fear, open the ears of their hearts, that they may exercise themselves in his law day and night; strengthen them in piety, unite them to and number them with his holy flock; vouchsafe them the laver of regeneration, and the garment of immortality, the true life;[19] and deliver them from all impiety, and give no place to the adversary against them; and cleanse them from all filthiness of flesh and spirit, and dwell in them, and walk in them by his Christ; *bless their goings out and*

---

18. A literary fiction. Eng. trans., ANF 7, 483-491.

19. For the same traditional expressions cf. Greg. Naz., **Sermon on Baptism, 4.**

their comings in, and order their affairs for their good (II *Cor.*
7, 1; 6, 16; *Ps.* 121, 8).

Let us then earnestly make our supplications for them, that
they may obtain the forgiveness of their transgressions by their
initiation, and so may be thought worthy to receive the holy
mysteries, and constant communion with the saints.

Rise up, you catechumens, beg for yourselves the peace of
God through his Christ, a peaceable day, and free from sin, and
the same for the whole span of your life; ask from a compassionate and merciful God a Christian death, and the forgiveness of your transgressions. Dedicate yourselves to the only unbegotten God, through his Christ. Bow down your heads, and
receive the blessing.

But at the naming of every petition by the deacon, as we
said before, let the people say, *Lord, have mercy,* and let the
children say it first.[20]

And as they have bowed down their heads, let the presiding
bishop bless them with this blessing:

O God Almighty, unbegotten and inaccessible, the only true
God, the Father of the Christ, your only begotten Son; the God
of the Comforter, and Lord of all things; who through Christ
did appoint your disciples to be teachers for the teaching of piety;
look down now also upon your servants, who are receiving instruction in the Gospel of your Christ, and *give them a new
heart, and renew a right spirit in their inward parts* (*Ps.* 51, 10),
that they may both know and do your will with full purpose
of heart, and with a willing soul.

Vouchsafe them a holy initiation, and unite them to your
holy Church, and make them partakers of your divine mysteries,
through Jesus Christ, who is our hope, and who died for them;
by whom glory and worship be given to you in the Holy Spirit
forever. Amen.

And after this, let the deacon say: Go out, you catechumens,
in peace.

Prayer for the Energumens [21]

And after they are gone out, let him say: For energumens and
those afflicted with unclean spirits, pray.

---

20. Cf. John Chrys. in Matt. hom. 71, 4.
21. Possessed of the devil.

Let us all earnestly pray for them, that God, the lover of mankind, will by Christ rebuke the unclean and wicked spirits, and deliver his suppliant from oppression and the dominion of the adversary. May he that rebuked the legion of demons, and the devil, the prince of wickedness (*Mark* 5, 9; *Zech.* 3, 2) even now rebuke these apostates from piety, and deliver his creatures from his power, and cleanse those creatures which he has made with great wisdom.

Let us still pray earnestly for them: Save them, O God, and raise them up by your power. Bow down your heads, you energumens, and receive the blessing.

And let the bishop add this prayer, and say: —

You, *who have bound the strong man,* and *spoiled all that was in his house,* who have given us *power over serpents and scorpions* to tread upon them, and *upon all the power of the enemy* (*Matt.* 12, 29; *Luke* 10, 19; *Ps.* 51, 12); who have delivered the serpent, that murderer of men, bound to us, *as a sparrow to children, whom all things dread, and tremble before the face of your power* (*Job* 11, 24), who have cast him down as *lightning from heaven* to earth (*Luke* 10, 18), not with a fall from a place, but from honor to dishonor, on account of his voluntary perversity; whose look dries the abysses, and threatening melts the mountains, and whose *truth remains forever;* whom the infants praise, and the sucking babes bless; whom angels sing hymns to, and adore; who *look upon the earth, and make it tremble; who touch the mountains, and they smoke; who threaten the sea, and dry it up, and make all its rivers as desert,* and the *clouds as the dust of your feet; who walk upon the sea as upon the firm ground* (*Ps.* 8, 3; 104, 32; *Job* 14, 11); You only begotten God, the Son of the great Father, rebuke these wicked spirits, and deliver *the works of your hands* from the harassment of the adverse spirit. For to you is glory, honor, and worship, and through you to your Father, in the Holy Spirit, forever. Amen. Then let the deacon say: *Go out, you energumens.*

Prayer for the Candidates for Baptism

And after their departure, let him cry aloud: You that are to receive the sacrament of illumination, pray. Let us all, the faithful, earnestly pray for them, that the Lord will vouchsafe that, being initiated into the death of Christ, they may rise with

him, and become partakers of his kingdom, and may be admitted to the communion of his mysteries; unite them to, number
them among, those that are saved in his holy Church. Pray then
earnestly for them: Save them, and raise them up by your grace.
And being sealed to God through his Christ, let them bow down
their heads, and receive this blessing from the bishop: —

You who have formerly said by your holy prophets to those
have appointed spiritual regeneration through Christ, do You
now also look down upon these that are candidates for baptism
and bless them, and sanctify them, and prepare them that they
may become worthy of your spiritual gift, and of true adoption,
of your spiritual mysteries, of being gathered together with those
that are saved through Christ our Savior; by whom glory, honor,
and worship be to you, in the Holy Spirit, forever. Amen.

And let the deacon say: *Go out, you that are preparing for
illumination.*

Prayer for Penitents

And after that let him proclaim: You penitents, pray:

Let us all earnestly pray for our brethren who are doing penance, that God, in his loving compassion, will show them the
way of repentance, and accept their return and their confession,
and *bruise Satan under their feet suddenly* (*Rom.* 16, 20), and
redeem them from the snare of the devil, and the violence of
the demons, and free them from every unlawful word, and every
shameful practice and wicked thought; forgive them all their
offences, both voluntary and involuntary, and *blot out that hand-
writing which is against them* (*Col.* 2, 14), and write them
in the book of life (*Phil.* 4, 3; *Dan.* 12, 1); cleanse them from
all filthiness of flesh and spirit (II *Cor.* 7, 1), and restore and
unite them to his holy flock. For he knows our frame. *For
who can glory that he has a clean heart? And who can boldly
say, that he is pure from sin?* (*Prov.* 20, 9). *For we are all
among the blameworthy* (*Ecclus.* 8, 5).

Let us still pray earnestly for them, for *there is joy in heaven
over one sinner that repents* (*Luke* 15, 7), that, being converted
from every evil work, they may be joined to all good practice; that
God, the lover of mankind, will quickly accept their petitions, will
restore to them the joy of His salvation, and strengthen them with
his free Spirit (*Ps.* 113); that they may not be any more

shaken, but be admitted to holy communion, and become partakers of his divine mysteries, that appearing worthy of his adoption, they may obtain eternal life. Let us all still earnestly say on their account: *Lord, have mercy.* Save them, O God, and raise them up by your mercy.

Rise up, and bow your heads to God through his Christ, and receive the blessing.

Let the bishop then add this prayer: Almighty, eternal God, Lord of the whole world, the Creator and Governor of all things, who have exhibited man as the ornament of the world through Christ, and did give him a law both naturally implanted and written, that he might live according to law, as a rational creature; and, when he had sinned, you gave him your goodness in order to incite him to repentance: Look down upon these persons who have bent the neck of their soul and body to you; for *you desire not the death of a sinner, but his repentance, that he turn from his wicked way, and live (Ezek.* 33, 11).

You who did accept the repentance of the Ninevites, who will that all men be saved, and come to the knowledge of the truth (*Jonah* 3; I *Tim.* 2, 4); who did accept of that son who had consumed his substance in riotous living (cf. *Luke* 15, 13, 20), with the bowels of a father, on account of his repentance; do you now accept the repentance of your suppliants; for *there is no man that will not sin; for if you, O Lord, mark iniquities, O Lord, who shall stand? For with you there is propitiation (Ps.* 130, 3-4). And do you restore them to your holy Church, into their former dignity and honor, through Christ our God and Savior, by whom glory and adoration be to you, in the Holy Spirit, forever. Amen. Then let the deacon say, *Depart, you penitents.*

MASS OF THE FAITHFUL

And let him add: Let none of those who ought not to come draw near. All we of the faithful, let us bend our knee: let us all entreat God through his Christ; let us earnestly beseech God through his Christ.

The Litany Prayer of the Deacon for the Faithful

Let us pray for the peace and tranquillity of the world, and of the holy churches; that the God of the universe may afford us his constant and stable peace, and such that may preserve us in a full prosecution of such virtue as is according to godliness.

Let us pray for the Holy, Catholic, and Apostolic Church which is spread from one end of the earth to the other; that God would preserve and keep it unshaken, and free from the waves of this life, until the end of the world, as founded upon a rock.

Let us pray for this holy parish: that the Lord of the whole world may vouchsafe us without failure to follow after his heavenly hope, and without ceasing to pay him the debt of our prayer.

Let us pray for every episcopacy throughout the world, who rightly divide the word of your truth (II *Tim.* 2, 15):

Let us pray for our bishop James, [22] and his parishes,

Let us pray for our bishop Clement, and his parishes,

Let us pray for our bishop Evodius, and his parishes,

Let us pray for our bishop Annianus, and his parishes:

That the compassionate God may guard them in his holy churches in health, honor, and long life, and afford them an honorable old age in godliness and justice.

Let us pray for our priests: that the Lord may deliver them from every disgraceful and wicked action, and afford them a priesthood in health and honor.

Let us pray for all the deacons and ministers in Christ: that the Lord may grant them a ministry without reproach.

Let us pray for the readers, chanters, virgins, widows, and orphans.

Let us pray for those that are in marriage and in child-bearing: that the Lord may have mercy upon them all.

Let us pray for the eunuchs who walk in holiness.

Let us pray for those who live in continence and piety.

Let us pray for those that give offerings in the holy Church, and give alms to the needy.

Let us pray for those who offer sacrifices and first fruits to the Lord our God: that God, the fountain of all goodness, may recompense them with his heavenly gifts, and *give them in this world an hundredfold, and in the world to come life everlasting* (*Matt.* 19, 29); and bestow upon them for their temporal things,

---

22. This is James, the Lord's brother; **Gal.** 1, 19.

those that are eternal; for earthly things, those that are heavenly.

Let us pray for our brethren newly baptized: that the Lord may strengthen and confirm them.

Let us pray for our sick brethren: that the Lord may deliver them *from every sickness and every disease (Matt.* 4, 23), and restore them in good health to His holy Church.

Let us pray for those that travel by sea or by land.

Let us pray for those that are in the mines, in exile, in prison, and in bonds, for the name of the Lord.

Let us pray for those that are afflicted with bitter slavery.

Let us pray for our enemies, and those that hate us.

Let us pray for *those that persecute us in the name of the Lord (Matt.* 5, 44; 10, 22), that the Lord may pacify their anger, and scatter their wrath against us.

Let us pray for those that are outside the Church and are wandering in error: that the Lord may convert them.

Let us be mindful of the infants of the Church: that the Lord may perfect them in his fear, and bring them to *a complete age (Eph.* 4, 13).

Let us pray for one another: that the Lord may keep us and preserve us by his grace to the end, and *deliver us from evil, and from all the scandals of those that work iniquity (Ps.* 141, 9), and lead us safely unto his heavenly kingdom.

Let us pray for every Christian soul: Save us and raise us up, O God, by your mercy.

Let us rise up, and let us pray earnestly, and dedicate ourselves and one another to the living God, through his Christ.

And let the bishop add this prayer, and say: —

O Lord, Almighty, the Most High, *who dwells on high,* the Holy One, *that rests among the saints (Isa.* 57, 15), you who are without beginning, the Omnipotent, who have given to us through Christ the preaching of knowledge, to the acknowledgment of your glory and of your name, which he has made known to us, for our comprehension; do you now also look down through him upon this your flock, and deliver it from all ignorance and wicked deeds, and grant that we may fear you in earnest, and love you with affection, and have a due reverence of your glory. Be gracious and merciful to them, and hearken to them when they pray unto you; and keep them, that they may be unmovable, irreproachable, and free of blame, that they may be holy in body and spirit, *not having spot or wrinkle, or any such thing* (*Col.* 1, 22; *Eph.* 5, 27); but that they may be complete and none of them may be defective or imperfect.

O God our powerful support, who are a defender and not a respecter of persons, be the assister of this Your people, which You have chosen from myriads, and You have redeemed with the precious blood of Your Christ; be their protector, aider, provider, and guardian, their strong wall of defense, their bulwark and security. For *none can snatch out of Your hand* (*John* 10, 29): for there is no other God like You, for on You is our reliance (*Isa.* 45, 5).

Sanctify them by your truth: for your word is truth (*John* 17, 17; *Ps.* 61, 6). You who do nothing for favor, you whom none can deceive, deliver them *from every sickness, and every disease* (*Matt.* 4, 23), and every offense, every injury and deceit, *from fear of the enemy, from the dart that flies in the day, from the mischief that walks about in darkness* (*Ps.* 64, 1; 91, 5, 6); and vouchsafe them that everlasting life which is in Christ, your only begotten Son, our God and Savior, through whom glory and worship be to you, in the Holy Spirit now and always, and forever and ever. Amen.

And after this let the deacon say: Let us attend.

And let the bishop salute the church, and say: *The peace of God be with you all.* And let the people answer: *And with your spirit.*

The Kiss of Peace

Let the deacon say to all: *Salute you one another with the holy kiss* (I *Cor.* 16, 20). And let the clergy salute the bishop, the laymen salute the men, the women the women.

And let the children stand at a given sign; and let another deacon stand by them, that they may not be disorderly. And let the other deacons walk about and watch the men and women, that no disturbance may be made, and that no one nod, or whisper, or slumber; and let the deacons stand at the doors of the men, and the sub-deacons at those of the women, that no one go out, nor a door be opened, although it be for one of the faithful, at the time of the oblation.

The Washing of the Hands

But let one of the sub-deacons bring water to wash the hands of the priests, which is a symbol of the purity of those souls consecrated to God.

And I, James, the brother of John, the son of Zebedee, prescribe that the deacon shall immediately say: Let none of the catechumens, let none of the hearers, let none of the unbelievers, let none of the heterodox, stay here. You who have prayed the foregoing prayer, approach.

Let the mothers take along their children; let no one have anything against any one; let no one come in hypocrisy; let us stand upright before the Lord with fear and trembling, to offer.

The Offertory

Then let the deacons bring the gifts to the bishop at the altar; and let the priests stand on his right hand, and on his left, as disciples stand by their master. But let two of the deacons, on each side of the altar, hold a fan, made up of thin membranes, or of peacock feathers or of fine cloth, and let them silently drive away the small animals that fly about, that they may not come near to the chalice. Let the high priest, therefore, together with the priests, pray by himself.

The Great Eucharistic Prayer

And let the bishop put on his splendid vestments, and stand at the altar, and make the sign of the cross upon his forehead and say: The grace of Almighty God and the love of our Lord Jesus Christ, and the fellowship of the Holy Spirit, be with you all.[23] And let all with one voice say:

And with your spirit.

The high priest: *Lift up your mind.*

All the people: *We lift it up unto the Lord.*

The high priest: *Let us give thanks to the Lord.*

All the people: *It is meet and right so to do.*

---

23. II **Cor.** 13, 13.   Later Eastern liturgies always employ this Trinitarian formula at the beginning of the Preface.

Then let the high priest say: It is truly meet and right before all things to sing an hymn to you, who are the true God, who are before all beings, *from whom the whole family in heaven and earth is named* (*Eph.* 3, 15); who alone are unbegotten, and without beginning, and without a ruler, and without a master; who stand in need of nothing, but bestow everything that is good; who are superior to all beginning and generation; who are always and immutably the same; from whom all things came into being, as from their proper origin.

For you are eternal knowledge, everlasting vision, unbegotten hearing, untaught wisdom, the first by nature, and the measure of being, and beyond all number; who did bring all things out of nothing into being by your only begotten Son, but did beget him before all ages by your will, your power, and your goodness, without any intermediary, the only begotten Son, God the Word, the living Wisdom, *the First-born of every creature, the angel of your Great Counsel* (*Col.* 1, 15; *Isa.* 9, 6), and your High Priest, the King and Lord of every intellectual and sensible nature, who was *before all things, by whom were all things* (I *Cor.* 8, 6).

For you, O eternal God, did make all things by him, and through him it is that you exercise your suitable providence over the whole world; for by him you bestowed being, and by him likewise bestowed well-being: the God and Father of your only begotten Son, who by him did make before all things the cherubim and the seraphim, the aeons and hosts, the powers and dominations, the principalities and thrones, the archangels and angels; and after all these, did by him make this visible world, and all things that are therein.

For you are he who did *frame the heaven as an arch, and stretch it out like the covering of a tent* (*Isa.* 40, 22; *Ps.* 104, 2), and did found the earth upon nothing by your mere will; who did fix the firmament, and prepare the night and the day; who did bring the light out of your treasures, and by its waning did bring on darkness, for the rest of the living creatures that move upon the world; who did appoint the sun in heaven to rule over the day, and the moon to rule over the night, and did establish in heaven the choir of stars to praise your glorious majesty;

Who did make the water for drink and for cleansing, the

air in which we live for respiration and the emission of sounds by means of the tongue, which strikes the air, and the hearing, which co-operates therewith, so as to perceive speech when it is received by it;

Who made fire for our consolation in darkness, for the supply of our want, and that we might be warmed and enlightened by it;

Who did separate the great sea from the land, and did render the former navigable and the latter fit for walking, and did replenish the former with small and great living creatures, and filled the latter with the same, both tame and wild; did furnish it with various plants, and adorn it with herbs, and beautify it with flowers, and enrich it with seeds;

Who did ordain the great deep, and on every side made a mighty cavity for it, which contains seas of salt waters heaped together, yet did you every way bound them with barriers of the finest sand (*Jer.* 5, 22; *Job* 38, 8); who sometimes does raise it to the height of mountains by the winds, and sometimes does smooth it like a plain; sometimes does enrage it with a tempest, and sometimes does still it with a calm, that it may be easy to seafaring men in their voyages;

Who did encompass this world, which was made by you through Christ, with rivers, and water it with currents, and moisten it with springs that never fail, and did gird it round with mountains for the firmness and security of the earth.

For you have replenished your world, and adorned it with sweet-smelling and with healing herbs, with many and various living creatures, strong and weak, for food and for labor, tame and wild; with the noises of creeping things, the sounds of various sorts of flying creatures; with the circuits of the years, the numbers of months and days, the order of the seasons, the courses of the rainy clouds, for the production of the fruits and the support of living creatures. You have also appointed the station of the winds, which blow when commanded by you, and the multitude of the plants and herbs.

And you have not only created the world itself, but have also made man for a citizen of the world, exhibiting him as the ornament of the world; for you did say to your Wisdom: *Let us make man according to our image, and according to our likeness; and let them have dominion over the fish of the sea, and over the fowls of the heaven* (*Gen.* 1, 26). Wherefore also you have made him of an immortal soul, and of a body liable to dissolution—the former out of nothing, the latter out of the four elements—and have given him as to his soul rational knowledge, the discerning of piety and impiety, and the observation of right and wrong; and as to his body, You have granted him five senses and progressive motion.

For you, O God Almighty, did by your Christ *plant a paradise in Eden in the east* (*Gen.* 2, 8), adorned with all plants fit for food, and did introduce him into it, as into a rich banquet. And when you made him, you gave him a law implanted in his nature, that so he might have at home and within himself the seeds of divine knowledge.

And when you had brought him into the paradise of pleasure, you allowed him the privilege of enjoying all things, only forbidding the tasting of one tree, in hopes of greater blessings; that in case he would keep that command, he might receive the reward of it, which was immortality.

But when he neglected that command, and tasted of the forbidden fruit, by the seduction of the serpent and the counsel of his wife, you did justly cast him out of paradise. Yet of your goodness you did not overlook him, nor suffer him to perish utterly, for he was your creature; but you did subject the whole creation to him, and did grant him liberty to procure himself food by his own sweat and labors, while you did cause all the fruits of the earth to spring up, to grow, and to ripen. But when you had laid him asleep for a while, you did with an oath call him to rebirth again, did loose the bond of death, and promise him life after the resurrection.

And not this only; but when you had increased his posterity to an innumerable multitude, those that continued with you you did glorify, and those who did apostatize from you you did punish. And while you did accept of the sacrifice of Abel as of an holy person, you did reject the gift of Cain, the murderer of his brother, as of a detestable wretch. And beside these, you did accept of Seth and Enos, and did translate Enoch.

For you are the Creator of men, and the giver of life, and the supplier of want, and the giver of laws, and the rewarder of those that observe them, and the avenger of those that transgress them; who did bring the great flood upon the world by reason of the multitude of the ungodly, and did deliver righteous Noah from that flood by an ark, with eight souls, the end of the foregoing generations, and the beginning of those that were to come; who did kindle a fearful fire against the five cities of Sodom, and *did turn a fruitful land into a salt lake for the wickedness of them that dwelt therein* (*Ps.* 107, 34), but did snatch holy Lot out of the conflagration.

You are he who did deliver Abraham from the impiety of his forefathers, and did appoint him heir of the world, and did manifest to him your Christ; who did ordain Melchisedech an high priest for your worship; who did render your patient servant, Job, the conqueror of that serpent who is the patron of wickedness; who made Isaac the son of the promise, and Jacob the father of twelve sons, and did increase his posterity to a multitude, and bring him into Egypt with seventy-five souls.

You, O Lord, did not overlook Joseph, but granted him, as a reward of his chastity for your sake, the government over Egypt. You, O Lord, did not overlook the Hebrews when they were afflicted by the Egyptians, on account of the promises made unto their fathers; but you did deliver them, and punish the Egyptians.

And when men had corrupted the law of nature, and had sometimes regarded creation as the result of chance, and sometimes honored it more than they ought, and equalled it to the God of the universe, you did not, however, allow them to go astray, but did raise up your holy servant Moses, and by him did give the written law for the assistance of the law of nature, and did show that the creation was your work, and did banish away the errors of polytheism. You did adorn Aaron and his posterity with the priesthood, and did punish the Hebrews when they sinned, and receive them again when they returned to you.

You did punish the Egyptians with the ten plagues, and did divide the sea, and bring the Israelites through it, and drown and destroy the Egyptians who pursued them. You did sweeten the bitter water with wood; you did bring water out of the rock of stone: You did rain manna from heaven, and quails as meat out of the air; you did afford them a pillar of fire by night to give them light, and the pillar of a cloud by day to shade them from the heat; you did declare Joshua to be the general of the army, and did overthrow the seven nations of Canaan by him; you did divide Jordan, and dry up the rivers of Etham; you did overthrow walls without instruments or the hand of man.

For all these things, glory be to you, O Lord Almighty. The innumerable hosts of angels, archangels, thrones, dominions, principalities, dominations, and powers, your everlasting armies, adore you. The cherubim and the six-winged seraphim, with two wings covering their feet, with two their heads, and with two flying, say, together with myriad thousands of archangels, and ten thousand times ten thousand angels, incessantly, and with constant and loud voices, and let all the people say it with them: *Holy, holy, holy, Lord of hosts, heaven and earth are full of your glory; be blessed forever. Amen.*

The Celebrant continues:

For you are truly holy, and most holy, the highest and most highly exalted forever. Holy also is your only begotten Son our Lord and God, Jesus Christ, who in all things ministered to his God and Father, both in your varied creation and your appropriate providence, and has not overlooked lost mankind. But after the law of nature, after the exhortations in the Law, after the reproofs of the prophets and the government of the angels (when men had perverted both the natural and the written law, and had cast out of their mind the memory of the flood, the burning of Sodom, the plagues of Egypt, and the slaughters of the inhabitants of Palestine), all being just ready to perish in an unparalleled manner, he was pleased by your good will to become man, who was man's Creator; to be under the laws, who was the Legislator; to be a sacrifice, who was an High Priest; to be a sheep, who was the Shepherd.

And he appeased you, his God and Father, and reconciled you to the world, and freed all men from the wrath to come, and was made of a virgin, and was incarnate, being God the Word, the beloved Son, *the first-born of the whole creation,* and was, according to the prophecies which were foretold concerning him by himself, of the seed of David and Abraham, of the tribe of Judah. And he was made in the womb of a virgin, who formed all mankind that are born into the world; he who was without flesh took flesh; he who was begotten before time was born in time;

He lived holily, and taught according to the law; he drove away every sickness and every disease from men, and wrought signs and wonders among the people; and he was partaker of meat, and drink, and sleep, who nourishes all that stand in need of food, and fills every living creature with his goodness; He manifested his name to those that knew it not (*Ps.* 145, 16; *John*

17, 6); He drove away ignorance; he revived piety, and fulfilled your will; *he finished the work which you gave him to do (John 17, 4).*

And when he had set all these things right, he was seized by the hands of the ungodly, of the priests and the high priests, falsely so called, and of the disobedient people, by the betraying of him who was possessed of wickedness as with a confirmed disease; he suffered many things from them, and endured all sorts of ignominy by your permission; he was delivered to Pilate the governor, and he that was the Judge was judged, and he that was the Savior was condemned, he that was impassible was nailed to the cross, and he who was by nature immortal died, and he that is the giver of life was buried, that he might loose those for whose sake he came from suffering and rescue them from death, and might break the bonds of the devil, and deliver mankind from his deceit.

He arose from the dead the third day; and, when he had continued with his disciples forty days, he was taken up into the heavens, and sits at the right hand of you, who are his God and Father.

Anamnesis

Being mindful, therefore, of those things that he endured for our sake, we give you thanks, O God Almighty, not in such a manner as we ought, but as we are able, and fulfill his command:

For in the same night that he was betrayed, he took bread in his holy and undefiled hands, and, looking up to you his God and Father, he broke it, and gave it to his disciples, saying: This is the mystery of the New Covenant: take of it, and eat. This is my body, which is broken for many, for the remission of sins.

In like manner also he took the cup, and mixed it of wine and water, and sanctified it, and delivered it to them, saying: Drink ye all of this; for this is my blood which is shed for many, for the remission of sins: do this in remembrance of me. For as often as ye eat this bread and drink this cup, ye do show forth my death until I come (I *Cor.* 11, 26).

Being mindful, therefore, of his passion, and death, and resurrection from the dead, and return into the heavens, and his future second coming, when he is to come with glory and power to judge the living and the dead, and to recompense every one according to his works, we offer to you, our King and our God, according to his command, this bread and this cup, giving you thanks, through him, that you have thought us worthy to stand before you and to exercise the priesthood.

And we beseech you that you will mercifully look down upon these gifts which are here set before you, O God, who stands in need of none of our offerings. And do you accept them to the honor of your Christ.

Epiclesis

Send down upon this sacrifice your Holy Spirit, the Witness of the Lord Jesus' sufferings (I *Pet.* 5, 1), that he may consecrate this bread to be the body of your Christ, and the cup to be the blood of your Christ, that those who are partakers thereof may be strengthened for piety, may obtain the remission of their sins, may be delivered from the devil and his deceit, may be filled with the Holy Spirit, may be made worthy of your Christ, and may obtain eternal life upon your reconciliation to them, O Lord Almighty.

Litany Prayer

We further pray unto you, O Lord, for your holy Church spread from one end of the world to another, which you have purchased with the precious blood of your Christ, that you will preserve it unshaken and free from disturbance until the end of the world; for the universal episcopate which rightly handles the word of truth.

We further pray to you for me, who am nothing, who offer to you, for the whole priesthood, for the deacons and all the clergy, that you will make them wise, and replenish them with the Holy Spirit.

We further pray to you, O Lord, for the king and all in authority, for the whole army, that we may be peaceable, that so, spending the whole span of our life in peace and quiet, we may glorify you through Jesus Christ, who is our hope.

We further offer to you also for all those saints who have

pleased you from the beginning of the world—patriarchs, prophets, righteous men, apostles, martyrs, confessors, bishops, priests, deacons, sub-deacons, lectors, chanters, virgins, widows, and laity, with all whose names you know.

We further offer to you for this people, that you will render them, to the praise of your Christ, *a royal priesthood, a holy nation* (I *Pet.* 2, 9); for those that are in virginity and chastity; for the widows of the Church; for those in honorable marriage and child-bearing; for the infants of your people; that you will not permit any of us to become castaways.

We further beseech you also for this city and its inhabitants; for those that are sick; for those in bitter servitude; for those in banishment; for those in prison; for those that travel by water or by land; that you, the helper and assister of all men, will be their supporter.

We further beseech you for those that hate us and persecute us for your name's sake; for those that are without, and wander in error; that you will convert them to goodness, and pacify their anger.

We further also beseech you first for the catechumens of the Church, secondly, for those that are vexed by the adversary, and thirdly for our brethren the penitents, that you will perfect the first in the faith, that you will deliver the second from the energy of the evil one, and that you will accept the repentance of the last, and forgive both them and us our offenses.

We further offer to you also for clement weather, and the fertility of the fruits, that so, partaking perpetually of the good things derived from you, we may praise you without ceasing, who gave food to all flesh.

We further beseech you also for those who are absent for a just cause, that you will keep us all in piety, and gather us together in the kingdom of your Christ, the God of all sensible and intelligent nature, our King; that you would keep us immovable, without fault and irreproachable; for to you belongs all glory, and veneration, and thanksgiving, honor and adoration, the Father, Son, and Holy Spirit, both now and always, and for everlasting and endless ages forever. And let all the people say, Amen.
And let all the people say, *And with your spirit.*

3 *The Mass*

Final Litany of the Deacon

And let the deacon proclaim again:

Let us still further beseech God through his Christ, and let us beseech him by the gift which is offered to the Lord God, that the good God will accept it, through the meditation of his Christ, upon his heavenly altar, for a sweet-smelling savor.

Let us pray for this congregation and people.

Let us pray for every episcopate, every priest, all the deacons and ministers in Christ, for the whole congregation, that the Lord will keep and preserve them all.

Let us pray *for kings and those in authority* (I *Tim.* 2, 1-2), that they may administer our affairs in peace, that so we may have and lead a quiet and peaceable life in all godliness and honesty.

Let us be mindful of the holy martyrs: that we may be thought worthy to be partakers of their trial.

Let us pray for those that are departed in the faith.

Let us pray for clement weather and the perfect maturity of the fruits.

Let us pray for those that are newly baptized, that they may be strengthened in the faith.

Let us all pray for one another.

Raise us up, O God, by your grace.

Let us stand up, and dedicate ourselves to God, through His Christ.

And let the bishop say: O God, who are great, and whose name is great, who are great in counsel and mighty in works, the God and Father of your holy child Jesus, our Savior; look down upon us, and upon this your flock, which you have chosen by him to the glory of your name; and sanctify our body and soul, and grant us the favor to be made pure from all filthiness of flesh and spirit, and to obtain the good things laid up for us, and do not account any of us unworthy; but be you our comforter, helper, and protecter, through your Christ, with whom glory, honor, praise, glorification, and thanksgiving be to you and to the Holy Spirit forever.   Amen.

And after all have said Amen, let the deacon say: Let us pay attention!

Communion

And let the bishop speak thus to the people:
Holy things for holy persons.
And let the people answer:

There is One that is holy; there is one Lord,
one Jesus Christ, blessed forever,
to the glory of God the Father.   Amen.
Glory to God in the highest,
and on earth peace, good-will among men.
Hosanna to the son of David!
Blessed be He that comes in the name of the Lord,
The Lord is God, He has appeared to us.
Hosanna in the highest.

And after that, let the bishop partake, then the priests, and deacons, and sub-deacons, and the lectors and the chanters, and the ascetics; and then of the women, the deaconesses, and the virgins, and the widows; then the children; and then all the people in order, with reverence and godly fear, without tumult.

And let the bishop give the oblation, saying, *The body of Christ;* and let him that receives say, *Amen.*

And let the deacon take the cup; and when he gives it, say, *The blood of Christ, the cup of life;* and let him that drinks say, *Amen.*   And let the thirty-third psalm be said, while the rest are receiving; and when all, both men and women, have received, let the deacons put what remains in the tabernacle. And when the psalm is finished, let the deacon say: —

The Litany Prayer after the Communion

Now that we have received the precious body and the precious blood of Christ, let us give thanks to him who has thought us worthy to partake of these his holy mysteries; and let us beseech him that it may not be to us for condemnation, but for salvation, to the advantage of soul and body, to the preservation of piety, to the remission of sins, and to the life of the world to come.

Let us rise, and in the grace of Christ let us dedicate ourselves to God, to the only begotten God, and his Christ.

The Thanksgiving

And let the bishop give thanks: —

O Lord God Almighty, the Father of your Christ, your blessed Son, who hear those who rightly call upon you, who also know the supplications of those who are silent; we thank you that you have thought us worthy to partake of your holy mysteries, which you have bestowed upon us, for the plenitude of the faith, for the preservation of piety, for the remission of our offenses; for the name of your Christ is invoked upon us, and we are joined to you.

O you that have separated us from the conspiracy of the ungodly, unite us with those that are consecrated to you in holiness; confirm us in the truth, by the coming of your Holy Spirit; reveal to us what things we are ignorant of, supply what things we are defective in, confirm us in what things we already know.

Preserve the priests blameless in your worship; keep the kings in peace, and the rulers in righteousness, and the weather at a good temperature, the fruits in fertility, the world in your all-powerful providence; pacify the warring nations, convert those that are gone astray, sanctify your people, preserve those that are in virginity, keep in fidelity those that are in marriage, strengthen those that are in purity, bring the infants to complete age, confirm the newly initiated; instruct the catechumens, and render them worthy of initiation; and gather us all together into your kingdom of heaven, in Jesus Christ our Lord, with whom glory, honor, and worship be to you, in the Holy Spirit, forever. Amen.

Final Blessing

And the deacon will say: Bow down to God through his Christ, and receive the blessing.

And let the bishop add this prayer, and say:

O God Almighty, the true God, to whom nothing can be compared, who are everywhere, and present in all things, and are in nothing as one of the things themselves; who are not bounded by place, nor grown old by time; who are not terminated by ages, nor deceived by words; who are not subject to generation, and want no guardian; who are above all corruption, free from all change, and immutable by nature; who dwell in light inaccessible; who are by nature invisible, and yet are known to all reasonable natures who seek you with a good mind, and are comprehended by those that seek after you with a good mind; the God of Israel, your people which truly see, and which have believed in Christ:

Graciously hear me, for your name's sake, and bless those that bow down their heads unto you, and grant them the petitions of their hearts, which are for their good, and do not reject any one of them from your kingdom; but sanctify, guard, protect, and assist them; deliver them from the adversary and every enemy; keep their houses, and guard their comings in and their goings out.

For to you belongs the glory, praise, majesty, worship, and adoration, and to your Son Jesus, your Christ, our Lord and God and King, and to the Holy Spirit, now and always, forever and ever. Amen.

And the deacon shall say, *Depart in peace.*

DERIVATIVES FROM THE SYRIAN TYPE:

THE BYZANTINE LITURGIES

In the fourth century Asia Minor was subject to the influence of Antioch. In the metropolitan sees the liturgy assumed a special character, especially at Caesarea in Cappadocia. Basil borrowed the liturgy of St. James at Antioch which should have been substantially the same as that of the *Apostolic Constitutions* but underwent a considerable revision. He drastically revised the *anaphora* (between 364 and 379), shortening the text. The "Liturgy of St. Basil" was in general use in the East at first, but is now used only on the Sundays of Lent, on Holy Thursday, Holy Saturday, the eves of Christmas and Epiphany, and the first of January (feast of St. Basil).

Antioch and Caesarea sent as bishops to Constantinople Gregory of Nazianzus, Nectarius, and John Chrysostom, who brought with them the liturgy of Cappadocia composed by St. Basil. From Constantinople it spread through the whole Byzantine world until it was supplanted by the considerably shorter version called *the Liturgy of St. John Chrysostom* at the end of the fourth century. The latter is still in common use in the East at the present day. We find the themes already encountered in the *Apostolic Constitutions.*

THE ANAPHORA OF ST. BASIL [24]

Preface

It is right and proper and a fitting tribute to your majesty that we should give you thanks and glory, O God in very truth, and with pure hearts and humble minds offer you this sacrifice of praise, for you have given us knowledge of your truth.

Who can adequately tell the extent of your power, or sound your praises, or describe your wonders? Sovereign Ruler of all that is, Lord of heaven and earth and of all other creatures, visible and invisible: you sit on your glorious throne and look down into the depths; you are eternal and invisible, O Father of our Lord Jesus Christ; and he is the Image of your glory, the Seal that presents a faithful copy of your own nature, O Father; the living Word, truly God,[25] eternal Wisdom, Life, Source of holiness and power.

He is the true Light, and through him has been revealed the Holy Spirit, the Spirit of truth, the Spirit of adoption, earnest of the inheritance that is to come and foretaste of the blessings of eternity. He is the power that gives life, the fount whence holiness flows; and in the strength that comes from him, every creature endowed with mind and spirit sings your praises and continually gives you glory.

All your servants prostrate themselves before you: the angels, archangels, thrones, dominations, principalities, virtues and powers. The cherubim with their many eyes stand round you, the six-winged seraphim too, hiding their faces with two of their wings, hiding their feet with two more, with the other two flying. They cry out to one another, never resting their voices, never sinking into silence as they proclaim your glory and say:

---

24. See W. E. Pitt, "The Origin of the Anaphora of St. Basil," **Jour. Eccl. Hist.** 12 (1961) 1-13.

25. The evident stress here laid on the divinity of Christ was prompted by the Christological controversies.

Sanctus

Holy, holy, holy is the God of hosts.   Heaven and earth are full of your glory.   Hosannah in high heaven.   Blessed is he that comes in the name of the Lord.   Hosannah in high heaven.

The priest continues:

Holy, holy, holy you are indeed, O Lord our God; no limit can be set to the splendor of your holiness; wise and judicious are all your ordinances.

The Works of the Father

You fashioned man from the dust of the earth, did him the honor of making him in your own image, set him in a delightful garden and promised that if he did what you told him, he should live for ever and enjoy the blessings of eternity. But he disobeyed your orders, true God though you were and his Creator; he was led astray by the cunning of the serpent and, becoming the victim of his own sins, was made subject to death. By that decree of yours, O God, he was driven out of paradise into this world and returned to the earth from which he had been taken.

But you provided a means of salvation for him: it would be possible for him to be born again through your Christ. You were too kind to cast off for ever the creature you had made; you promoted his welfare in many different ways, so great was your mercy. You sent him prophets; you worked miracles through the saints, who generation after generation gave you pleasure; you gave the law for our assistance; you set angels over us to guard us.

The Mission of the Son

When the appointed time came, you spoke to us through your only Son, through whom you had created this temporal world. He is the radiance of your splendor and the full expression of your being; he upholds all things by his powerful word; he thought it no usurpation to claim equality with God, for he was God himself from all eternity. Your Son appeared on earth and lived among men; he took flesh of Mary, the virgin; he accepted the lot of a slave and assumed the body that is the sign of man's humble condition, as a prelude to assuming us into his own glorious body.

Since through man sin came into the world and through sin death, your only Son, who was in your bosom throughout eternity, yet was born of a woman, was pleased to condemn sin in flesh of his own that they who died because of Adam were to receive life because of Christ. He lived in the world as a citizen of it and told us what to do to obtain salvation; he placed us where the errors of idolatry could not reach us and he taught us to know you, the true God; so that he acquired in us a chosen people, a royal priesthood, a consecrated nation.

He cleansed us with water and sanctified us with the Holy Spirit; he gave himself to ransom us from death, whose prisoners we were—for we had been sold, because we had sinned. From the cross he went down into hell, bent on giving fulfilment himself to every single thing. On the third day he rose again, opening the way for all flesh to follow him (for it could not be that the Source of life should fall a prey to corruption); he became the first-fruits of them that had fallen asleep, the first-born of the dead: in every way he was to have the primacy. He went up to heaven and took his seat at your Majesty's right hand, in the highest place; and he will come back and give us all the reward our conduct deserves.[26] He left us these reminders of his saving passion which we have set before you.

Institution of the Eucharist

As he was going, of his own accord, to that ever memorable death which brought us life, on the night when he gave himself up that the world might live, he took bread in his hands, those pure and holy hands, and offering it to you, O Father, gave thanks, blessed, consecrated and broke it, and gave it to his holy disciples and apostles, saying:

Take it and eat it: this is my body, broken for you, to remit your sins.

---

26. Note the insertion of an explicit confession of faith in the anaphora.

In the same way, he took the chalice with the fruit of the vine; he diluted it, gave thanks, blessed and consecrated it, and gave it to his holy disciples and apostles, saying:

Drink some of it, all of you: this is my blood, shed for you and for the multitudes, to remit your sins. Do this in memory of me. Every time you eat this bread and drink this cup, you will be proclaiming my death and confessing my resurrection.

Anamnesis

We too, then, Lord, call to mind his saving sufferings and his life-giving cross, the three days he spent in the tomb, his resurrection from the dead, his going up to heaven, where he sits at your right hand, O Father, and the second visit he has yet to make us, an occasion of glory and fear. And of all the things that are yours we offer you these, which are yours especially.

The people:

For all your blessings, for every one, we sing your praises, bless you, thank you, and offer you our prayers, O God.

The priest:

Therefore we too, all-holy Lord—whom you have enabled to serve at your holy altar, not for any virtue of ours (for never in our lives have we done any good) but because your mercy and compassion are so great—we too make bold to approach your altar and offer you the sacrament of the holy body and blood of your Christ.

We beg and beseech you, holiest of all the holy, in your kindness and benevolence send your Holy Spirit upon us and upon these gifts, to bless and sanctify them. May he make this bread the precious body of our Lord and Savior, Jesus Christ—

The deacon:

Amen.

The priest:

—and this chalice the precious blood of our Lord and Savior, Jesus Christ,

The deacon:

Amen.

The priest:

—shed that the world may have life.

The deacon:

Amen.

The priest:

May all of us that share the one bread and the one chalice be united with one another and have fellowship in the one Holy Spirit. May the reception of the holy body and blood of your Christ bring judgment and condemnation to none of us. May we find mercy and grace with all the saints who have ever given you pleasure since the beginning of time.

Then comes the Great Intercession.

And grant that with one voice and heart we may praise and glorify your name in the fulness of its holiness and splendor, O Father, Son and Holy Spirit, now and for ever, age after age. Amen.

THE ANAPHORA OF ST. JOHN CHRYSOSTOM

Preface

It is right and proper that we should give you praise and thanks and worship wherever your power is felt, *for no word can express you, O God, no mind understand you, no eye behold you, no intelligence grasp you—you who have existed from all eternity and have always been the same*: [27] you and your only Son and your Holy Spirit. You it was that drew us out of nothingness into existence, and when we fell, raised us up again; you spared no effort until you had brought us to heaven and bestowed upon us the kingdom that is to come.

We thank you for all these blessings—you and your only Son and your Holy Spirit; we thank you, too, for all the other blessings you have given us, *those we are aware of and those of which we know nothing, those that we see and those that we cannot see. We thank you for this offering, which you have consented to accept at our hands,* O God round whom *the archangels* throng *in their thousands and the angels in their tens of thousands,* the cherubim *also* and the seraphim, each with his six wings and his many eyes, each borne aloft and flying, each one chanting the hymn of triumph. Loud and full it echoes as they say:

The people:

Holy, holy, holy is the Lord of hosts. Heaven and earth are full of your glory. Hosannah in high heaven. Blessed is he that comes in the name of the Lord. Hosannah in high heaven.

The priest:

With these blessed powers we too cry out to you, Lord, for we know how you love men. Holy you are, we say, all-holy: you and your only Son and your Holy Spirit. Holy you are, and splendid indeed is your glory. Such was your love for the world that you gave up your only Son; no one who believed in him was to perish: they were all to have eternal life.

So, then, he came; and when he had done all that he was meant to do for us, on the night when he was given up—or rather, when he gave himself up—he took bread in his holy hands, gave thanks, blessed it, broke it and gave it to his disciples and apostles, saying:

Take it and eat it: this is my body, broken for you, to remit your sins.

When the meal was over, he did the same with the chalice, saying:

---

27. The passages in italics are later additions.

Drink some of it, all of you: this is my blood, the blood of the new testament, shed for you and for the multitudes, to remit your sins.

Anamnesis

Calling, then, to mind, the holy rite he told us to perform and all that has been done for us; remembering the cross, the burial, the resurrection on the third day, Christ's going up to heaven, where he sits, Father, at your right hand, and the second visit he will come again in his glory to make us: of all the things that are yours we offer you these, which are yours especially; gladly we offer them to you.

The people:

We sing your praises, bless you, thank you and offer you our prayers, O God.

Epiclesis

The priest:

We offer you, too, this spiritual sacrifice, which requires no shedding of blood. We beg and beseech you, we implore you, send down your holy Spirit upon us and upon these gifts; make this bread the precious body of your Christ (*send your Holy Spirit to change it*) and make what is in this chalice your Christ's precious blood (*send your Holy Spirit to change that too*). To those who receive them may these gifts bring spiritual purity, forgiveness of sins, the bestowal of the Holy Spirit, full possession of the kingdom of heaven and a confident approach to you; may they not lead to judgment and condemnation.

We offer you [28] this spiritual sacrifice for those of our ancestors and fathers who had the faith and are now at rest; in memory of the patriarchs, prophets, apostles, preachers, evangelists, martyrs and confessors and those who lived continently; and for the spirits of all the just who died in possession of the faith.

---

28. The following passage has no parallel in the Syriac.

Especially do we offer it in honor of our lady Mary, the all-holy, unspotted, more than blessed, glorious, mother of God and ever virgin.

At this point the diptychs containing the names of the dead are read.

We offer the sacrifice in honor of Saint John, the prophet, precursor and baptist; of the holy apostles, glorious and illustrious; of Saint N., whose feast we are celebrating; and of all your other saints. May their prayers prevail upon you to regard us with favor. Remember, too, all who have fallen asleep confident of rising again and living for all eternity; give them rest where the light shines from your face.

Again we pray you, remember, Lord, all the orthodox bishops who faithfully teach your word, the true word, remember all their priests, the deacons serving Christ, and every other degree of the hierarchy.

Again, we offer you this spiritual sacrifice for the whole world, for the holy, catholic, and apostolic Church, for those whose lives are dignified by chastity, for our eminently faithful and Christ-loving kings, and for all their household and army. Grant them a peaceful reign, O Lord, that sharing in their tranquillity we too may live calm and tranquil lives, with devotion and dignity.

Here the diptychs with the names of the living are read.

Remember, Lord, the city where we live, and every other city and district; remember those dwelling in them according to the orthodox faith.

Remember, Lord, those who are travelling, whether by land or by sea; remember the sick, the suffering and those who are held in captivity; remember to grant them all salvation.

Remember, Lord, all who are bearing fruit and doing good works in your holy churches and seeing to the needs of the poor; and send down your mercy on us all.

And grant that with one voice and heart we may praise and glorify your name in the fulness of its holiness and splendor, O Father, Son and Holy Spirit, now and for ever, age after age. Amen.

PART TWO

Commentary on Biblical Texts

1. THE PASSOVER NARRATIVE
   Exodus 12, 1-12; 14.
2. THE INSTITUTION OF THE EUCHARIST
   Matthew 26, 26-29.
3. THE BREAD OF LIFE
   John 6, 48-59.
4. CELEBRATION OF THE EUCHARIST AT CORINTH
   I Cor. 10, 16-17; 11, 17-34.

As stated in the introduction, the eucharistic catechesis applied itself to the books of the Old and New Testament, particularly to the Institution narrative found in the Liturgy of the Eucharist.

1. *From the Jewish Pasch to the Eucharistic Pasch*

It was Christ's intention to situate the Last Supper in the perspective of the Jewish Passover: "I have greatly desired to eat this passover with you before I suffer: for I say to you that I will eat of it no more, until it has been fulfilled in the kingdom of God" (*Luke* 22, 15-16). John testifies to the same thing: "Before the feast of the Passover, Jesus, knowing that the hour had come for him to pass out of this world to the Father . . ." (*John* 13, 1). And St. Paul says: "Christ our passover has been sacrificed" (I *Cor.* 5, 7). The Apocalypse establishes a parallel between the deliverance of the people of the Exodus and the celebration of the Christian liturgy, the sacrament of the new and definitive covenant. The Fathers, e.g., pseudo-Chrysostom and Ephrem, allude to this.

At the Last Supper Jesus, like the master of the house, comments on the Jewish delivery. He utilizes ritual prayers. He gives thanks; the hour is come to pass from this world to the Father. The time of preparation is past, the hour of fulfillment has arrived.

2. *The Institution of the Eucharist*

In the Jewish pasch the immolation preceded the meal. At the Supper the meal preceded the immolation of the morrow and took its meaning from it: the oblation of the cross is the work confided to Christ, the action *par excellence* of His life, sorrowful but efficacious, the one which re-establishes the covenant between God and his people and congregates men without distinction in the universal community of the Church. The sacrifice of the cross, ritualized at the Supper, achieved in the bare simplicity of its action the whole history of salvation and is the consummation of the life and teaching of Jesus.

At the moment where the Synoptics recount the Institution, the new economy is established, the victory of the risen Christ attesting that the work of restoration and reconciliation has been realized. The celebration, then, expresses the act of thanksgiving in joy; it is the sacrament of the Eucharist of the people of the New Covenant, en route for the final stage of history.

3. *The Bread of Life*

Chapter Six of St. John's Gospel, frequently commented on by the Fathers, is a catechesis which presents baptism and the Eucharist as a new Exodus. The bread of the Eucharist fulfills the promise and the figure of the manna in the desert. John calls it *living* bread, *shed* blood, to express the sacrificial character of the mystery.

The death of Christ represents the rejection of the Messiah by his people, and also the victorious struggle against the prince of darkness. The paschal meal, like the exaltation of the cross, is for John already triumphant: love conquers hate and liberates the messianic people in the blood and death.

Finally, the eucharistic pasch celebrates the great delivery of the history of salvation. It is preeminently the eucharistic act of the Coming, the passage from figure to reality, from old to new covenant. The Eucharist, in the Johannine perspective, is the consummation of the redemptive incarnation and the cause of its fruitfulness. He who eats it is established, so to speak, in the life of God: *He who eats my flesh abides in me and I in him.* By this compenetration the faithful, like the Church, is "incorpo-

rated" in the Son of God. Augustine and Cyril of Alexandria
furnish us with especially fine developments of this Johannine
theme.

4. *Celebration of the Eucharist at Corinth*

St. Paul speaks frequently of the Eucharist in his Epistle to
the faithful of Corinth and enables us to gauge its place in the
life of an apostolic community.   It links the celebration with
tradition: *For I myself have received from the Lord what I also
delivered to you* (I *Cor.* 11, 23).   For St. Paul the sacrificial meal
is at once a memorial of (which renders active and present) the
death of Chrsit and the anticipation of his return in glory.

Another text from the same Epistle, commented on by John
Chrysostom, situates the Christian rite in the continuation of the
people of the Exodus which prefigured it: *And all ate the same
spiritual food—they drank from the spiritual rock which followed
them, and the rock was Christ* (I *Cor.* 10, 3-4).

Idol offerings, or food sacrificed to idols, provide St. Paul
with an occasion to establish a parallel between pagan and Christian
sacrifices.   As the pagan ones received their sacred character from
the altar, the body and blood of Christ are consecrated on the
"table of the Lord."   The one bread assembles the Church and
reduces to unity the multiplicity of members because, although
broken, it remains ideally one: it is the body of Christ.   The
Eucharist makes perceptible to Paul the mystery of the Church:
we form one body in living the same life of Christ.

1. THE PASSOVER NARRATIVE
EXODUS 12, 1-12, 14

And the Lord said to Moses and Aaron in the land of Egypt:
"This month shall be to you the beginning of months: it shall be
the first in the months of the year.   Speak ye to the whole assembly
of the children of Israel, and say to them: on the tenth day of
this month let every man take a lamb by their families and houses.
But if the number be less than may suffice to eat the lamb, he
shall take unto him his neighbor that joins to his house, according to the number of souls which may be enough to eat the lamb.
And it shall be a lamb without blemish, a male of one year:
according to which rite you shall also take a kid.   And you shall

keep it until the fourteenth day of this month: and the whole multitude of the children of Israel shall sacrifice it in the evening. And they shall take of the blood thereof, and put it upon both the side posts, and on the upper door posts of the houses, wherein they shall eat it.   And they shall eat the flesh that night roasted at the fire, and unleavened bread with wild lettuce.   You shall not eat thereof anything raw, nor boiled in water, but only roasted at the fire: you shall eat the head with the feet and entrails thereof. Neither shall there remain anything of it until morning.   If there be anything left, you shall burn it with fire.   And thus you shall eat it: you shall gird your reins, and you shall have your shoes on your feet, holding staves in your hands, and you shall eat in haste; for it is the Passover (that is the Passage) of the Lord . . . . And this day shall be for a memorial to you: and you shall keep it a feast to the Lord in your generations with an everlasting observance."

CHRIST IS THE PASCHAL LAMB — I CORINTHIANS 5, 7-8

Purge out the old leaven, that you may be a new dough, as you really are without leaven.   For Christ, our passover, has been sacrificed.   Therefore let us keep festival, not with the leaven of malice and wickedness, but with unleavened bread of sincerity and truth.

PSEUDO-CHRYSOSTOM [1]

On the Pasch

The paschal lamb without blemish signified the holiness of Christ; the salvation of the first-born achieved by the paschal sacrifice signified the salvation of men in the passion of Christ and the supper signified sanctification as we have said already. Today when we touch on the rest of the Law we must consider, first, how the one who seeks to be sanctified should prepare himself; secondly, how he ought to approach Holy Communion; and thirdly, how he ought to live once he has entered into participation and communion with what is holy.

---

1. For text, cf. PG 59, 729-732; SC 36, 103-117; Trans., T. Halton.

1. *Preparation involves circumcision of the flesh*

The Law, in speaking of circumcision, figuratively describes the preparation which the person should make who is approaching Communion, saying: *These are the regulations for the Passover. No foreigner may partake of it. However, any slave who has been bought for money may partake of it provided you have first circumcised him* (*Exod.* 12, 43-44). Circumcision at that time was partial and its utility was not self-evident. A man in virtue of circumcision was no better than the uncircumcised. On the contrary God addressed this reproach to the Israelites: *All the people are uncircumcised of the flesh, but the people of Israel are uncircumcised of heart* (*Jer.* 9, 25). True circumcision, however, concerns the whole flesh: it puts the circumcised of heart and body on friendly and familiar terms with God. We have inherited this covering of the flesh and we need circumcision; this was hinted at in advance by the Law in circumcising the genitals, taking the symbols of generation as symbols of the veil over our soul as a consequence of being born in sin.

No one, then, if he is not circumcised from the ways of the flesh, can come to intimate communion with Christ; but it is we *who are his circumcision,* says the followers of Christ, *we who are the servants of the spirit of God without suffering in the flesh* (*Phil.* 3, 3).

A heart stripped of all carnal desires can render true worship to God, and can be in communion with Christ spiritually. The passion of Christ is the principal of this circumcision. He laid down his flesh for us, and has even accepted circumcision itself for us; and the mystery [2] is typified in us by baptism and realized by a truly Christian life. *In him you have been circumcised with a circumcision not wrought by hand, but through putting off the body of the flesh, a circumcision which is of Christ. For you were buried together with him in baptism* (*Col.* 2, 11, 12). As long as you do not "put off" your fleshly ways, you will be an alien and a stranger and you should not participate in or communicate with what is holy, Christ come down from heaven. To approach what is from heaven, you must be heavenly yourself, and heavenly implies rejection of what is earthly.

---

2. "Mystery" has the same meaning here as our word "sacrament."

2. *Dispositions for approaching Communion*

Thus you will approach and commune with Christ after circumcising the old man beforehand in the grace of baptism and in the love of spiritual works. But we must see in the second place the prescriptions of the Law for those people who participate in the Pasch in order to know what we must be like ourselves who receive Christ. It is said, *This is how you are to eat it; with your loins girt, sandals on your feet and your staff in hand* (*Exod.* 12, 11). The garb of travellers, girt, travelling light, indicates that we ought to be ready to run unimpeded to the promise of God, just as then Israel, a ready traveller, set out for the fair promised land.

Notice the superiority of the spiritual traveller to the earlier one, not just hastening to an earthly promised land, not just pursuing transient blessings, not just exchanging one country for another, Judea for Egypt. On the contrary, how does one traveller describe his journey? *Forgetting what is behind, I strain forward to what is before. I press on toward the goal, to the prize of God's heavenly call* (*Phil.* 3, 13-14).

The loins are *girded with truth* (*Eph.* 6, 14) according to the Apostle. You will be well girded for the good race if like David you regard all things as *vanity and falsehood* (cf. *Ps.* 4, 2), if you seek only the truth that is to come and desire it with all your heart.

Having feet shod with the readiness of the gospel of peace (*Eph.* 6, 15), we are ready for every good race through which we confirm for ourselves our peace with God as the Apostle says: *Let us have peace with God through our Lord Jesus Christ* (*Rom.* 5, 1); and: *Let us run with patience to the fight set before us* (*Heb.* 12, 1), and *I so run as to obtain the prize* (I *Cor.* 9, 24).

Staff in hand: faith and hope in God which are applied to our soul and do not allow us to fall in tribulations as Paul has said, but confirm us and make us unshakable.

Eat in haste; it is the passover of the Lord. It is nourishment without delicacy or luxury, not for races who are sluggish or somnolent, but alert and prompt, because the passover of the avenging destroyer is upon us and the Lord gives us this gift. Therefore it says: *It is the Pasch of the Lord;* which another translator [3] reads: *It is the Passover of the Lord.*

---

3. The Aquila translation.

3. *Conduct after Communion*

After such reception of the divine food, let us examine the third point: What kind of life should one lead who has partaken of this holy nourishment? The unleavened bread and the days of the unleavened bread provide the answer. Let the Jews be preoccupied with their days of unleavened bread and let them feel that these seven days provide something wonderful for them, because they do not eat or have leavened bread. They have nothing to show for this, for it is a type of the future not a truth in its own right.

But let you look on the unleavened bread as has been foretold by the apostle and explained by us as the pure soul free of all evil, the new conduct which holds on to none of the ancient evil, to which the saying seems especially applicable: *Anyone who eats leavened bread shall be cut off from the community of Israel* (*Exod.* 12, 19). For a return to the old ways of wickedness spells destruction for him who has passed to a new life; *for if you live according to the flesh you will die* (*Rom.* 8, 13).

What do the seven days symbolize, *the seven days during which you will eat unleavened bread?* (*Exod.* 12, 15) The seven days denote the totality of time. The first day returns after the seventh, which is the Sabbath day, and so there is a recurrence of a cycle of seven days. You must live then for all time *in simplicity and sincerity* (II *Cor.* 1, 12), a truly salutary attitude: for if *by the spirit you put to death the deeds of the flesh you will live* (*Rom.* 8, 13). Simple is the way of life of the man who does not seek after the things of the flesh; he is without guile, without malice, without evil, without bitterness.

And why has Scripture given to the first day or the seventh the epithet "holy": *And the first day shall be called holy, and the seventh day will be called holy to you* (*Exod.* 12, 16). It is because the first day represents the beginning of time, when we were sanctified by the coming of the Holy Spirit, while the seventh day marks the end when we are freed from the body and rejoin Christ to dwell with the Lord, quitting this earthly exile and passing completely to what is holy: *To remain in the body is to live in exile far from the Lord* (II *Cor.* 5, 6).

4. *Observance of the Sabbath*

The Law demands that no work be done on these holy days: *no work may be done then* (*Exod.* 20, 10). We see, then, that the soul should not weary itself with earthly concerns, nor endure a slavery incompatible with the service of God. The only works on which the soul should employ its zeal and occupy its efforts are those which further its spiritual good. This has been signified to us in the words: *but what every one must eat that only may be prepared by you* (*Exod.* 12, 16). To make us understand that the legal observance of rest is to be interpreted of works which lead to vanity, not those which contribute to our spiritual good, he addresses this question to the Pharisees: *Is it lawful on the Sabbath to do good or to do evil? to save a life or to destroy it?* (*Luke* 6, 9).

If you wish to observe the sabbath in all justice and according to Christ, and the rest which is enjoined on the feast, then abstain from concern and from worldly tasks, that your thoughts and actions may be consecrated to God and to the care of your soul, and so that you will observe a truly holy sabbath: the feast that you celebrate will become holy, an image of that celebrated in the presence of Christ, to whom be glory for ever and ever, Amen.

2. THE INSTITUTION OF THE EUCHARIST [4]

Saint Luke

And having taken bread, he gave thanks and broke, and gave it to them, saying, "This is my body, which is being given for you; do this in remembrance of me." In like manner he took also the cup after the supper, saying, "This cup is the new covenant in my blood, which shall be shed for you."

Saint Mark

And while they were eating, Jesus took bread, and blessing it, he broke and gave it to them, and said, "Take; this is my body."

---

4. Luke 22, 19-20; Mark 14, 22-24; Matt. 26, 26-29; I Cor. 11, 23-25.

And taking a cup and giving thanks, he gave it to them, and they all drank of it; and he said to them, "This is my blood of the new covenant, which is being shed for many."

Saint Matthew

And while they were at supper, Jesus took bread, and blessed and broke, and gave it to his disciples, and said, "Take and eat; this is my body." And taking a cup, he gave thanks and gave it to them, saying, "All of you drink of this; for this is my blood of the new covenant, which is being shed for many unto the forgiveness of sins."

Saint Paul

The Lord Jesus, on the night in which he was betrayed, took bread, and giving thanks broke, and said, "This is my body which shall be given up for you; do this in remembrance of me." In like manner also the cup, after he had supped, saying, "This cup is the new covenant in my blood; do this as often as you drink it, in remembrance of me."

EPHRAEM († 373)

Ephraem, the most celebrated Doctor of the Syrian church, was born in Nisibis, north-west of Mossoul, in Mesopotamia. He wrote in Syriac. His immense productivity in poetry and theology has earned him the title, "Lyre of the Holy Spirit." A witness to the Eastern catechesis, he is closer to Jewish than to Greek antecedents.

His "Mimré"—of which we publish a text commenting on the Last Supper—enables us to form an idea of a literary *genre* at once poetical and lyrical, the "inspired" homily which already existed in the synagogue.

MIMRÉ 4: ON THE PASSION [5]

When the Scriptures were fulfilled according to which Jesus was to take the form of a slave, after he became the slave of the

---

5. Edition Lamy, **Sti Ephrem syri hymni et sermones,** 1, 413; Trans., T. Halton.

apostles and abased himself to wash and dry their feet, when he had persuaded them to learn humility themselves and teach it to others, then Jesus concluded a second covenant to abolish the ancient pasch; he instituted a new pasch for all the people unto eternal life.

Consecration of the Bread

Jesus our Lord took bread in his hands—at the beginning it was only bread—blessed it, making the sign of the cross over it, consecrated it in the name of the Father and of the Holy Spirit. Then he broke and distributed it in pieces to his disciples, in his bounteous mercy calling bread his living body and filling it with himself and his Holy Spirit; stretching out his hand he gave his disciples the bread which his right hand had consecrated; take it, he said, eat all of this which my word has consecrated. That which I have now given you is not just bread, believe me; take it, eat it, do not break it in pieces. I have called it and it really is my body. The smallest part of this particle can sanctify thousands of souls and is sufficient to give life to those who receive it. Receive; eat it with faith, and without hesitation, because it is my body, and he who eats it with faith receives with it the fire of the Holy Spirit. For him who eats it without faith it is merely ordinary bread; but he who eats with faith the bread consecrated in my name, if he is pure maintains his purity, and if he is a sinner obtains his pardon. He who spurns, despises, and outrages it, let him be certain that he outrages the Son who has called the bread his body and effected this transformation in it.

Take and eat all of you, and eat with it the Holy Spirit, for it is truly my body, and he who eats it will live forever. This is the bread from heaven; the bread come down from on high. This manna which the Israelites have eaten in the desert, this manna which they collected and which they had spurned although it had fallen on them from heaven, was a figure of the spiritual bread which you now have received; *take and eat all of you,* for the bread you eat is my body, a true source of forgiveness. *I am the bread of life.*

The Prophecy of Isaiah

I am the burning coal which touched and sanctified the lips of Isaiah (*Isa.* 6, 6), I who am now carried to you as bread and sanctify you. The prophet saw a pincers seize the burning coal from the altar; I have been prefigured in this raised symbol. The prophecy has preceded the event. Isaiah saw me as you see me now raising my hand and offering the living bread to your lips. The pincers is my right hand; the seraphim is myself; the burning coal is my body; Isaiah is all of you; the altar is this table; the temple is the Supper room; the master is myself. Here is the fulfillment of the prophecy of old. It is of my spirit that Isaiah has received, of me he has spoken.

The Exclusion of Judas

After the disciples had eaten the new, holy bread and had grasped by faith that they had eaten the body of Christ, Jesus proceeded to give an extended explanation of the whole sacrament. *He took the chalice of wine* mingled with water; then he blessed it, making the sign of the cross over it, consecrated it and said, *This is my blood which is about to be shed.* Stretching his hand toward Simon he presented the chalice to him so that he might be the first to drink the divine blessing; then he presented it to his neighbor. They all approached and drank; all, that is to say, of the eleven without distinction. Judas approached to receive the consecrated bread as his colleagues had done, but Jesus dipped the bread in water and gave it to him, in this way washing away and removing the blessing, and separating from the others the piece given to Judas. By that the disciples knew that Judas would betray him. Jesus then dipped his bread to remove the consecration before giving it to him. And so Judas did not drink of the cup of life. Understanding by this dipping in water that he was unworthy to receive the author of life, Judas, irritated and fired with anger of the sort which does not drink of the chalice of the blood of Jesus, [6] went out and without seeing the consecrated cup betook himself to those who were going to crucify Christ. The devil hastened to separate Iscariot from his colleagues so that he might not participate in the living and lifegiving sacrament.

The Consecration of the Wine

When the disciples had received from the right hand of Jesus the cup of salvation, they approached and all drank of it in turn.

---

6. An exegesis not commonly accepted, but peculiar to Ephrem.

In giving them the cup to drink Christ explained to them that the chalice which they were drinking was his blood: *This is my blood which shall be shed for you. Take and drink you all. This is the new covenant in my blood: do this in remembrance of me* (*Luke* 22, 19 f). When you are united in the Church in every country in my name, do what I have done in remembrance of me. Eat my body and drink my blood, a covenant new and old. My Father has sent his ark in the clouds in order to keep at a distance the waters of the deluge (cf. *Gen.* 9, 13-17) by means of this visible ark. I am the son of the living Father descended after five thousand years from heaven to make with my church a new covenant, to abolish through the memorial of my body and blood the judgment of destruction levelled by me against the impious who offend me as in former times.

The New Covenant

Our Lord gave to his disciples his final teaching in life this evening when he distributed his body to them and made them drink his blood. This was a perfect evening when Christ completed the true Pasch. This was the evening of evenings on which Christ put the seal to his teaching, the evening when obscurity vanished and darkness changed to light, when the fourteenth moon changed to the day of the new sun. The Lord had ordained that each year on the 14th of Nisan [7] the synagogue would immolate a lamb and prepare the unleavened bread. He laid down a law for his church, the same evening of this pasch, to make as a memorial of the lamb the Son of our God who before immolating himself for us gave us his body and blood. O evening ever celebrated, during which the mysteries have been explained, the Old Covenant sealed, and the Church of the nations enriched! Blessed is that evening, blessed the time during which the Supper has been consecrated! Blessed be the table which is become an altar for the apostles! During the Supper our Lord produced spiritual nourishment and blended with this nourishment a heavenly drink as Isaiah had predicted (*Isa.* 6, 6). He took the nature of a slave to fulfill the oracle of the son of Amos.

---

7. **Exod.** 12, 18. Nisan corresponded to March-April.

The Greatest Humility

During this same supper the universal teacher discoursed on humility, on the occasion of the discussion that followed at table concerning which of them was the greatest. He who knows all secret things penetrated their thoughts and said to them with persuasiveness and without reproach, with kindness and without haughtiness, *the kings of the Gentiles lord it over them and they who exercise authority over them are called Benefactors.* For you, that it may not be similar, do not be like the rest of nations. *But let him who is greatest among you become as the least and him who is the chief as the servant (Luke 22, 25).* You know that I, being your Lord and Master, am the greatest. Now I have chosen you as disciples: receive and keep my commandments. Because you have been constantly with me in my trials I have given you the promise that my Father has made to me. I will give to you the kingdom of heaven, I will heap up for you delicacies on my table, and the heavenly virtues will be in ecstasy. You will not eat and drink with me if you are not my disciples. I will set you as judges over twelve cities, and I will make the twelve tribes of Israel appear before you. You will judge your brothers in my place and pronounce sentence upon them. Such were the words of Jesus. After the Eucharist they left and went to the mount of Olives, that all the prophecies of Scripture might be fulfilled.

SAINT JOHN CHRYSOSTOM

HOMILY 82 ON MATTHEW [8]
(Matt. 26, 26-28)

And while they were at supper, Jesus took bread, and blessed, and broke, and gave it to his disciples, and said, Take and eat; This is my body. Then taking a cup, he gave thanks, and gave it to them, saying, All of you drink of this; this is my blood of the New Covenant, which is being shed for many unto the forgiveness of sins (Matt. 26, 26-28).

---

8. For text cf. MG 57, 737-746. English trans.: NPNF (Ser. 1) 10, 491-97.

1. How great is the blindness of the traitor! Even partaking
of the mysteries, he remained the same; and admitted to the most
holy table, he changed not. And this Luke shows by saying that
after this Satan entered into him, not as despising the Lord's body,
but thenceforth laughing to scorn the traitor's shamelessness.
For indeed his sin became greater from both causes, as well in that
he came to the mysteries with such a disposition, as that having
approached them, he did not become better, either from fear, or
from the benefit, or from the honor.

But Christ forbade him not, although he knew all things, so
that you might learn that he omits none of the things that pertain
to correction. Wherefore both before this, and after this, he
continually admonished him, and checked him, both by deeds,
and by words; both by fear, and by kindness; both by threatening,
and by honor. But none of these things withdrew him from the
grievous pest.

Wherefore thenceforth he leaves him, and by the mysteries
again reminds the disciples of his being slain, and in the midst of
the meal his discourse is of the cross, by the continual repeating
of the prediction, making his passion easy to receive. For if,
when so many things had been done and foretold, they were
troubled; if they had heard none of these things, what would
they not have felt?

And as they were eating, He took bread and broke it.

From Old to New Testament

Why can it have been that he ordained this sacrament, then,
at the time of the Passover? That you might learn from everything, both that he is the lawgiver of the Old Testament, and that
the things therein are foreshadowed because of these things.
Therefore, I say, where the type is, there he puts the truth.

But the evening is a sure sign of the fullness of times, and
that the things were now come to the very end.

And He gives thanks, to teach us how we ought to celebrate
this sacrament, and to show that he comes to the passion without
reluctance, and to teach us to bear whatever we may suffer thank-
fully, thence also suggesting good hopes. For if the type was
a deliverance from such bondage, how much more will the truth
set free the world, and be delivered up for the benefit of our race!

Wherefore, I would add, neither did he appoint the sacrament before this, but when henceforth the rites of the law were to cease. And thus the very chief of the feasts he brings to an end, removing them to another most awful table, and he says, *Take, eat, This is my body, which is broken for many.*

And how were they not confounded at hearing this? Because he had previously told them many great things concerning this. Wherefore he establishes that no more, for they had heard it sufficiently, but he speaks of the cause of his passion, namely, the *taking away of sins.* And he calls it *blood of a New Testament,* that of the undertaking, the promise, the new law. For this he undertook also of old, and this comprises the Testament that is in the new law. And just as the Old Testament had sheep and bullocks, so this has the Lord's blood.

Hence also he shows that he is soon to die, wherefore also he made mention of a *Testament,* and he reminds them also of the former Testament, for that also was dedicated with blood. And again he tells the cause of his death, *which is shed for many for the remission of sins;* and he adds, *Do this in remembrance of me.* See how he removes and draws them off from Jewish customs. For just as you did that, he says, in remembrance of the miracles in Egypt, so do this likewise in remembrance of me. That was shed for the preservation of the first-born, this for the remission of the sins of the whole world. For, *This,* says he, *is my blood, which is shed for the remission of sins.*

But this he said, indicating thereby, that his passion and his cross as a mystery, by this too again comforting his disciples. And just as Moses says, *This shall be to you for an everlasting memorial (Exod.* 3, 15), so he says too, *in remembrance of me, until I come.*[9] Therefore he also says, *With desire I have desired to eat this passover (Luke* 22, 15), that is, to deliver you the new rites, and to give a passover, by which I am to make you spiritual.

And he himself drank of it. For lest on hearing this, they should say, What then? do we drink blood and eat flesh? and then be perplexed (for when he began to discourse concerning these things, even at the very sayings many were offended, cf. *John* 6, 60, 61, 66) therefore lest they should be troubled then

---

9. See I Cor. 11, 26.

likewise, he first did this himself, leading them to the calm participation of the mysteries. Therefore he himself drank his own blood.

Refutation of Heresies

What then, you will say; must we observe that other ancient rite also? By no means. For on this account he said, *Do this,* that he might withdraw them from the other. For if this works remission of sins as it surely does work it, would not the other be now superfluous?

As then in the case of the Jews, so here also he has bound up the memorial of the benefit with the mystery, by this again stopping the mouths of heretics. For when they say, whence is it manifest that Christ was sacrificed? together with the other arguments we stop their mouths from the mysteries also. For if Jesus did not die, of what are the rites the symbols?

2. See how much diligence has been used, that it should be ever borne in mind that he died for us? For since the Marcionists, and Valentinians, and Manichaeans were to arise, denying this dispensation, he continually reminds us of the passion even by the mysteries, (so that no man should be deceived); at once saying, and at the same time teaching by means of that sacred table. For this is the chief of the blessings; wherefore Paul also is in every way pressing this.

Then, when he had delivered it, he said, *I will not drink of the fruit of this vine, until that day when I drink it new with you in my Father's kingdom (Matt.* 26, 29). For because he had discoursed with them concerning the passion and cross, he again introduces what he has to say of his resurrection, having made mention of a "kingdom" before them, and so calling his own resurrection.

And wherefore did he drink after he was risen again? Lest the grosser sort might suppose the resurrection was an appearance. For the common sort made this an infallible test of his having risen again. Wherefore also the apostles also persuading them concerning the resurrection say this, *We who did eat and drink with him (Acts* 10, 41).

To show therefore that they should see him manifestly risen

again and that he should be with them once more, and that they themselves shall be witnesses to the things that are done, both by sight, and by act, he said, *Until I drink it new with you, you bearing witness. For you shall see me risen again.*

But what is *new?* In a new, that is, a strange manner, not having a passible body, but now immortal and incorruptible, and not needing food.

It was not then for want that he both ate and drank after the resurrection, for neither did his body need these things any more, but for all the full guarantee of his resurrection.

And wherefore did he not drink water after he was risen again, but wine? To pluck up by the roots another wicked heresy. For since there are certain ones who use water in the mysteries; to show that both when he delivered the mysteries he had given wine, and that when he had risen and was setting before them a mere meal without mysteries, he used wine, *of the fruit,* he said, *of the vine.* But a vine produces wine, not water.

The Fear of the Apostles is a Proof of the Mystery

And when they had sung a hymn, they went out unto the Mount of Olives (Matt. 26, 30). Let them hear this, as many as, like swine eating at random, rudely spurn the natural table, and rise up in drunkenness, whereas it were meet to give thanks, and end with a hymn.

Hear this, as many as wait not again for the last prayer of the mysteries, for this is a symbol of that. He gave thanks before he gave it to his disciples, that we also may give thanks. He gave thanks, and sang a hymn after the giving, that we also may do this selfsame thing.

But for what reason does he go forth unto the mountain? Making himself manifest, that he may be taken, in order not to seem to hide himself. For he hastened to go to the place which was also known to Judas.

Then he said unto them, *All you shall be offended in me (Matt. 26, 31).* After this he mentions also a prophecy, *For it is written, I will smite the shepherd, and the sheep shall be scattered abroad:* [10] at once persuading them ever to give heed

---

10. See **Zech.** 13, 7.

to the things that are written, and at the same time making it plain that he was crucified, according to God's purpose; and by everything showing he was no alien from the Old Covenant, nor from the God preached therein, but that what is done is a dispensation, and that the Prophets all proclaimed all things beforehand from the beginning that are comprised in the matter, so that they be quite confident about the better things also.

And he teaches us to know what the disciples were before the crucifixion, what after the crucifixion. For indeed they who, when he was crucified, were not able so much as to stand their ground, these after his death were mighty, and stronger than adamant.

And this selfsame thing is a demonstration of his death, the fright and cowardice, I mean, of his disciples. For if when so many things have both been done and said, still some are shameless, and say that he was not crucified; if none of these things had come to pass, to what pitch of wickedness would they not have proceeded? So for this reason, not by his own sufferings only, but by what took place with respect to the disciples, he confirms the word concerning his death, and by the mysteries also, in every way confounding those that are diseased with the pest of Marcion. For this reason he suffers even the chief apostle to deny him. But if he was not bound or crucified, whence sprung the fear of Peter, and to the rest of the apostles?

He suffers them not however, on the other hand, to wait until the sorrows, but what does he say? *But after I am risen again, I will go before you into Galilee* (Matt. 26, 32). For not from heaven does he appear at once, neither will he depart into any distant country, but in the same nation, in which he had also been crucified, nearly in the same place, so as hereby again to assure them that he that was crucified was the very same that rose again, and in this way to comfort them more abundantly when in sorrow. Therefore also he said "in Galilee," that being freed from the fears of the Jews they might believe his saying. For which cause indeed he appeared there.

The Presumption of Peter

But Peter answered and said, *Though all men should be offended because of you, yet will I never be offended* (Matt. 26, 33).

3. What do you say, O Peter? The Prophet said: "The sheep shall be scattered"; Christ has confirmed the saying, and do you say, No? Is not what passed before enough, when you said, *Far be it from you (Matt.* 16, 22), and your mouth was stopped? For this then he suffers him to fall, teaching him thereby to believe Christ in all things, and to account his declaration more trustworthy than one's own conscience. And the rest too reaped no small benefit from his denial, having come to know man's weakness, and God's truth. For when he foretells anything, we must no longer be subtle, nor lift up ourselves above the common sort. For, *your rejoicing,* it is said, *you shall have in yourself, and not in another (Gal.* 6, 4). For where he should have prayed, and have said, Help us, that we be not cut off, he is confident in himself, and says, *Though all men should be offended in you, yet will I never;* though all should undergo this, I shall not undergo it, which led him on by little and little to self-confidence. Christ then, out of a desire to put down this, permitted his denial. For since he neither submitted to him nor the prophet (and yet for this intent he brought in the prophet besides, that they may not gainsay), but nevertheless since he submitted not to his words, he is instructed by deeds.

For in proof that for this intent he permitted it, that he might amend this in him, hear what he says, *I have prayed for you, that your faith fail not (Luke* 22, 32). For this he said sharply reproving him, and showing that his fall was more grievous than the rest, and needed more help. For the matters of blame were two; both that he gainsaid; and that he set himself before the other; or rather a third too, namely, that he attributed all to himself.

To cure these things then, he suffered the fall to take place, and for this cause also leaves the others, and addresses himself earnestly to him. For, *Simon,* says he, *Simon, behold Satan has desired to have you that he may sift you as wheat (Luke* 22, 31); that is, that he may trouble, confound, tempt you; but *I have prayed for you, that your faith fail not.*

And why, if Satan desired all, did he not say concerning all, I have prayed for you? Is it not quite plain that it is this, which I have mentioned before, that it is as reproving him, and showing that his fall was more grievous than the rest, that he directs his words to him?

And wherefore said he not, "But I did not suffer it," rather than, "I have prayed?" He speaks from this time lowly things, on his way to his passion, that he may show his humanity. For he that has built his Church upon Peter's confession, and has so fortified it, that ten thousand dangers and deaths are not to prevail over it; he that has given him the keys of heaven, and has put him in possession of so much authority, and in no manner needed a prayer for these ends (for neither did he say, I have prayed, but with his own authority, *I will build my church, and I will give you the keys of heaven*), how should he need to pray, that he might brace up the shaken soul of a single man? Wherefore then did he speak in this way? For the cause which I mentioned, and because of their weakness, for they had not as yet the becoming view of him.

Man's Weakness without Grace

How then was it that he denied? He said not, that you may not deny, but *that your faith fail not,* that you perish not utterly. For this came from his care.

For indeed fear had driven out all else, for it was beyond measure, and it became beyond measure, since God had to an exceeding degree deprived him of his help, and he did exceedingly deprive him thereof, because there was to an exceeding degree in him the passion of self-will and contradiction. In order then that he might pluck it up by the roots, therefore he suffered the terror to overtake him.

For in proof that this passion was grievous in him, he was not content with his former words, gainsaying both prophet and Christ, but also after these things when Christ had said unto him, *Verily I say unto you, that this night, before the cock crow, you shall deny me thrice,* he replied, *Though I should die with you, I will not deny you in any wise (Matt.* 26, 34, 35). And Luke signifies moreover, that the more Christ warned him, so much the more did Peter exceedingly oppose him.

What mean these things, O Peter? When he was saying, "One of you shall betray me," you did fear lest you should be the traitor, and did constrain the disciple to ask, although conscious to yourself of no such thing; but now, when he is plainly crying out, and saying, "All shall be offended," are you gainsaying it, and not once only, but twice and often? For this is what Luke says.

Whence then did this come to him? From much love, from much pleasure. I mean, that after that he was delivered from that distressing fear about the betrayal, and knew the traitor, he then spoke confidently, and lifted himself up over the rest, saying, *Though all men shall be offended, yet will I not be offended* (*Matt.* 26, 33). And in some degree too his conduct sprung from jealousy, for at supper they reasoned "which of them is the greater," to such a degree did this passion trouble them. Therefore He checked him, not compelling him to the denial, God forbid! but leaving him destitute of his help and convicting human nature.

See at any rate after these things how he was subdued. For after the resurrection, when he had said, *And what shall this man do?* (*John* 21, 22) and was silenced, he ventured no more to gainsay as here, but held his peace. Again, towards the ascension, when he heard, *It is not for you to know times and seasons* (*Acts* 1, 7), again he holds his peace, and contradicts not. After these things, on the house, and by the sheet, when he heard a voice saying to him, *What God has cleansed, do not you call common* (*Acts* 1, 15,), even though he knew not for the time what the saying could be, he is quiet, and strives not.

All these things did that fall effect, and whereas before that he attributes all to himself, saying, "Though all men shall be offended, yet will I not be offended"; and, "if I should die, I will not deny you" (when he should have said, if I receive the assistance from you)—yet after these things altogether the contrary, *Why do you give heed to us, as though by our own power or holiness we had made him to walk?* [11]

4. Hence we learn a great doctrine, that a man's willingness is not sufficient, unless one receive the succor from above; and that again we shall gain nothing by the succor from above, if there be not a willingness. And both these things do Judas and Peter show; for the one, though he had received much help, was profited nothing, because he was not willing, neither contributed his part; but this one, though he was ready in mind, because he received no assistance, fell. For indeed of these two things is virtue's web woven.

Wherefore I entreat you, neither (when you have cast all upon God) to sleep yourselves, nor, when laboring earnestly, to think

---

11. **Acts** 3, 12. (Slightly altered).

to accomplish all by your own toils. For neither is it God's will that we should be supine ourselves, therefore he works it not all himself; nor yet boasters, therefore he did not give all to us; but having removed what was hurtful in either way, left that which is useful for us. Therefore he suffered even the chief apostle to fall, both rendering him more humbled in mind, and training him thenceforth to greater love. *For to whom more is forgiven,* it is said, *he loves more (Luke 7, 47).*

The Presence of Jesus Christ

Let us then in everything believe God, and gainsay him in nothing, though what is said seem to be contrary to our thoughts and senses, but let his word be of higher authority than both reasonings and sight. Thus let us do in the mysteries also, not looking at the things set before us, but keeping in mind His sayings.

For his word cannot deceive, but our senses are easily beguiled. His word never failed, but our senses in most things go wrong. Since then the word says, "This is my body," let us both be persuaded and believe, and look at it with the eyes of the mind.

For Christ has given nothing sensible, but though in things sensible yet all to be perceived by the mind. So also in baptism; the gift is bestowed by a sensible thing, that is, by water; but that which is done is perceived by the mind, the birth, I mean, and the renewal. For if you had been incorporeal, he would have delivered you the incorporeal gifts bare; but because the soul has been locked up in a body, he delivers you the things that the mind perceives, in things sensible.

How many now say, I would wish to see his form, his face, his clothes, his shoes? Lo! you see him. And you indeed desire to see his clothes, but he gives himself to you not to see only, but also to touch and eat and receive within you.

Fervent Communion

Let, then, no one approach it with indifference, no one faint-hearted, but all with burning hearts, all fervent, all aroused. For if Jews standing, and having on their shoes and their staves in their hands, ate with haste, much more ought you to be watchful.

For they indeed were to go forth to Palestine, wherefore also they had the garb of pilgrims, but you are about to go to heaven.

5. Wherefore it is needful in all respects to be vigilant, for indeed no small punishment is appointed to them that partake unworthily.

Consider how indignant you are against the traitor, against them that crucified him. Look therefore, lest you also yourself become guilty of the body and blood of Christ. They slaughtered the all-holy body, but you receive it in a filthy soul after such great benefits. For neither was it enough for him to be made man, to be smitten and slaughtered, but he also commingles himself with us, and not by faith only, but also in very deed makes us his body. What, then, ought not he to exceed in purity, that has the benefit of this sacrifice, than what sunbeam should not that hand be more pure which is to sever this flesh, the mouth that is filled with spiritual fire, the tongue that is reddened by that most awful blood? Consider with what sort of honor you were honored, of what sort of table you are partaking. That which when angels behold, they tremble, and dare not so much as look up at it without awe on account of the brightness that comes thence, with this we are fed, with this we are commingled, and we are made one body and one flesh with Christ.

Christ is Our Food

Who shall declare the mighty works of the Lord, and cause all his praises to be heard? (*Ps.* 106, 2) What shepherd feeds his sheep with his own limbs? And why do I say shepherd? There are often mothers that after the travail of birth send out their children to other women as nurses; but he endures not to do this, but himself feeds us with his own blood, and by all means entwines us with himself.

Mark it, he was born of our substance. But, you say, this is nothing to all men; though it does concern all. For if he came unto our nature, it is quite plain that it was to all; but if to all, then to each one. And how was it, you say, that all did not reap the profit therefrom. This was not of his doing, whose choice it was to do this on behalf of all, but the fault of them that were not willing.

With each one of the faithful does he mingle himself in the mysteries, and whom he begot, he nourishes by himself, and puts not out to another; by this also persuading you again, that he had taken your flesh. Let us not then be remiss, having been counted worthy of so much both of love and honor. See you not the infants with how much eagerness they lay hold of the breast? With what earnest desire they fix their lips upon the nipple? With the like let us also approach this table, and the nipple of the spiritual cup. Or rather, with much more eagerness let us, as infants at the breast, draw out the grace of the spirit; let it be our one sorrow not to partake of this food.

The Same Supper

The works set before us are not of man's power. He that then did these things at that supper, this same now also works them. We occupy the place of servants. He who sanctifies and changes them is the same. Let then no Judas be present, no covetous man. If anyone be not a disciple, let him withdraw, the table receives not such. For *I keep the passover,* he says, *with my disciples* (*Matt.* 26, 18).

This table is the same as that, and has nothing less. For it is not so that Christ wrought that, and man this, but he does this too. This is that upper chamber, where they were then; and hence they went forth unto the mount of Olives.

Let us also go out unto the hands of the poor, for this spot is the mount of Olives. For the multitude of the poor are olive-trees planted in the house of God, dropping the oil, which is profitable for us there, which the five virgins had, and the others that had not received perished thereby. Having received this, let us enter in, that with bright lamps we may meet the bridegroom; having received this, let us go forth hence.

Let no inhuman person be present, no one that is cruel and merciless, no one at all that is unclean.

Counsels to Priests

6. These things I say to you that receive, and to you that minister. For it is necessary to address myself to you also, that you may with much care distribute the gifts there. There is no small punishment for you, if being conscious of any wickedness in

any man, you allow him to partake of this table. *His blood shall be required at your hands (Ezek. 33, 8).* Though anyone be a general, though a deputy, though it be he himself who is invested with the diadem, and come unworthily, forbid him; the authority you have is greater than his. You, if you were entrusted to keep a spring of water clean for a flock, and then were to see a sheep having much mire on its mouth, you would not suffer it to stoop down unto it and foul the stream: but now being entrusted with a spring not of water, but of blood and of spirit, if you see any having on them sin, which is more grevious than earth and mire, coming unto it, are you not displeased? Do you not drive them off? And what excuse can you have?

For this end God has honored you with this honor, that you should discern these things. This is your office, this your safety, this your whole crown, not that you should go about clothed in a white and shining vestment.

And when do I know, you may say, this person, and that person? I speak not of the unknown, but of the notorious.

Shall I say something more fearful? It is not so grievous a thing for the energumens [12] to be within, as for such as these, whom Paul affirms *to trample Christ under foot,* and to *account the blood of the covenant unclean, and to do despite to the grace of the Spirit.* [13] For he that has fallen into sin and draws nigh, is worse than one possessed with a devil. For they, because they are possessed are not punished, but those, when they draw nigh unworthily, are delivered over to undying punishment.

Exclusion of the Unworthy from Communion

Let us not, therefore, drive away these only, but all without exception, whomsoever we may see coming unworthily.

Let no one communicate who is not of the disciples. Let no Judas receive, lest he suffer the fate of Judas. This multitude also is Christ's body. Take heed, therefore, you that minister at the mysteries, lest you provoke the Lord, not purging this body. Give not a sword instead of meat.

Nay, though it be from ignorance that he comes to communicate, forbid him, be not afraid. Fear God, not man. If you

---

12. i.e., vexed with devils.
13. **Heb.** 10, 29. (Slightly altered).

should fear man, you will be laughed to scorn even by him, but if God, you will be an object of respect even to men.

But if you dare not to do it yourself, bring him to me; I will not allow any to dare do these things. I would give up my life rather than impart of the Lord's blood to the unworthy; and will shed my own blood rather than impart of such awful blood contrary to what is meet.

But if any has not known the bad man, after much inquiry, it is no blame. For these things have been said about the open sinners. For if we amend these, God will speedily discover to us the unknown also; but if we let these alone, wherefore should He then make manifest those that are hidden?

But these things I say, not that we repel them only, nor cut them off, but in order that we may amend them, and bring them back, that we may take care of them. For thus shall we both have God propitious, and shall find many to receive worthily; and for our own diligence, and for our care for others, receive great reward; unto which God grant we may all attain by the grace and love towards man of our Lord Jesus Christ, to whom be glory world without end. Amen.

3. THE BREAD OF LIFE

"I am the living bread which came down from heaven. If anyone eats this bread, he will live forever. And the bread that I will give is my own flesh for the life of the world."

At this the Jews started to quarrel among themselves, saying, "How can he give us his flesh to eat?" Therefore Jesus said to them,

"I solemnly assure you, if you do not eat the flesh of the Son of Man and drink his blood, you have no life in you. He who eats on my flesh and drinks my blood has life eternal. And I shall raise him up on the last day. For my flesh is real food, and my blood, real drink. The man who eats on my flesh and drinks my blood abides in me and I in him.

Just as the Father who has life sent me and I have life because of the Father, so the man who feeds on me will have life because of me. This is the bread which came down from heaven. Unlike your ancestors who ate and yet died, the man who feeds on this bread will live forever."

Thus Jesus taught in the synagogue at Capharnaum.

SAINT JOHN CHRYSOSTOM

HOMILY 46 ON JOHN [14]
(John 6, 41-53)

"The Jews therefore murmured about him because he had said: I am the bread that has come down from heaven." And they kept saying: *Is this not the son of Joseph, whose father and mother we know? How, then, does he say: I have come down from heaven? (John 6, 41-42)*

1. *Their god is their belly, their glory is in their shame (Phil. 3, 19)*, said Paul, writing to the Philippians about certain men among them. Now, it is clear from what had gone before that the Jews were just like these men, and this is likewise clear from the words they addressed to Christ as they approached him. When, indeed, he gave them bread and satisfied their hunger, they kept calling him a prophet and sought to make him king. But when he taught them about their spiritual food, about life everlasting, when he led them away from things of sense, when he spoke to them of the resurrection, and elevated their thoughts, when, in short, they ought most of all to have admired him, then they murmured and went away.

The Human and Divine Birth of Christ

Now, if he was in truth the Prophet, as they had just said: This is indeed he about whom Moses said: *The Lord your God will raise up to you a prophet of your brethren like unto me: him shall you hear (Deut. 18, 15)*; they ought to have listened to him when he said: "I have come down from heaven." On the contrary, they did not listen to him, but murmured. Of course, they still held him in awe because of the recent miracle of the loaves. That if why they did not oppose him openly, but by murmuring they showed that they resented it, because he did not give them the table which they desired. And as they murmured, they kept saying: "Is this not the son of Joseph?"

From this it is clear that they did not yet know his marvelous and strange generation. That is why they still called him the

14. Greek text: PG 59, 257-262. Eng. trans., FC. 33, 462.

son of Joseph. Yet, he did not reprove them or say to them:
"I am not the son of Joseph." This was not, to be sure, because he was the son of Joseph, but because they were not yet
able to hear of his wonderful Incarnation. And if they were
not ready for a clear revelation of his birth according to the flesh,
much more was that the case with that ineffable one from above.
If he did not reveal the humble one, much less would he have
treated of the other. And though it scandalized them very much
to think that he was of a lowly and ordinary father, he nevertheless did not reveal his true parentage, in order that, in removing
one scandal, he might not cause another.

How God Draws Men

What, then, did he reply when they murmured? *No one
can come to me unless the Father who sent me draw him.*

The Manichaeans pounce on this and say that no action
lies within our power,[15] though the statement actually proves
conclusively that we are in possession of free will. "If a man has
the power to come to him," they say, "what need has he of
being drawn?" In reality, Christ's words do not dispense with
free will, but underline our need for assistance (in exercising free
will), because he here was pointing out that it is not anyone who
happens to do so that comes to him, but that it is a person enjoying the benefit of much assistance who comes.

In the next place, he also pointed out the manner by which
he draws him. In order that they might not suspect God of
some purely material operation, he added: *Not that anyone has
seen the Father except him who is from God, he has seen the
Father.*

"How, then, does he draw him?" you will ask. The Prophet
foretold this of old, prophesying in the words: "They all shall
be taught of God." Do you see the high dignity of faith? And
do you see how he predicted that they were going to learn, not
from men, nor through a man, but through God himself? Indeed,
that is why he dispatched them to the Prophets, namely, to
corroborate his words.

---

15. The heresy of the Manichaeans came to the zenith of its power in
the Eastern Roman Empire during the period when St. John was preaching
these Homilies; cf. art., "Manichaeism," in New Catholic Encyclopedia.

"But," you say, "if he says, 'They all shall be taught of God,' how is it that not all men are believers?" Because his words were spoken of the majority of men. Besides, even apart from this, the prophecy refers not to all men in general, but to all who will to be taught. For, as a teacher, he is at the disposal of all men, ready to give them his teachings, pouring out his teaching in abundance unto all.

And I will raise him up on the last day. In this text the Son has no inconsiderable dignity, for if, to be sure, the Father draws men, the Son it is who raises them up, not, of course, separating his works from those of the Father (for how could that be?), but showing that Their power is the same. Therefore, just as in the place where he said: *And the Father, who has sent me, bears witness to me,* in order that none might contend against his words, he thereupon referred them to the Scriptures; so also in this text, in order that they might not conceive the same suspicion, he referred them to the Prophets, to whom he repeatedly turned to prove that he was not in opposition to the Father.

"But," you will say, "what of those before this time? Were they not 'taught of God'? Then, what is better here?" The fact is that, before this, people learned the things of God through men, while now they learn them through the only-begotten Son of God and through the Holy Spirit. Next he added: "Not that anyone has seen the Father except him who is from God," not saying this here in the sense of causality, but of the mode of His existence. Because, if he had said it in the sense of causality, we are all, likewise, "from God." Where then would be the superiority and preeminence of the Son? "But why," you will say, "did he not make it clearer?" Because of their weakness. If they were scandalized to such a degree when he said: "I have come down from heaven," what scandal would they not have taken if he added this?

He called himself *living bread* because he welds together for us this life and the life to come. Therefore, he added: *If anyone eat of this bread he shall live forever.* Surely, "bread" here means the teachings of salvation, and faith in him, or else his body, for both strengthen the soul. Yet, when he said elsewhere: *If anyone hear my word, he will not taste death (John 8, 52),* they were scandalized, while here they did not have any such reaction, perhaps because they still were in awe of him

on account of the loaves he had [miraculously] brought into being.

The Manna and the True Bread of Life

2. Moreover, notice what a distinction he made between the
living bread and the manna, by telling them the kind of effect
that each of these foods produces. To show that the manna had
no unusual effect he added: "Your fathers ate the manna in the
desert and have died." Next, He placed before them very con-
vincing evidence that they themselves were deemed worthy of
much greater blessings than their fathers, by referring indirectly
to those well-known and wonderful men who lived at the time
of Moses. Therefore, when he had said that they who had eaten
the manna had died, he added: *If anyone eat of this bread, he
will live forever.* And he did not use the words "in the desert"
without design, but to imply that the manna was not provided
for a long period of time and did not accompany them into the
Promised Land.

This bread, however, is not such. *And the bread that I will
give is my flesh that I will give for the life of the world.* With
good reason at this point someone might inquire in perplexity
whether that was a good time for him to say these words, which
were not then constructive or profitable, but rather were even
injurious to what had already been built up. "From this time,"
Scripture says, "many of his disciples turned back, saying, 'This
is a hard saying. Who can listen to it?'" It seems that these
teachings ought to have been given to the disciples alone, as
Matthew [16] has said: "He explained privately to them."

What reply, then, shall we make to this objection? That even
now these teachings were both very profitable and very necessary.
Since they were urgently asking for food, but bodily food—and
in recalling to him the nourishment provided for their forefathers
were stressing the greatness of the manna—in order to prove
that all this was type and figure, while the reality thus fore-
shadowed was actually present, he made mention of spiritual
nourishment.

"But," you will say, "he ought to have said: 'Your fathers
ate the manna in the desert, and I have provided bread for you.'"

---

16. Actually, **Mark** 4, 34; but cf. **Matt.** 13, 36.

However, there was a great difference between the two. The latter, indeed, seemed inferior to the former, because this was brought from above, while the other, the miracle of the loaves, took place on earth. Therefore, since they were seeking for food brought down from heaven, for this reason he kept saying repeatedly: "I have come down from heaven."

Now, if someone should inquire: "Why in the world did he shroud the explanation in mystery?" we should say this in reply to him: It was just the right time for such words, for the obscurity of the meaning of what is said always attracts the attention of the listener and makes him listen more carefully.

They ought not, therefore, to have been scandalized, but they should have asked questions and made inquiries. Instead, they went away. If, indeed, they thought he was a Prophet, they ought to have believed his words. The scandal, then, consisted in their perversity, not in the doubtful meaning of his words. And notice, too, how he had gradually bound his disciples to himself, for it was they who said: "You have words of life; where else shall we go?" This was notwithstanding the fact that he here represented himself as the giver, not his Father: *The bread that I will give is my flesh.* However, the crowd did not react as his disciples did, but quite the contrary: *This is a hard saying.* And they therefore went away.

Yet, the teaching was not strange and new. John the Baptist, in truth, had implied it when he addressed him as "Lamb." "Even so, they did not know, what John the Baptist meant," you will say. I am fully aware they did not, but even the disciples did not completely understand. If they did not know anything clearly about the resurrection, and for that reason were ignorant of the meaning of the words: *Destroy this temple, and in three days I will raise it up (John 11, 19)*, much more would they not understand the words said here, for the former were less obscure than these. They did, indeed, know that Prophets had raised people from the dead, even if the Scriptures did not say this clearly, but no Scripture had ever said that someone ate flesh. Nevertheless, they believed and followed him and confessed that he had the words of eternal life. It is the part of a disciple not to inquire impertinently into the teachings of his master, but to listen and believe and await the proper time for explanation.

"Why is it, then," you will say, "that the contrary also happened and [the others] turned back and went away?" This was because of their perversity. When the question "how" comes in, unbelief also accompanies it. Nicodemus likewise was disturbed in this way when he said: *How can a man enter into his mother's womb?* (cf. *John* 3, 4). And these men were similarly perturbed when they said: "How can this man give us flesh to eat?" Now, if you really are looking for the "how," why did you not say this in the case of the loaves: "How has he multiplied the five into so many?" Because then they were concerned only with being filled, not with witnessing the miracle. "But on that occasion," you will say, "experience taught them." Well, then, as a result of that, these words also ought to have been readily accepted. It was for this reason that he first worked that wonder, so that, having been instructed by it, they might no longer fail to believe what was said afterwards.

At that time, then, they actually derived no profit from his words, but we have enjoyed the benefit of the very realities. Therefore, we must learn the wonder of the mystery, what it is, why it was given, and what is the benefit to be derived from it. *We are one body,* Scripture says, *and members made from his flesh and from his bones* (*Eph.* 5, 30). Let the initiated attend studiously to these words.

3. Therefore, in order that we may become of his body, not in desire only, but also in very fact, let us become commingled with that body. This, in truth, takes place by means of the food which he has given us as a gift, because he desired to prove the love which he had for us. It is for this reason that he has shared himself with us and has brought his body down to our level, namely, that we might be one with him as the body is joined with the head. This, in truth, is characteristic of those who greatly love.

Job, indeed, was implying this when he said of his servants —by whom he was loved with such an excess of love—that they desired to cleave to his flesh. In giving expression to the great love which they possessed, they said: *Who will give us of his flesh that we may be filled?* (Job 31, 31) Moreover, Christ has done even this to spur us on to greater love. And to show the love he has for us he has made it possible for those who desire, not merely to look upon him, but even to touch him and to consume him and to fix their teeth in his flesh and to be commingled with him; in short, to fulfill all their love.

The Virtue of Christ's Blood

Let us, then, come back from that table like lions breathing out fire, thus becoming terrifying to the Devil, and remaining mindful of our Head and of the love which he has shown to us.

"Parents, it is true, often entrust their children to others to be fed, but I do not do so," he says; "I nourish mine on my own flesh. I give myself to you, since I desire all of you to be of noble birth, and I hold out to you fair hopes for the future. He who gives himself to you here will do so much more in the life to come. I wished to become your brother. When for your sake I had assumed flesh and blood, I gave back again to you that very flesh and blood through which I had become your kinsman." This blood makes the seal of our King bright in us; it produces an inconceivable beauty; it does not permit the nobility of the soul to become corrupt, since it refreshes and nourishes it without ceasing.

The blood which we receive by way of food is not immediately a source of nourishment, but goes through some other stage first; this is not so with this blood, for it at once refreshes the soul and instills a certain great power in it. This blood, when worthily received, drives away demons and puts them at a distance from us, and even summons to us angels and the Lord of angels. Where they see the blood of the Lord, demons flee, while angels gather. This blood, poured out in abundance, has washed the whole world clean. The blessed Paul has uttered many truths about this blood in the Epistle to the Hebrews (cf. *Heb.* 9). This blood has purified the sanctuary and the holy of holies.

Now, if its type had so much power, both in the Temple of the Hebrews and in the midst of the Egyptians, when sprinkled on the doorposts (cf. *Exod.* 12, 7, 13), much more power does the reality have. In its types this blood sanctified the golden altar; without it, the High Priest did not dare to enter the sanctuary. This blood has ordained priests; in its types it has washed away sins. And if it had such great power in its types, if death shuddered so much at the figure, how would it not be in terror of the reality itself, pray tell? This blood is the salvation of our souls; by it the soul is cleansed; by it, beautified; by it, inflamed. It makes our intellect brighter than fire; it renders our soul more radiant than gold. This blood has been poured forth and has opened the way to heaven.

The Mysteries of the Church

4. Awe-inspiring, in truth, are the mysteries of the Church; awesome, in truth, her altar. A fountain sprang up out of paradise, sending forth sensible streams; a fountain arises from this table, sending forth spiritual streams. Beside this fountain there have grown, not willows without fruit, but trees reaching to heaven itself, with fruit ever in season and incorrupt. If someone is intensely hot, let him come to this fountain and cool down the feverish heat. It dispels parching heat and gently cools all things that are very hot; not those inflamed by the sun's heat, but those set on fire by burning arrows. It does so because it takes its beginning from above, and has its source from there, and from there it is fed. Many are the streams of this fountain, streams which the Paraclete sends forth; and the Son becomes its Custodian, not keeping its channel open with a mattock, but making our hearts receptive.

This fountain is a fountain of light, shedding abundant rays of truth. And beside it the Powers from on high have taken their stand, gazing on the beauty of its streams, since they perceive more clearly than we the power of what lies before us and its unapproachable flashing rays. Just as if one were to put one's hand or tongue into molten gold—if that were possible—he would at once make the object golden, the mystery lying before us here affects the soul, but much more so. The stream gushes up more vigorously than fire; it does not burn, however, but only cleanses what it touches.

This blood was formerly foreshadowed continually in altars, in sacrifices of the Law. This is the price of the world; by it Christ purchased the Church; by it he adorned her entirely. Just as a man in buying slaves gives gold and, if he desires to beautify them, does this with gold, so also Christ has both purchased us with his blood and adorned us with his blood. Those who share in this blood have taken their stand with angels, and archangels, and the Powers from on high, clad in the royal livery of Christ and grasping spiritual weapons. But I have not yet mentioned anything great, for they are wearing the King himself.

However, since it is a great and wonderful thing, if you approach with purity you come unto salvation, but if with conscious unworthiness, unto punishment and dishonor. *For he that eats and drinks the Lord unworthily,* Scripture says, *eats and drinks judgment to himself* (I *Cor.* 11, 29). If, then, those who defile the royal purple are punished in the same way as those who have rent it, why is it unfitting that those who receive the [sacred] body with unworthy dispositions have in store for them the same punishment as those who pierced it through with nails? Indeed, see how Paul has described the fearful punishment in the words:

A man making void the law of Moses dies without any mercy on the word of two or three witnesses; how much worse punishments do you think he deserves who has trodden under foot the Son of God, and has regarded as unclean the blood of the covenant through which he was sanctified (*Heb.* 10, 28-29).

Let us who enjoy such blessings, beloved, take heed to ourselves, and when we are tempted to utter a sinful word, or when we find ourselves being carried away by anger or some other such passion, let us reflect on what privileges we have been granted, what Spirit it is whose presence we enjoy, and this thought will check in us the unruly passions. How long, in truth, shall we be attached to present things? How long shall we remain asleep? How long shall we not take thought for our own salvation? Let us remember what privileges God has bestowed on us, let us give thanks, let us glorify him, not only by faith, but also by our very works, in order that we may obtain blessings also in the world to come, by the grace and mercy of our Lord Jesus Christ with whom glory be to the Father, together with the Holy Spirit, now and always, and forever and ever. Amen.

ST. AUGUSTINE OF HIPPO

TRACTATE 27 ON ST. JOHN [17]
(c. 6, 60-72)

A Strange Nourishment

1. We have just heard out of the Gospel the words of the Lord which follow the former discourse. From these a discourse is due to your ears and minds, and it is not unseasonable today; for it is concerning the body of the Lord which he said that he gave to be eaten for eternal life. And he explained the mode

---

17. Latin text: PL 35. 1615-21. Eng. trans. NPNF (ser. 1) 7, 174-178.

of this bestowal and gift of his, in what manner he gave his flesh to eat, saying, *he that eats my flesh, and drinks my blood, dwells in me, and I in him.*

The proof that a man has eaten and drank is this, if he abides and is abode in, if he dwells and is dwelt in, if he adheres so as not to be deserted. This, then, he has taught us, and admonished us in mystical words that we may be in his body, in his members under himself as head, eating his flesh, not abandoning our unity with him. But most of those who were present, by not understanding him, were offended; for in hearing these things, they thought only of flesh, that which they themselves were. But the Apostle says, and says what is true, *To be carnally minded is death (Rom.* 1, 6). The Lord gives us his flesh to eat, and yet to understand it according to the flesh is death; while yet he says of his flesh, that therein is eternal life. Therefore we ought not to understand the flesh carnally. As in these words that follow:

The Astonishment of the Disciples

2. *Many therefore,* not of his enemies, but *of his disciples, when they had heard this, said, this is a hard saying; who can hear it?* If his disciples found this saying hard, what must his enemies have thought? And yet so it behooved that to be said which should not be understood by all. The secret of God ought to make men eagerly attentive, not hostile. But these men quickly departed from him, while the Lord said such things: they did not believe him to be saying something great, and covering some grace by these words; they understood just according to their wishes, and in the manner of men, that Jesus was able, or was determined upon this, namely, to distribute the flesh with which the Word was clothed, piecemeal, as it were, to those that believe in him. *This,* say they, *is a hard saying: who can hear it.*

3. *But Jesus, knowing in himself that his disciples murmured at it*—for they so said these things with themselves that they might not be heard by him; but he who knew them in themselves, hearing within himself—answered and said, *This offends you;* because I said, I give you my flesh to eat, and my blood to drink, this forsooth offends you. "Then what if you shall see the Son of Man ascending where he was before?" What is this? Did he hereby solve the question that perplexed them? Did he hereby uncover the source of their offense? He did

clearly, if only they understood. For they supposed that he was going to deal out his body to them; but he said that he was to ascend into heaven, of course, whole: *When you see the Son of man ascending where he was before;* certainly then, at least, you will see that in the manner you suppose does he dispense his body; certainly then, at least, you will understand that his grace is not consumed by tooth-biting.

The Son of Man comes from Heaven

4. And he said, *It is the Spirit that quickens; the flesh profits nothing.* Before we expound this, as the Lord grants us, that other must not be negligently passed over, where he says, *Then what if you shall see the Son of Man ascending where He was before?* For Christ is the Son of man, of the Virgin Mary. Therefore Son of man he began to be here on earth, where he took flesh from the earth. For which cause it was said prophetically, *Truth is sprung from the earth* (*Ps.* 85, 12). Then what does he means when he says, *when you shall see the Son of man ascending where he was before?* For there had been no question if he had spoken thus: "If you shall see the Son of God ascending where he was before." But since he said, "The Son of man ascending where he was before," surely the Son of man was not in heaven before the time when he began to have a being on earth? Here, indeed, he said, *where he was before,* just as if he were not there at this time when he spoke these words. But in another place he says, *No man has ascended into heaven but he that came down from heaven, the Son of man who is in heaven* (*John* 3, 13). He said not "was," but says he, "the Son of man who is in heaven." He was speaking on earth, and he declared himself to be in heaven. And yet he did not speak thus: "No man has ascended into heaven but he that came down from heaven," the Son of God, "who is in heaven." Whither tends it, but to make us understand that which even in the former discourse I commended to your minds, my beloved, that Christ, both God and man, is one person, not two persons, lest our faith be not a trinity, but a quaternity?

Christ, therefore, is one; Word, soul and flesh: one Christ; the Son of God and Son of man, one Christ; Son of God always, Son of man in time, yet one Christ in regard to unity of person. He was in heaven when he spoke on earth. He was Son of man in heaven in the manner in which he was Son of God on earth; Son of God on earth in the flesh which he took, Son of man in heaven in the unity of person.

A Profitable Flesh

5. What is it, then, that he adds? *It is the Spirit that quickens; the flesh profits nothing.* Let us say to him (for he permits us, not contradicting him, but desiring to know), O Lord, good Master, in what way does the flesh profit nothing, whilst you have said, *Except a man eat my flesh, and drink my blood, he shall not have life in him?* Or does life profit nothing? And why are we what we are, but that we may have eternal life, which you have promised by your flesh? Then what means "the flesh profits nothing?" It profits nothing, but only in the manner in which they understood it. They indeed understood the flesh, just as when cut to pieces in a carcass, or sold in the shambles; not as when it is quickened by the Spirit. Wherefore it is said that *the flesh profits nothing,* in the same manner as it is said that *knowledge puffs up.* Then, ought we at once to hate knowledge? Far from it! And what means *knowledge puffs up?* Knowledge alone, without charity. Therefore he added, *but charity edifies* (I *Cor.* 8, 1). Therefore, add to knowledge charity, and knowledge will be profitable, not by itself, but through charity. So also here, "the flesh profits nothing," only when alone. Let the Spirit be added to the flesh, as charity is added to knowledge, and it profits very much.

For if the flesh profits nothing, the Word would not be made flesh to dwell among us. If through the flesh Christ has greatly profited us, does the flesh profit nothing? But it is by the flesh that the Spirit has done somewhat for our salvation. Flesh was a vessel; consider what it held, not what it was.

The apostles were sent forth; did their flesh profit us nothing? If the apostles' flesh profited us, could it be that the Lord's flesh should have profited us nothing? For how should the sound of the Word come to us except by the voice of the flesh? Whence should writing come to us? All these are operations of the flesh, but only when the spirit moves it, as if it were its organ. There fore *it is the Spirit that quickens; the flesh profits nothing,* as they understood the flesh, but not so do I give my flesh to be eaten.

Spirit and Unity

6. Hence *the words,* says he, *which I have spoken to you are Spirit and life.* For we have said, brethren, that this is what the Lord has taught us by the eating of his flesh and drinking of his blood, that *we should abide in him and he in us.* But we abide in him when we are his members, and he abides in us when we are his temple. But unity joins us together that we may be his members. And what but love can effect that unity should join us together? And the love of God, whence is it? Ask the Apostle: *The love of God,* says he, *is shed abroad in our hearts by the Holy Spirit which is given to us (Rom. 5, 5).* Therefore *it is the Spirit that quickens,* for it is the Spirit that makes living members. Nor does the Spirit make any members to be living except such as it finds in the body, which also the Spirit itself quickens. For the Spirit which is in you, O man, by which it consists that you are a man, does it quicken a member which it finds separated from the flesh? I call your soul your spirit. Your soul quickens only the members which are in your flesh; if you take one away, it is no longer quickened by your soul, because it is not joined to the unity of your body.

These things are said to make us love unity and fear separation. For there is nothing that a Christian ought to dread so much as to be separated from Christ's body. For if he is separated from Christ's body, he is not a member of Christ, he is not quickened by the Spirit of Christ. *But if any man,* says the Apostle, *have not the Spirit of Christ, he is none of his (Rom. 8, 9). It is the Spirit,* then, *that quickens; the flesh profits nothing. The words that I have spoken to you are spirit and life.* What means are *spirit and life?* They are to be understood spiritually. Have you understood spiritually? They are spirit and life. Have you understood carnally? So also are they *spirit and life,* but are not so to you.

The Gift of Faith

7. *But,* says he, *there are some among you that believe not.* He said not, there are some among you that understand not; but he told the cause why they understand not. *There are some among you that believe not,* and therefore they understand not, because

they believe not. For the Prophet has said, *If you believe not, you shall not understand* (*Isa.* 7, 9). We are united by faith, quickened by understanding. Let us adhere to him through faith, that there may be that which may be quickened by understanding. For he that adheres not, resists; he that resists, believes not. And how can he that resists be quickened? He is an adversary to the ray of light by which he should be penetrated: he turns not away his eye, but shuts his mind. *There are,* then, *some who believe not.* Let them believe and open, and be illuminated.

For Jesus knew from the beginning who they were that believed, and who should betray him. For Judas also was there. Some indeed, were offended; but he remained to watch his opportunity, not to understand. And because he remained for that purpose, the Lord kept not silence concerning him. He described him not by name, but neither was he silent about him, that all might fear through only one should perish . But after he spoke, and distinguished those that believe from those that believe not, He clearly showed the cause why they believed not. *Therefore I said unto you,* says he, *that no man can come unto me except it were given unto him of my Father.* Hence to believe is also given to us; certainly to believe is something. And if it is something great, rejoice that you have believed, yet be not lifted up; for *What have you that you did not receive?* (I *Cor.* 4, 7)

The Abandonment by His Disciples

8. *From that time many of his disciples went back, and walked no more with hm.* Went back, but after Satan, not after Christ. For Christ our Lord once addressed Peter as Satan, rather because he wished to precede his Lord, and to give counsel that he should not die, that we might not die forever; and he says to him, *Get you behind me, Satan; for you savor not the things that be of God, but the things that be of men* (*Matt.* 16,23). He did not drive him back to go after Satan, and so called him Satan; but he made him go behind himself, that by walking after his Lord he should not be a Satan.

But these went back in the same manner as the apostle says of certain women: *For some are turned back after Satan* (I *Tim.* 5, 15). They walked not further with him. Behold, cut off from the body, for perhaps they were not in the body, they have lost life. They must be reckoned among the unbelieving, not-

withstanding they were called disciples.   Not a few, but many
went back.

This happened, maybe, for our consolation.   For sometimes
it happens that a man may declare the truth, and that what he
says may not be understood, and so they that hear it are offended
and go away.   Now the man regrets that he had spoken that truth,
and he says to himself, "I ought not to have spoken so, I ought
not to have said this."   Behold, it happened to the Lord: he
spoke, and lost many; he remained with few.   But yet he was
not troubled, because he knew from the beginning who they were
that believed and that believed not.   If it happen to us, we are
sorely perplexed.   Let us find comfort in the Lord, and yet
let us speak words with prudence.

To Whom Shall We Go?

9. And now, addressing the few that remained: *Then said
Jesus to the twelve* (namely, those twelve who remained), *Will you
also,* said he, *go away?* Not even Judas departed.   But it was
already manifest to the Lord why he remained: to us he was
made manifest afterwards.   Peter answered in behalf of all, one
for many, unity for the collective whole: *Then Simon Peter
answered Him, Lord, to whom shall we go?* You drive us from
you; give us your other self.   "To whom shall we go?"   If we
abandon you, to whom shall we go?   *You have the words of
eternal life.*   See how Peter, by the gift of God and the renewal
of the Holy Spirit, understands him.   How other than because he
believed?   *You have the words of eternal life.*   For you have
eternal life in the ministration of your body and blood.

And we have believed and have known.   Not have known
and believed, but *believed and known.*   For we believed in order
to know; for if we wanted to know first, and then to believe, we
should not be able either to know or to believe.   What have we
believed and known?   *That you are Christ, the Son of God;* that
is, that you are that very eternal life, and that you give in your
flesh and blood only that which You are.

God's Handiwork

10. Then said the Lord Jesus: *Have not I chosen you twelve,
and one of you is a devil?*   Therefore should he have said, "I

have chosen eleven": or is a devil also chosen, and among the elect? Persons are wont to be called "elect" by way of praise: or was man elected because some great good was done by him, without his will and knowledge? This belongs peculiarly to God; the contrary is characteristic of the wicked. For as wicked men make a bad use of the good works of God, so, on the contrary, God makes a good use of the evil works of wicked men. How good it is that the members of the body are as they can be disposed only by God, their author and framer! Nevertheless what evil use does wantonness make of the eyes? What ill use does falsehood make of the tongue? Does not the false witness first both slay his own soul with his tongue, and then, after he has destroyed himself, endeavor to injure another? He makes bad use of the tongue, but the tongue is not therefore an evil thing; the tongue is God's work, but iniquity makes an ill use of that good work of God. How do they use their feet who run into crimes? How do murderers employ their hands? And what bad use do wicked men make of those good creatures of God that lie outside of them? With gold they corrupt judgment and oppress the innocent. Bad men make a bad use of the very light; for by evil living they employ even the very light with which they see into the service of their villanies. A bad man, when going to a bad deed, wishes the light to shine for him, lest he stumble; he who has already stumbled and fallen within, that which he is afraid of in his body has already befallen in his heart.

Hence, to avoid the tediousness of running through them separately, a bad man makes a bad use of all the good creatures of God: a good man, on the contrary, makes a good use of the evil deeds of wicked men. And what is so good as the one God? Since, indeed, the Lord himself said, *There is none good, but the one God* (*Mark* 10, 18). By how much he is better, then, by so much the better use he makes of our evil deeds. What worse than Judas? Among all that adhered to the Master, among the twelve, to him was committed the common purse; to him was allotted the dispensing for the poor. Unthankful for so great a favor, so great an honor, he took the money, and lost righteousness: being dead, he betrayed life: him whom he followed as a disciple, he persecuted as an enemy. All this evil was Judas'.

But the Lord employed his evil for good. He endured to be

betrayed, to redeem us. Behold, Judas' evil was turned to good. How many martyrs has Satan persecuted! If Satan left off persecuting, we should not today be celebrating the very glorious crown of Saint Laurence. If then God employs the evil works of the devil himself for good, what the bad man effects, by making a bad use, is to hurt himself, not to contradict the goodness of God. The Master makes use of that man. And if he knew not how to make use of him, the Master contriver would not have permitted him to be. Therefore, he says, *One of you is a devil,* whilst I have chosen you twelve. This saying, *I have chosen you twelve,* may be understood in this way, that twelve is a sacred number. For the honor of that number was not taken away because one was lost, for another was chosen into the place of the one that perished (*Acts* 1, 26). The number remained a sacred number, a number containing twelve: because they were to make known the Trinity throughout the whole world, that is, throughout the four quarters of the world. That is the reason of the three times four. Judas, then only cut himself off, not profaned the number twelve: he abandoned his Teacher, for God appointed a successor to take his place.

The Grains are Intermingled

11. All this that the Lord spoke concerning his flesh and blood—and in the grace of that distribution he promised us eternal life, and that he meant those that eat his flesh and drink his blood to be understood, from the fact of their abiding in him and he in them; and that they understood not who believed not; and that they were offended through their understanding spiritual things in a carnal sense; and that, while these were offended and perished, the Lord was present for the consolation of the disciples who remained, for proving whom he asked, *Will you also go away?* that the reply of their steadfastness might be known to us, for he knew that they remained with him;—let all this, then, avail us to this end, most beloved, that we eat not the flesh and blood of Christ merely in the sacrament, as many evil men do, but that we eat and drink to the participation of the Spirit, that we abide as members in the Lord's body, to be quickened by his Spirit, and that we be not offended, even if

many do now with us eat and drink the sacraments in a temporal manner, who shall in the end have eternal torments.

For at present Christ's body is as it were mixed on the threshing-floor: *But the Lord knows them that are His* (2 *Tim.* 2, 19). If you know what you thresh, that the substance is there hidden, that the threshing has not consumed what the winnowing has purged; certain we are, brethren, that all of us who are in the Lord's body, and abide in him, that he also may abide in us, have of necessity to live among evil men in this world even unto the end.   I do not say among those evil men who blaspheme Christ; for there are now few found who blaspheme with the tongue, but many who do so by their life.   Among those, then, we must necessarily live even unto the end.

12. But what is this that he says: *He that abides in me, and I in him?* What, but that which the martyrs heard: *He that perseveres unto the end, the same shall be saved.* How did Saint Laurence, whose feast we celebrate today, abide in him? He abode even to temptation, abode even to tyrannical questioning, abode even to bitterest threatening, abode even to destruction; —that were a trifle, abode even to savage torture.   For he was not put to death quickly, but tormented in the fire: he was allowed to live a long time; nay, not allowed to live a long time, but forced to die a slow, lingering death.   Then, in that lingering death, in those torments, because he had well eaten and well drunk, as one who had feasted on that meat, as one intoxicated with that cup, he felt not the torments.   For he was there who said, *It is the Spirit that quickens.*   For the flesh indeed was burning, but the Spirit was quickening the soul.   He shrunk not back, and he mounted into the kingdom.   But the holy martyr Xystus, whose day we celebrated five days ago, had said to him, "Mourn not, my son"; for Xystus was a bishop, he was a deacon. "Mourn not," said he; "you shall follow me after three days."   He said three days, meaning the interval between the day of Saint Xystus's suffering and that of Saint Laurence's suffering, which falls on today.   Three days is the interval.   What comfort!   He says not, "Mourn not, my son; the persecution will cease, and you will be safe"; but, "do not mourn: whither I precede you shall follow; nor shall your pursuit be deferred: three days will be the interval, and you shall be with me."   He accepted the oracle, vanquished the devil, and attained to the triumph.

SAINT CYRIL OF ALEXANDRIA

THAT THE HOLY BODY OF CHRIST IS LIFEGIVING, WHEREIN HE SPEAKS OF HIS OWN BODY AS OF BREAD.[18]

I am the bread of life. Your fathers ate the manna in the wilderness, and died: This is the bread which came down from heaven, that a man may eat thereof and not die.

Christ, the Bread of Life (6, 48-64)

Full clearly may one herein behold that which was foretold by the Prophet Isaiah, *I was made manifest to them that seek me not, I was found of them that asked not for me. I said, Behold me, unto a nation that was not called by my name: all the day spread I out my hands unto a rebellious and gainsaying people.* For, removing the whole pod from his speech, and having taken away (so to say) all that cloaked it, he at length reveals himself unveiled to them of Israel, saying, *I am the bread of life,* that they may now learn that if they would be superior to corruption and would put off the death which from the transgression fell upon us, they must approach to the participation of him who is mighty to give life, and destroy corruption, and bring to nought death: for this is a work proper and most fit for that which is by nature life.   But since they, affirming that the manna was given to their fathers in the wilderness, received not the bread which in truth came down from heaven, that is, the Son, he made a necessary comparison between the type and the truth that so they might know that the manna is not the bread which is from heaven, but he whom the trial shows to be so by nature.

Manna and Eucharist

For your fathers (he says) and ancestors by eating the manna, gave to the bodily nature its need, gaining thereby life for a season, and imparting to the flesh its daily sustenance therefrom, with difficulty effected that it should not die at once.   But it will

---

18. Commentary on St. John 4, 2 and 3.   Greek text, PG 73, 560-605. English trans., LFC 43, 406-438.

be (he says) the clear proof of its not being the bread which is from heaven in a truer sense, that they who partook were no way benefitted thereby unto incorruption: a token again in like way that the Son is properly and truly the bread of life, that they who have once partaken, and been in some way commingled with him through the communion with him have been shown superior to the very bonds of death. For that the manna again is taken rather as an image or shadow of Christ, and was typifying the bread of life, but was not itself *the bread of life*, has been often said by us: and the Psalmist supports us, crying out in the Spirit, *he gave them bread of heaven, man did eat angels' bread* (*Ps.* 78, 24, 25). For it seems to have been said to them of Israel by the Spirit clad, but in truth it is not so, but to us rather is the aim of the words directed.

Bread of Men and Bread of Angels

For is it not foolish and utterly naive to suppose that the holy angels in heaven, although they have an incorporeal nature, should partake grosser food, and need such aid in order to prevail unto life, as this body of earth desires? But I think it nothing hard to conceive, that, since they are spirits, they should need like food, spiritual (I mean) and of wisdom. How then is angels' bread said to have been given to the ancestors of the Jews, if the Prophet speaks truly in so crying? But it is manifest, that since the typical manna was an image of Christ, which contains and upholds all things in being, nourishing the angels and quickening the things on earth, the Prophet was calling that which is signified by shadows by the name of the truth,—from the fact that the holy angels could not partake of the more earthly food, drawing off his hearers even against their will from any gross conception as to the manna, and bringing them up to the spiritual meaning, that of Christ, who is the food of the holy angels themselves also.

They then who *ate the manna* (he says) *are dead*, not having received any participation of life therefrom (for it was not truly lifegiving, but rather taken as an aid against carnal hunger and in type of the true); but they who receive in themselves the bread of life, will have immortality as their prize, wholly setting at nought corruption and its consequent evils, and will mount up unto boundless and unending length of life in Christ. Nor will it at all damage our words on this subject that they who have been made partakers of Christ, need to taste bodily death on account of what is due to nature; for even though they, falling into this end, undergo the lot of humanity, yet, as Paul says (*Rom.* 6, 10), *they that shall live, live to God.*

Necessity to Insist on This Teaching (v. 51)

To say the same things unto you, to me indeed is not grievous, but for you it is safe (*Phil.* 3, 1), writes the divine Paul, in this too (I suppose) instructed by these very words of the Savior. For as those who are diseased with wounds need not the application of a single plaster, but manifold tending, and that not once applied, but by its continuance of application expelling the pain: so for the soul most rugged, and withered mind, should many aids of teaching be contrived and come one after the other, for one will avail to soften it not by one and the first leading, but through its successive coming to it, even if it comes to the same words. Oftentimes then does the Savior bringing round the same manner of speech to the Jews set up before them manifoldly, sometimes darkly, and clad in much obscurity, at other times freed, delivered, and let loose from all double meaning, that they, still disbelieving, might lack nothing yet unto their condemnation, but being evil evilly might be destroyed, themselves thrusting the sword of perdition against their own soul.

Christ therefore no longer concealing anything says, *I am the living bread which came down from heaven.* That manna was (he says) a type and a shadow and an image. Hear him now openly and no more veiled, *I am the living bread; if any man eat of this bread, he shall live for ever.* Those who ate of that died, for it was not lifegiving: he that eats of this bread, that is me, or my flesh, *shall live forever.*

Warning to Unbelievers

We must then beware of and reject alike hardening ourselves to the words of piety, since Christ not once only but oftentimes persuades us. For there is no doubt, that they will surely be open to the severest charges, who turn aside to the uttermost folly, and through boundless unbelief, refuse not to rage against the Author of the most excellent things. Therefore says he of the Jews, *If I had not come and spoken unto them, they had not had sin, but now they have no cloak for their sin* (*John* 15, 22). For they who have never by hearing received the word of salvation into their heart, will haply find the Judge milder, while they plead that they heard not at all, even though they shall especially give account for not having sought to learn: but they who when instructed by the same admonitions and words to the seeking after what is profitable, senselessly imagine that they ought to deprive themselves of the most excellent good things, shall undergo most bitter punishment, and shall meet with an offended judge, not able to find an excuse for their folly which may shame him.

Christ Offers a Victim for All Men

I die (he says) for all, that I may quicken all by myself, and I made my flesh a ransom for the flesh of all. For death shall die in my death, and with me shall rise again (he says) the fallen nature of man. For for this became I like to you, Man (that is) and of the seed of Abraham, that I might *be made like in all things unto my brethren* (*Heb.* 2, 17). The blessed Paul himself also, well understanding what Christ just now said to us says, *Forasmuch then as the children have partaken of flesh and blood, he also himself likewise took part of the same, that through death he might destroy him that had the power of death, that is, the devil* (*Heb.* 2, 14). For no otherwise was it possible that he that has the power of death should be destroyed, and death itself also, had not Christ given himself for us, a ransom, One for all, for he died in behalf of all. Wherefore he says in the Psalms, too, offering himself as a spotless sacrifice to God the Father, *Sacrifice and offering you would not, but a body you prepared for me. In burnt-offerings and offerings for sin you took no pleasure: then said I, Lo I come (in the chapter of the book it is written of me) to do your will, O God, was my choice.*[19] For since *the blood of bulls and of goats and the ashes of an heifer* (*Heb.* 10, 5-7) sufficed not unto the purging away of sin, nor yet would the slaughter of brute beasts ever have destroyed the power of death, Christ himself came in some way to undergo punishment for all. For *with his stripes we were healed* (*Isa.*

---

19. **Ps.** 40, 7-8 cited in **Heb.** 10, 5-7.

53, 5), as says the Prophet, and *his own self bare our sins in his own body on the tree* (I *Pet.* 2, 24); and he was crucified for all and on account of all, that if One died for all, all we might live in him. For it was not possible that he should be holden by death, neither could corruption over-master that which is by nature life.

But that Christ gave his own *flesh for the life of the world,* we shall know by his words also, for he says, *holy Father keep them* (*John* 17, 11); and again, *For their sakes I sanctify myself* (*John* 17, 19). He here says that he sanctifies himself, not aiding himself unto sanctification for the purification of the soul or spirit (as it is understood of us), nor yet for the participation of the Holy Spirit, for the Spirit was in him by nature, and he was and is holy always, and will be so ever. He here says, *I sanctify myself,* for, I offer myself and present myself as a spotless sacrifice for an odor of a sweet smell. For that which is brought to the divine altar was sanctified, or called holy according to the law.

Christ Establishes Life in Us

Christ therefore gave his own body for the life of all, and again through it he makes life to dwell in us; and how, I will say as I am able. For since the life-giving Word of God indwelt in the flesh, he transformed it into his own proper good, that is life, and by the unspeakable character of this union, coming wholly together with it, rendered it life-giving, as himself is by nature. Wherefore the body of Christ gives life to all who partake of It. For it expels death, when it comes to be in dying men, and removes corruption, full in itself perfectly of the Word which abolishes corruption.

The Life Promised by Christ Should not Be Confused with the Resurrection of the Dead

But a man will perhaps say, fixing the eye of his understanding upon the resurrection of them that have slept: They who received not the faith in Christ, and were not partakers of him, will not live again at the time of the resurrection. What? Shall not every created thing that has fallen into death return again to life?

To these things we say, Yes, all flesh shall live again: for prophecy foretells that *the dead shall be raised.* For we consider that the mystery through the resurrection of Christ extends over the whole nature of man, and in him first we believe that our whole nature has been released from corruption. For all shall rise, after the likeness of him that was raised for our sakes, and has all in himself, in that he is Man. And as in the first-formed we fell down into death, so in the First-born again, who was so for our sakes, all shall rise again from the dead: but *they that did good, unto the resurrection of life* (as it is written), *and they that wrought evil, unto the resurrection of doom.* And I will grant, that in no passing degree bitterer than death is the resurrection unto punishment, and the receiving life again unto disgrace alone. In the stricter sense then we must understand the Life that is really so, the life in Christ, in holiness and bliss and unfailing delight. For that this is truly life the wise John too knows, saying, *He that believes in the Son has everlasting life, and he that believes not the Son shall not see life, but the wrath of God shall abide in him.* For lo, he says that he who is in unbelief shall not see life: although every creature looks to return again to life, and to rise again. It is then manifest, that the Savior with reason called that the life which is prepared for the saints, I mean that in glory and in holiness, which no right-minded person will doubt that we ought to pursue by coming to the participation of the Life-giving Flesh.

A Figure of the Eucharist

But since the Savior called himself bread in many of the passages that have already been before us, let us see whether he would not hereby too bring to our mind any one of the things fore-announced and is reminding us of the things in Holy Writ, wherein he was long ago signified under the form of bread. It is written then in Numbers, *And the Lord spoke unto Moses, saying, Speak unto the children of Israel, and you shall say unto them, when you come into the land whither I bring you, then it shall be, that when you eat of the bread of the land, you shall offer up an heave-offering a separation unto the Lord: a cake the first-fruit of your dough shall you offer for an heave-offering: as an heave offering of the threshing floor, so shall you heave it, a first fruit of*

*your dough, and you shall give unto the Lord an heave offering un-
to your generations (Num. 15, 17-21).*

Obscurely then, and bearing a gross covering as of the letter,
did the law typify these things: yet did it proclaim afore the true
very bread that comes down from heaven, i.e., Christ, and gives
life unto the world. For observe how he made Man like us by
reason of his likeness to us, a certain first-fruits of our dough
and heave offering, as it is written, was offered up to God the
Father, set forth *the first-Begotten of the dead,* and the first-fruits
of the resurrection of all ascending into heaven itself. For he
was taken of us, *He took hold of the seed of Abraham,* as Paul
says, he was offered up, as of all, and in behalf of all, that he
might quicken all, and might be offered to God the Father, as it
were the first handful of the floor. But as he being in truth
light, put that grace upon his disciples; for he says, *You are
the light of the world:* so too he being the living bread, and
that quickens all things and keeps them in being, by a likeness
and through the shadow of the Law, was typifying in the twelve
loaves the holy choir of the apostles. For thus he says in
Leviticus, *And the Lord spoke unto Moses, saying, Command
the children of Israel, that they bring unto you oil olive pure beaten
for the light, to cause the lamp to burn continually without the veil
in the tabernacle of the testimony.* And then he proceeds, *And
you shall take fine flour, and make twelve cakes thereof: two tenth
deals shall be in one cake. And you shall set them in two rows,
six in a row, upon the pure table before the Lord, and shall put
pure frankincense upon each row, and salt, and it shall be on the
loaves for a memorial unto the Lord (Lev. 24, 5-7).*

The lamp then in the holy tabernacle, and giving light without
the veil, we said in the foregoing was the blessed John the Baptist,
nourished with the purest oil, that is, the illumination through
the Spirit: outside the veil, because his doctrine was catechetic:
for he says, *Prepare you the way of the Lord, make straight the
paths of our God.*[20] But the things within the veil, that is, the
hidden mystery of Christ, he shows not much. For I (he says)
*baptize you with water unto repentance, but he that comes
after me is mightier than I, whose shoes I am not worthy to bear,
he shall baptize you with the Holy Spirit and with fire (Matt.*

---

20. **Isaiah** 40, 3 and **Matt.** 3, 3.

3, 11). See then how he shines, as in simpler speech calling
unto repentance; but the things within the veil he commits to
him that baptizes with fire and the Spirit, to lay open? And these
things we have set forth more at large, on the words, at the beginning of the book, *He was the burning and the shining light* (*John*
5, 35); yet we touched on them now cursorily, since it was
necessary, on John's passing away, to show that the preaching of
the holy Apostles was near and straightaway present.

For this reason, I suppose, the Scripture, having first signified
him by the lamp puts before us the consideration of the twelve
loaves. *You shall make* (it says) *twelve cakes: two tenth deals
shall be in one cake.* It is the custom of the Divine Scripture, to
receive ever the number ten as perfect, and to acknowledge it as
the fullest, since the series and order of the consecutive numbers,
receiving a kind of revolution and multiplication of the same
into the same, advances and is extended to whatsoever one will.
He commands then that each cake be of two tenth deals, that you
may see perfection in the disciples, in the even pair, I mean both
active virtue, and that of contemplation. He bids two rows to
be made (and profitably so) well nigh indicating the very position,
which it was (as is like) their custom to take, ever receiving the
Lord in the midst of them, and accustomed ever to surround him
as their Master. And that we may know that, as Paul says, they
are unto God the Father a sweet savor of Christ (II *Cor.* 2, 15),
he bids frankincense to be put on the cakes, and that they be
sprinkled also with salt. For it is said to them, *You are the salt
of the earth* (*Matt.* 5, 13). Indeed and with reason does he bid
it be offered upon the Sabbath day, for they were made manifest
in the last times of the world: and the last day of the week is the
Sabbath. And not only so, but because at the time of our
Savior's coming we held a Sabbath spiritually: for we rested
from sin. And then the holy apostles were also made manifest
unto us, by whose divine writings also we nourished attain unto
the life of holiness. Therefore on the Sabbath day especially does
he bid the cakes to be set out upon the holy table, that is, in
the Church. For the whole is often signified by a part. But
what is holier than the holy Table of Christ? Therefore the
Savior was pre-typified as bread by the Law: the apostles again
as cakes by their likeness to him. For all things were in verity
in Christ, but by likeness to him, they belong to us too through
his grace.

The insolence of the question of the Jews (v. 52)

All things are plain to him that understands, and right to them that find knowledge (Prov. 8, 9), as it is written, but darksome to the foolish is even that which is exceeding easy. For the truly wise hearer shuts up the more obvious teaching in the treasury of his understanding, not admitting any delay in respect of this: but as to the things the meaning whereof is hard, he goes about with his inquiries, and does not cease asking about them; and he seems to me profitably to press on to do much the same as they say that the fleetest dogs of the chase do, who having from nature great quickness of scent, keep running round the haunts of their game. And does not the wise and prophetic oracle call to some similar habit, *Seeking seek and dwell with me?* For the seeker must seek, that is, must bring a most unflinching zeal thereto, and not go astray after empty speculations, but in proportion as anything is more rugged in its difficulty, with so much the more vigorous mind must he apply himself and carry by storm with more resolute onset of his thoughts that which is concealed. But the unpracticed and unteachable mind, whatever starts up before it, rages at it with its unbelief, rejects the word "conquering" as spurious, from undisciplined daring mounting up to the last degree of arrogance. For that which will give away to none, nor think that ought is greater than it, how will it not at last be, what we have just said?

And we shall find by looking into the nature of the thing that the Jews too fell into this disorder. For when they ought to have accepted unhesitatingly the words of the Savior, having already through many things marvelled at his God-befitting power and his incontestable authority over all, and to have inquired what was hard of attainment, and to have besought instruction wherein they were perplexed: they senseless repeat *How* to God, as though they knew not that it is a word replete with all blesphemy. For the power of accomplishing all things without toil belongs to God, but they, *being natural men,* as the blessed Paul says, *received not the things of the Spirit of God* (I *Cor.* 2, 14), but the so dread mystery seems *folly* to them.

We then ought to derive benefit herefrom, and reestablishing our own life by others' falls, to hold without question our faith in the teaching of the divine mysteries and not to apply *How* to ought that is told us (for it is a Jewish word, and therefore deserving of extremest punishment). And when the ruler of the synagogue of the Jews, Nicodemus by name, on hearing the Divine words, said, *How can these things be?* with justice was he ridiculed hearing, *Are you a master of Israel, and know not these things?* (*John* 3, 10)

The Christian Attitude to Mystery

Let us then, found more skillful in the search after what is profitable, even by others' folly, beware of saying *How,* to what God works, but rather study to attribute to him the knowledge of the mode of his own works. For as no one will know what God is by nature, but he is justified who believes that he is and that he is a rewarder of them that diligently seek him: so again will one be ignorant of the mode of his several acts, but by committing the issue to faith, and by confessing the almighty power of God who is over all, will he receive the not contemptible reward of so good a decision. For the Lord of all himself willing us so to be affected says by the Phophet Isaiah, *For my counsels are not as your counsels, neither as your ways are my ways, says the Lord, but as the heaven is far from the earth, so are my ways far from your ways, and your thoughts from my mind* (*Isa.* 55, 8-9). But he that so greatly surpasses us in wisdom and might, how shall he not also work wonderfully, and surpass our understanding?

I would introduce yet an other argument besides, no mean one, as I think. For they who in this life take up the knowledge of mechanics (as it is called) often engage to perform some great thing, and the way of doing it is hidden from the mind of hearers, till they have seen it done; but they looking at the skill that is in them, even before the trial itself, accept it on faith, not venturing to gainsay. How then (may one say) will not they with reason be open to heavy charges, for daring to dishonor with their un-belief God the chief worker of all things, who refuse not to say *how* to those things which he works, albeit they acknowledge him to be the giver of all wisdom, and are taught by the whole divine Scripture that he can do all things?

Nothing is Impossible to God

But if you persist O Jew, saying *How!* I too will imitate for your sake your ignorance, and say to you, *how* came you out of

Egypt? *How* (tell me) was the rod of Moses changed into a serpent? *How* became the hand leprous, and was again restored, as it is written? *How* passed the water into the nature of blood? *How* passed you through the Red Sea, as through dry land? *How* by means of a tree was the bitter water of Mara changed into sweet? *How* too was water supplied to you from the breasts of the rocks? *How* was the manna brought down to you? *How* again stood the Jordan in his place? Or *how* through a shout alone was the impregnable wall of Jericho shattered?   And will that *how* never fail you?   For you will be detected, already amazed at many mighty works, to which if you apply the *how,* you will wholly disbelieve all divine Scripture, and will overthrow all the words of the holy Prophets, and, above all, the holy writings of thine own Moses himself.   It were therefore far meeter, that, believing in Christ and assenting unhesitatingly to his words, you should be zealous to learn the mode of the blessing, and not be inconsiderately intoxicated saying, *How can this man give us his flesh to eat?* for the word *this man* too they say in disdain.   For some such meaning again does their arrogant speech hint at.

The Flesh of Christ is the Source of Life (v. 53)

Long-suffering, truly, and of great mercy is Christ, as one may see from the words now before us. For in no wise reproaching the littleness of soul of the unbelievers, he again richly gives them the life-giving knowledge of the mystery, and having overcome, as God, the arrogance of them that grieve him, he tells them those things whereby they shall (he says) mount up to endless life. And how he will give them his flesh to eat, he tells them not as yet, for he knew that they were in darkness, and could never avail to understand the ineffable: but how great good will result from the eating he shows to their profit, that haply inciting them to a desire of living in greater preparation for unfading pleasures, he may teach them faith. For to them that have now believed there follows suitably the power too of learning. For so says the prophet Isaiah, *If you will not believe neither yet shall you understand* (*Isa.* 7, 9). It was therefore right, that faith having been first rooted in them, there should next be brought in understanding of those things whereof they are ignorant, and that the investigation should not precede faith.

For this cause (I suppose) did the Lord with reason refrain

from telling them how he would give them his flesh to eat, and calls them to the duty of believing before seeking. For to them that had at length believed he *broke bread, and gave to them, saying, Take, eat, This is my Body* (*Matt.* 26, 26). Likewise handing round the cup to them all, he says, *Drink of it all of you, for this is my blood of the New Testament, which is being shed for many for the remission of sins* (*Matt.* 26, 27). See how to those who were yet senseless and thrust from them faith without investigation, he explains not the mode of the mystery, but to those who had now believed, he is found to declare it most clearly? Let them, then, who of their folly have not yet admitted the faith in Christ, hear, *except you eat the flesh of the Son of man and drink his blood, you have no life in you* (*John* 6, 54). For wholly destitute of all share and taste of that life which is in sanctification and bliss, do they abide who do not through the mystical blessing receive Jesus. For he is life by nature, inasmuch as he was begotten of a living Father: no less quickening is his holy body also, being in a manner gathered and ineffably united with the all-quickening word. Wherefore it is accounted his, and is conceived of as one with him. For, since the Incarnation, it is inseparable; except as regards the knowledge that the Word which came from God the Father, and the temple from the Virgin, are not indeed the same in nature (for the body is not consubstantial with the Word from God), yet are they one by that coming-together and ineffable concurrence. And since the flesh of the Savior has become life-giving (as being united to that which is by nature life, the Word from God), when we taste it, then have we life in ourselves, we too united to it as it to the indwelling Word.

Proof through the Miracles of the New Testament

For this cause also, when he raised the dead, the Savior is found to have operated, not by word only, or God-befitting commands, but he laid a stress on employing his holy flesh as a sort of co-operator unto this, that he might show that it had the power to give life, and already made one with him. For it was in truth his own body, and not another's. And verily when he was raising the little daughter of the chief of the synagogue saying,

Maid, arise,[21] he laid hold of her hand, as it is written, giving life, as God, by his all-powerful command, and again, giving life through the touch of his holy flesh, he shows that there was one kindred operation through both.   Indeed, and when he went into the city called Naim, and one was being carried out dead, the only son of his mother, again he touched the bier, saying, *Young man, to you I say, Arise (Luke* 7, 14).   And not only to his word gives he power to give life to the dead, but that he might show that his own body was life-giving (as I have said already), he touches the dead, thereby also infusing life into those already decayed.   And if by the touch alone of his holy flesh, he gives life to that which is decayed, how shall we not profit yet more richly by the life-giving blessing when we also taste it?   For it will surely transform into its own good, i.e., immortality, those who partake of it.

And wonder not thereat, nor ask yourself in Jewish manner, *How?* but rather consider that water is cold by nature, but when it is poured into a kettle and brought to the fire, then it all but forgets its own nature, and goes away unto the operation of that which has mastered it.   We too then in the same way, even though we be corruptible through the nature of our flesh, yet forsaking our own infirmity by the intermingling of life, are transformed to Its property, that is, life.   For it needed, it needed that not only should the soul be re-created through the Holy Spirit into newness of life, but also that this gross and earthly body should by the grosser and kindred participation be sanctified and called to incorruption.

Proof through the Figures of the Old Testament

But let not the Jew, sluggish of understanding, ever suppose that a mode of some new mysteries has been discovered by us. For he will see it in the older books, I mean those of Moses, already fore-shadowed and bearing the force of the truth, for that it was accomplished in outward forms too.   For what (tell me) shamed the destroyer?   What provided that their forefathers also should not perish along with the Egyptians, when death, the con-

---

21. **Mark** 5, 41; **Luke** 8, 54.

queror of all, was arming himself against the first-born? Is it not manifest to all, that when they, in obedience to the divine Law sacrificed the lamb, and having tasted of its flesh anointed the door-posts with the blood, death was compelled to pass them by, as sanctified? For the destroyer, that is, the death of the body, was arrayed against the whole nature of man, by reason of the transgression of the first-formed man. For then first did we hear, *Dust you are, and unto dust you shall return (Gen.* 3, 19). But since Christ was about to overthrow so dire a tyrant, by existing in us as life through his holy flesh, the mystery was typified to them of old, and they tasted of the flesh of the lamb, and were sanctified and preserved by its blood, he that was appointed to destroy passing by, by the appointment of God, those who were partakers of the lamb. Why then are you angry, O Jew, at being now called from the types to the truth, when Christ says, *Except you eat the flesh of the Son of man and drink his blood, you have not life in you?* albeit you ought to come with more confidence to the comprehending of the mystery, pre-instructed by the books of Moses, and by most ancient figures led most undoubtingly to the duty of faith.

The Word and the Flesh are Inseparable in the Incarnation (v. 54)

Herein too ought we specially to admire the holy Evangelist openly crying, *And the Word was made Flesh (John* 1, 14). For he shrank not from saying, not that he was made in flesh, but that he was made flesh, that he might show the Union. And we do not say either that God the Word, of the Father, was transformed into the nature of the flesh, or that the flesh passed into the Word (for each remains that which it is by nature, and one Christ of both); but in a manner unspeakable and passing human understanding, the Word united to his own flesh, and having, as it were, transformed it all into himself (according to the operation which lies in his power of quickening things lacking life) drove forth of our nature the corruption, and dislodged too death which of old prevailed by means of sin. He therefore that eats the holy flesh of Christ, has eternal life: for the flesh has in itself the Word which is by nature life. Wherefore he says, *I will raise him up on the last day.* Instead of saying, my body shall raise him up, i.e., him that eats it, he has put I: not as though he were other than his own flesh (and not wholly so by nature), for after the union he cannot at all be severed into a pair of sons. I therefore (he says) who am become in him, through mine own flesh, that is, will raise up him who eats thereof, in the last day. For it were indeed even impossible that he who is by nature life, should not surely overcome decay, and master death. Wherefore even though death which by the transgression sprang on us compel the human body to the debt of decay, yet since Christ is in us through his own flesh, we shall surely rise. For it is incredible, indeed rather impossible, that Life should not make alive those in whom It is. For as if one took a spark and buried it amid much stubble, in order that the seed of fire preserved might lay hold on it, so in us too our Lord Jesus Christ hides life through his own flesh, and inserts it as a seed of immortality, abolishing the whole corruption that is in us.

For My Flesh is True Meat and My
Blood True Drink (v. 55)

Again does he contrast the mystic blessing with the supply of manna, and the savor of the cup with the founts from rocky beds. And what he said before in other words, this he again says here, manifoldly fashioning the same discourse. For he does not advise them to marvel overmuch at the manna, but rather to receive him, as bread from heaven, and the giver of eternal life. For *your fathers* (he says) *ate the manna in the wilderness and died: this is the bread which comes down from heaven, that a man may eat thereof and not die.* For the food of manna (says he) having for a very little time sported with the need of the body, and driven away the hurt of want, was again powerless, and did not engraft eternal life in them that had eaten thereof. That then was not the true food, and bread from heaven, that is; but the holy body of Christ, which nourishes to immortality and life everlasting, is verily the true food. Indeed and they drank water also from the rock. "And what then" (he says) "or what the profit to them who drank? for they have died." That too then was not true drink; but true drink in truth is found to be the precious blood of Christ, which uproots from the foundation all corruption, and dislodges death which dwelt in the flesh of man. For it is not the blood of any chance man, but of the very life that is by nature. Wherefore we are entitled both the body and the members of Christ, as receiving through the blessing the Son himself in ourselves.

He that eats My Flesh and drinks My Blood
dwells in Me and I in him (v. 56)

Clearly Christ initiates us by these words, and since his discourse is hard of attainment by the more unlearned, asking for itself rather the understanding of faith than investigation, He revolving again and again over the same ground makes it easy in divers ways, and from all parts illuminates what is useful therein, fixing as a kind of foundation and groundwork the most excellent desire for it. For *he that eats my flesh* (says he) *and drinks my blood abides in me and I in him.* For as if one should join wax with other wax, he will surely see (I suppose) the one in the other; in like manner (I deem) he who receives *the flesh* of our Savior Christ and *drinks his precious blood,* as he says, is found one with him, commingled as it were and intermingled with him through the participation, so that he is found in Christ, Christ again in him.

Leaven in the Dough

Thus was Christ teaching us in the Gospel too according to Matthew, saying, *The Kingdom of heaven is like unto leaven, which a woman took and hid in three measures of meal, till the whole was leavened* (*Matt.* 13, 33). Who then is the woman, what the three measures of meal, or what the measure at all, shall be spoken of in its proper place: for the present we will speak only of the leaven. As then Paul says that a *little leaven leavens the whole lump* (I *Cor.* 5, 6), so the least portion of the blessing blends our whole body with itself, and fills it with its own mighty working, and so Christ comes to be in us, and we again in him. For one may truly say that the leaven is in the whole lump, and the lump by like reasoning is in the whole leaven: you have in brief the sense of the words. And if we long for eternal life, if we pray to have the giver of immortality in ourselves, let us not like some of the more heedless refuse to be blessed nor let the devil, deep in wickedness, lay for us a trap and snare a perilous reverence.

Indeed (says he) for it is written, *he that eats of the bread, and drinks of the Cup unworthily, eats and drinks doom unto himself* (I *Cor.* 11, 29): and I, having examined myself, see that I am not worthy.

When then will you be worthy (will he who thus speaks hear from us) when will you present yourself to Christ? For if you are always going to be scared away by your stumblings, you will never cease from stumbling (for *who can understand his errors?* [*Ps.* 19, 12] as says the holy Psalmist) and will be found wholly without participation of that wholly-preserving sanctification. Decide then to lead a holier life, in harmony with the law, and so receive the blessing, believing that it has power to expel, not death only, but the diseases in us. For Christ thus coming to be in us lulls the law which rages in the members of the flesh, and kindles piety to God-ward, and deadens our passions, not imputing to us the transgressions in which we are, but rather, healing us, as sick. For he binds up that which was crushed, he raises, what had fallen, as a Good Shepherd and one that has laid down his life for his sheep.

THAT THE SON IS NOT A PARTAKER OF LIFE FROM ANY OTHER,
BUT RATHER LIFE BY NATURE, AS BEING BEGOTTEN OF
GOD THE FATHER WHO IS LIFE BY NATURE

The Holy Trinity and the Incarnation (v. 57)

The meaning of this passage is obscure and enveloped in no passing difficulty: but it will not entirely attain to impenetrability: for it will be apprehended and got at by those who choose to think aright. When then the Son says that he was sent, he signifies his Incarnation, and nothing else. And when we speak of his Incarnation, we mean that he was made man complete. As then *the Father* (he says) has made me man, and since I God the Word, was begotten life of that which is by nature life, and, made man, have filled my temple, that is, my body, with mine own nature; in like manner shall he also *who eats my flesh live because of me.* For I took mortal flesh: but, having dwelt in it, being by nature life, because I am of the living Father, I refashioned it wholly into mine own life, I have not been overcome of the corruption of the flesh but have rather overcome it, as God. As then (for again I will say it shrinking not for profit's sake) although I was made (he says) flesh (for this the *being sent means*), *I live again because of the living Father,* that is, retaining in myself the natural excellence of him that begot me, so he too who, by the participation of my flesh, receives me in himself *shall live,* wholly transformed entire into me, who am able to give life, because I am (as it were) of life-giving root, that is God the Father.   But he says that he was Incarnate by the Father, although Solomon says, *Wisdom builded her a house* (*Prov.* 1, 9):   and the blessed Gabriel attributes the creation of the divine body to the operation of the Spirit, when he was speaking with the holy Virgin (for *the Holy Spirit,* he says, *shall come upon you and the power of the Highest shall overshadow you*) (*Luke* 1, 35) that you may again understand, that the Godhead being by nature one, conceived of both in the Father and the Son and in the Holy Spirit — not severally will each inwork as to ought of things that are, but whatever is said to be done by one, this is wholly the work of the whole divine nature.   For since the Holy Trinity is one in respect of consubstantiality, one full surely will be also its power in respect to every thing.   For all things are of the Father through the Son in the Spirit.   But what we have often said, this we will again say.   For to say the same things, though it be burdensome, yet it is safe.   It was the habit of our Savior Christ for our profit to attribute those things which surpass the power suitable to man, to the operation of the Father.   For he has humbled himself being made man: and since he accepted the form of a servant, he spurns not the measure of servants, yet will he not be excluded from doing all things with the Father. And he that begot him works all things through him, according to the word of the Savior himself, *The Father* (he says) *that dwells in me, himself does the works.*   Having then given to the dispensation of the flesh what befits it, he attributes to God the Father what is above man's power.   For the buidling a Temple in the Virgin surpasses man's power.

Against the Nestorian Heresy

But our opponent will again reply: "And in what other mode did the Son reveal what he is by nature, or how did he show clearly that the Father is greater, save by saying, *I live because of the Father?*"   For if the Father is the giver of life to the Son, who will rush on to so great stupidity as not full surely to conceive that that which partakes of life, will not be the same by nature as life or that which is mighty to give life?

To such things we too will array in turn the word of the truth, and opportunely say, *the fool will speak folly, and his heart will conceive vain things, to practice transgression, and to utter error against the Lord* (*Isa.* 32, 6). For what can be more wicked than such a conception of the heretics? How is not the deepest error uttered by them against Christ who quickens all things, since those most foolish ones blush not to say, that he lives by partaking of life from another, just like his creatures? Will then the Son at last be a creature too, inasmuch as it is a partaker of life, but is not very life by nature? For the creature must needs be wholly other than that which is the life in it. But if they suppose that they may be the same, let them call every creature life. But I do not suppose that any one in his senses would do that. Therefore neither is the Only-Begotten a creature, but will be conceived of as by nature life: for how would he be true in saying, I am the resurrection and the life? (*John* 11, 25). For life is that which gives life, not that which needs to receive it from another, just as wisdom too is understood to be that which can make wise, not that which receives wisdom. Therefore according to you the truth will be false, and Christ will not be true, who says "I am the life." Indeed and the brilliant choir of saints again will speak falsely, uttering words through the Spirit, and calling the only-begotten life. For the divine Psalmist is found saying to the Father, *with you is the fountain of life* (*Ps.* 36, 9). And the wondrous Evangelist John in his Epistles thus says, *that which was from the beginning, which have heard, which we have seen with our eyes, which we beheld, and our hands handled, of the Word of life: and the Word was manifested, and we have seen and bear witness and declare unto you the eternal life, which was with the Father, and was manifested unto us* (I *John* 1, 1-2). See that the Psalmist speaks true, even by the testimony of John, when he says to God the Father of all, *with you is the fountain of life.* For the Son was and is with him the fountain of life. For that the inspired writer says these things of him, he will again prove by his words: for he thus writes, *and we know that the Son of God is come, and has given us an understanding, that we may know him that is true, and we are in his true Son Jesus Christ. This is the true God and eternal life* (I *John* 5, 20).

The Son, Source of Life on the Same Plane as the Father

Then who (tell me) will any longer endure the trifling of the heretics? Or who will not justly cry out against their impiety, in daring to say that the Son is partaker of life from another, albeit the holy and God-inspired Scripture says no such thing of him; but rather openly cries aloud, that he is both God by nature, and truth, and the fountain of life, and again life eternal. For how will he be conceived of as very God, who needs life from another, and is not rather himself life by nature? Or how will he any more be called fountain of life, if he is helped by another's gifts to be able to live?

But indeed (says the opponent) we grant that the Son is so far life, that he too can give life, as having in himself the living Father.

Yet this will not suffice, most noble sirs, to exempt you from blasphemy against the Only-Begotten: but in this too shall your argument be proved untutored and every way falling to pieces. For to have to say that the Son is called life, because he can quicken things recipient of life, by reason he has in himself the Father, how is it not replete with unmeasured folly? For you know not (it seems) what *by nature* means, or what "being of any thing by nature" means as compared with so being by circumstances. As fire is hot by nature, and other things too are hot, by partaking of its operation, as iron or wood: but not because they are heated, are they said to be fire: for they have an external and not a physical operation in them. But our argument will proceed by means of illustrations in regard to ourselves too.

Grammar for instance, or Geometry, are held to be species of reasoning science, but when any one becomes skilled in grammar or the other, he is not himself conceived of as Grammar or Geometry, but from the Grammar that is in him, he is called a Grammarian, and similarly with regard to the other: so too that which is by nature life, is something altogether different from the things wherein it is, transforming to itself what is not so by nature. When therefore you say that the Father is in the Son, as he might be in matter (for instance), in order that, since he is life by nature, he too may be able to give life to you foolishly grant still that he is life, and not rather participant of it from another, yet by relation, and not by essence called to the dignity of a dispenser thereof. And as one would not reasonably call the heated iron fire, albeit it has the operation of the fire, in that it is heated from it: or again a man skillful in grammar is not called grammar, because he can lead others also unto the science, so I do not imagine that any man of sense would call the Son life because he can quicken others also, though he have not by nature, according to them, the being life, but as from the engrafted operation of the Father, or by reason of the indwelling Father. For what (tell me) is to hinder us at last from conceiving of the Son as one of us, that is, of corruptible nature, if he *live because of the Father,* that is, having received the gift of life from the Father, as they understand it? For he would perish, according to the analogy of their notions, if he had not the living Father in himself. And if we confess that he speaks truly, *I am in the Father and the Father in me;* he indeed has in himself the Father who is life by nature, and is himself in the Father though not life by nature. I pass over the blasphemy, though one must utter it to convict the fighters against God of their impiety: for the Father will be found to have in himself that which is destitute of life, that is, decay, or a decaying nature. For since the nature of the matter in hand compels us so to conceive of the Son, we must investigate further, and go through various considerations, since our aim is by due precision to refine the question.

The Son, exactly like the Father, is Life by Nature

You say that God the Father is by nature life. Well, so he is, but he is in the Son also. For this your argument too allows. I would now with reason ask you, desiring to learn it, "What will he work in respect of his Son, being in him? Will he impart of his own life to his offspring, as though he needed it and had not life of himself? How then must we not suppose the Son to be void of life? That which is void of life, what is it, but subject to decay? But he will not impart of his own life to his offspring: for he is life, even though he receive it not from him."

How then do some unguardedly babbling still accuse him and say that the Son therefore lives, because he has in himself the Father who is by nature life? For if he live also apart from the Father, as being essentially life's very self, he will never live *because of the Father,* that is, because of participation of the

Father. But if he have the Father the giver of his own life, manifestly he has no life of his own. For he borrows it of another, and is (as we said at first) a creature rather than life, and of a nature subject to decay. How then does he call himself life? For either we too may safely say, *I am the life*, or if this be no safe word (for it is not lawful for the creature to mount up to God-befitting dignities), the Son knows that he is by nature life: since how will he be the *impress* of the *Person* (*Heb.* 1, 3) of him that begot him, how the *Image and accurate likeness?* Or how was not Philip right in saying, *show us the Father, and it suffices us?* (*John* 14, 8) For in truth one ought to consider, that he that had seen the Son, had not yet seen the Father, since the one is by nature life, the other participant of life from him. For one will never see that which quickens in that which is quickened, him that lacks not in him that lacks. Hence in another way too will he be untrue in saying, *he that has seen me has seen the Father* (*John* 14, 9).

But he who loves the pious doctrines of the Church sees what great absurdities will follow their partings. Let him then *turn from* them, *and pass away* (*Prov.* 4, 15), as it is written, and let him *make straight paths, and direct his ways* (*Prov.* 4, 26), and look to the simple beauty of the truth, believing that God the Father is by nature life, the Son begotten of him life too. For as he is said to be light of light, so too life of life: and as God the Father lightens things lacking light by his own light, his Son, and gives wisdom to things recipient thereof, through his own wisdom, and strengthens things needing strength, again through his own strength, so too he quickens things whatever lack the life from him, by his own life which flows forth from him, his Son. When then he says, *I live because of the Father,* do not suppose that he confesses that he lives because he receives life from the Father, but asserted that because he was begotten of a living Father, that therefore he also lives. For it were impossible that he who is of a living Father, should not live. As though any of us were to say, I am a reasonable man on account of my father, for I was born the child of a reasonable man: so do you conceive in respect of the Only-Begotten also. *I live* (he says) *because of the Father.* For since the Father who begot me is life by nature, and I am his natural and proper offspring, I gain by nature what is his, i.e., being life: for this the Father too is. For since he is conceived to be and is one of one (for the Son is from the Father, even though he were with him eternally); he with reason glories in the natural attributes of him that begot him, as his own.

This is the Bread Which Came Down from Heaven, not as Your Fathers ate the Manna and Died; He That eats of This My Bread shall Live Forever(v. 58)

Great (says he) ought to be the effects of great things, and the gifts of the grace from above should appear God-befitting and worthy of the divine munificence. For if you have wholly received in faith that *the bread came down from heaven,* let it produce continuous life in them that long after it, and have the unceasing operation of immortality. For this will be a clear proof of its being *the bread from heaven,* that is from God: since we say that it befits the eternal to give what is eternal, and not the enjoyment of temporary food, which is barely able to last for just the least moment. For one will no longer wisely suppose that that was the bread from God and from above, which our forefathers eating, were overcome by death, and repelled not the evil of corruption, and no wonder; for that was not the bread which avails to render immortal. Hence neither will it be rightly conceived and said by any to be from heaven. For it was a work befitting that which came down thence, to render the partakers of It superior to death and decay. By undoubted proof again will it be confirmed, that this was *the bread from heaven,* that to wit through Christ, i.e., his body. For it makes him that tastes thereof to live forever. Herein too is seen a great pledge of the divine nature, which vouchsafes not to give a little thing, but everything wonderful, even surpassing our understanding, so as for the greatness of the grace, to be even disbelieved by the more simple. For with so wealthy a hand how should not the will to give largely be present? Wherefore Paul too says in amazement, *eye has not seen, nor ear heard, neither has it entered into the heart of man, to conceive the things which God prepared for them that love him* (I *Cor.* 2, 9). By little examples was the Law typifying great ones, *having the shadow of the good things to come, not the very image of the things* (*Heb.* 10, 1), as it is written: as in the food of manna is seen the blessing that is through Christ. For *the shadow of the good things to come* was prefigured to them of old.

The Public Nature of Christ's Teaching (v. 59)

The most wise Evangelist introducing to us the exposition of marvellous mysteries, with reason attributes to our Savior, Christ, the commencement of the doctrine thereof, by the clear view of his person shaming the gainsayer, and scaring off beforehand those who should come with a view to gainsay: for sometimes the renown of the teachers makes the hearer more ready to believe, and demands a more earnest assent on the part of the learners. Full well too does he add, *in the synagogue.* For the expression shows that not one chance person, or two, heard Christ say these things: but he is seen teaching openly in the synagogue to all, as himself says by the Prophet Isaiah too, *Not in secret have I spoken nor in a dark place of the earth (Isa. 45, 19).* For he was discoursing openly of these things, rendering their judgment without excuse to the Jews, and rendering the charges of not believing on him heavier to the disobedient. For they, if not instructed in so dread a mystery, might reasonably have deprecated punishment, and pleading utter ignorance, have undergone a lighter sentence from the Judge: but since they knowing, and often initiated, still outraged him with their unbelief, how will they not reasonably be punished, all mercy at last taken away, and pay most bitter penalty to him that was dishonored of them? Some such thing has the Savior himself too said of them, *If I had not come* (he says) *and spoken unto them, they had not had sin, but now they have no cloak for their sin (John 15, 22).*

We must then guard against, indeed rather renounce, disobedience, as the bringer in of death, and look upon faith in what Christ teaches, as the giver of life. For thus shall we escape being punished with them. But he adds that Christ had spoken *these things in Capernaum,* that he may be proved to have remembered accurately. For he that knows both place and village, how shall he fail in the relation of the things taught?

The Incredulity of the Disciples Prefigured by the Increduity of the Jews (vv. 60-61)

This is the custom of the simple: they ever find fault with the more subtle doctrines and foolishly tear in pieces any thought that is above them, because they themselves understand it not: although they ought rather to have been eager to learn, and to have loved to search diligently the things spoken, not on the contrary to rise up against so wise words, and call that *hard,* which they ought to have marvelled at. For they are somewhat in the same plight as one may see those in who have lost their teeth. For the one, hurrying to the more delicate food, often reject the more wholesome, and sometimes blame the more excellent, not acknowledging the disease, whereby they are compelled to decline it: and these, the foster-brethren of unlearning and bereft of sound mind, shrink from knowledge, which they ought to have pursued with exceeding much toil, and to have attained by intent zeal.

The spiritual man, then, will delight himself in the words of our Savior, and will justly cry out, *How sweet are thy words unto my throat, yea, above honey and the comb to my mouth* (*Ps.* 119, 103); while the carnal Jew ignorantly esteeming the spiritual mystery to be foolishness, when admonished by the words of the Savior to mount up to the understanding befitting man, ever sinks down to the folly which is his foster-brother, *calling evil good, and good evil* (*Isa.* 5, 20), according to the Prophet's voice. He follows again his fathers, and herein too is he detected imitating the unlearning of his forefathers. For the one on receiving the manna from God, and being made partakers of the blessing from above, were dragged down to their wonted coarseness, and sought for the unsavorinesses of Egypt, desiring to behold onions, leeks, and kettles of fish: and these on being exhorted to receive the life-giving grace of the Spirit, and taught to feed on the very bread, which comes from God the Father, turn aside after their own error, *lovers of pleasure rather than lovers of God*: and as their forefathers used to find fault with the very food of manna, daring to say, *And our soul is dried away* with this manna: so do these too again reject the very bread, and blush not to say, *Hard is this saying.*

The hearers therefore of the divine mysteries must be wise, they must be *approved exchangers,* so as to know the approved and counterfeit coin, and neither unseasonably to bring inextricable questioning on those things which are to be received in faith, nor to lavish a faith sometimes harmful upon those things that require investigation, but to render to every thing that is said its due, and to advance as it were by a straight path, refusing to turn aside on either hand. For by a royal road beseems it him to travel who runs to uprightness of faith which is in Christ.

Does This Offend You? What and If You Shall See the Son of Man Ascend up Where He was Before? (v. 62)

From utter ignorance, certain of those who were being taught by Christ the Savior, were offended at his words. For when they heard him saying, *Amen, amen, I say unto you, except you eat the flesh of the Son of man and drink his blood, you have no life in you* (*John* 6, 53), they supposed that they were invited to some brutish savageness, as though they were enjoined to eat flesh and to sup up blood, and were constrained to do things which are dreadful even to hear. For they knew not the beauty of the Mystery, and that fairest economy devised for it. Besides, this, they surely reasoned thus with themselves. How can the human body implant in us everlasting life, what can a thing of like nature with ourselves avail to immortality? Christ therefore understanding their thoughts (*for all things are naked and bared to his eyes*) (*Heb.* 4, 13), heals them again, leading them by the hand manifoldly to the understanding of those things of which they were yet ignorant. Very foolishly, sirs, (says he) are you offended at my words. For if you cannot yet believe, albeit oftentimes instructed, that my body will infuse life into you, how will you feel (he says) when you shall see it ascend even into heaven? For not only do I promise that I will ascend even into heaven itself, that you may not again say, *How?* but the sight shall be in your eyes, shaming every gainsayer. *If then you shall see* (says he) *the Son of man ascending into heaven, what will you say then?* For you will be convicted of no slight folly. For if you suppose that my flesh cannot put life into you, how can it ascend into heaven like a bird? For if it cannot quicken, because its nature is not to quicken, how will it soar in air, how mount up into the heavens? For this too is equally impossible for flesh. But if it ascends contrary to nature, what is to hinder it from quickening also, even though its nature be not to quicken, of its own nature? For he who made that heavenly which is from earth, will render it life-giving also, even though its nature be to decay, as regards its own self?

We must observe how he does not endure to be divided into two christs, according to the folly of some. For he keeps himself every way undivided after the Incarnation. For he says that *the Son of man ascends up where he was before,* although the earthly body was not above before this, but only the Word by itself before his concurrence with flesh. Well then has Paul put in his Epistle, *one Lord Jesus Christ* (*I Cor.* 8, 6). For he is one Son, both before the Incarnation and after the Incarnation, and we do not reckon his own body as alien from the Word. Wherefore he says that the Word which came down from above from heaven is also the Son of man. For he was made flesh, as the blessed Evangelist says (*John* 1, 14), and did not pass into flesh by change (for he is without turning and unchangeable by nature as God) but as it were dwelling in his own Temple, I mean that from the Virgin, and made man in very deed. But by saying that he will *ascend up where he was before* also, he gives his hearers to understand that he has come down from heaven. For thus it was like that they, understanding the force of the argument, should give heed to him not as to a man only, but should at length know that he is God the Word in the flesh, and believe that his body too is life-giving.

It is the Spirit That Quickens, the Flesh Profits Nothing (v. 63)

It is not unreasonably (he says) that you have clothed the flesh in no power of giving life. For when the nature of the flesh is considered alone and by itself, plainly it is not life-giving. For never will ought of things that are give life, but rather it has itself need of him who is mighty to quicken. But when the mystery of the Incarnation is carefully considered, and you then learn who it is who dwells in this flesh, you will then surely feel (he says) unless you would accuse *the divine Spirit* itself also, that it can impart life, although of itself *the flesh profits* not a bit. For since it was united to the life-giving Word, it has become wholly life-giving, hastening up to the power of the higher nature, not itself forcing unto its own nature him who cannot in any wise be subjected. Although then the nature of the flesh be in itself powerless to give life, yet will it effect this, when it has the life-working Word, and is replete with his whole operation. For it is the body of that which is by nature life, not of any earthly

being, as to whom one might rightly hold, *The flesh profits nothing.*
For not the flesh of Paul (for instance) nor yet of Peter, or any
other, would work this in us; but only and especially that of our
Savior Christ in whom dwelt *all the fulness of the Godhead bodily*
(*Col.* 2, 9).

For it would be a thing most absurd that honey should
infuse its own quality into things which naturally have no sweetness, and should have power to transfer into itself that wherewith
it is mingled, and that the life-giving nature of God the Word
should not be able to elevate to its own good that body which
it indwelt. Wherefore as to all other things the saying will be
true, that *the flesh profits nothing;* but as to Christ alone it holds
not, by reason that life, that is the only-begotten, dwelt therein.
And he calls himself Spirit, for *God is a Spirit* and as the blessed
Paul says, *For the Lord is the Spirit* (II *Cor.* 3, 17). And we do
not say these things, as taking away from the Holy Spirit his
proper existence; but as he calls himself Son of man, since
he was made man, so again he calls himself Spirit from his
own Spirit. For not other than he is his Spirit.

The Unity of the Person of Christ (v. 64)

He fills whole his own body with the life-giving operation
of the Spirit. For he now calls the flesh *Spirit,* not turning it
aside being flesh: but because by reason of its being perfectly united to him, and now endued with his whole life-giving
power, it ought to be called Spirit too. And no wonder, for be
not offended at this. For if *he that is joined unto the Lord is one
spirit* how shall not his own body rather be called one with him?
Something of this kind then he means in the passage before us:
I perceive from your reasoning within you (says he) that you
foolishly imagine that I am telling you, that the body of earth
is of its own nature life-giving: but this is not the drift of my
words. For my whole exposition to you was of the divine Spirit
and of eternal life. For it is not the nature of the flesh which
renders the Spirit life-giving, but the might of the Spirit makes
the body life-giving. *The words* then *which I* have discoursed
with *you, are spirit,* that is spiritual and of the Spirit, *and are life,*
i. e., life-giving and of that which is by nature life. And not
as repudiating his own flesh does he say these things, but
as teaching us what is the truth.

Christ and the Spirit

For what we have just said, this will we repeat for profit sake. The nature of the flesh cannot of itself quicken (for what more is there in him that is God by nature?) yet will it not be conceived of in Christ as alone and by itself: for it has united to it the Word, which is by nature life. When therefore Christ calls it life-giving, he does not testify the power of quickening to it so much, as to himself, or to his Spirit. For because of him is his own body too life-giving, since he re-fashioned it to his own power. But the "how" is neither to be apprehended by the mind, nor spoken by the tongue, but honored in silence and faith above understanding.

But that the Son too is often called by the name of Spirit by the God-inspired Scriptures, we shall know by what is enjoined. The blessed John then writes of him, *This is he that came by water and Spirit, Jesus Christ, not by water only, but by water and the Spirit: and it is the Spirit that bears witness, because the Spirit is truth* (I *John* 5, 6). Lo, he calls the Spirit truth, albeit Christ openly cries out, *I am the truth* (*John* 14, 6). Paul again writes to us saying, *They that are in the flesh cannot please God: but you are not in the flesh, but in the Spirit, if so be that the Spirit of God dwells in you, but if any man have not the Spirit of Christ, he is not his. But if Christ be in you, the body is dead because of sin, the Spirit is life because of righteousness* (*Rom.* 8, 8-10). Lo again, herein having proved that the Spirit of God dwells in us, he has said that Christ himself is in us. For insepa-rable from the Son is his Spirit, according to the count of identity of nature, even though he be conceived of as having a personal existence. Therefore he often names indifferently, sometimes the Spirit, sometimes himself.

4. CELEBRATIONS OF THE EUCHARIST AT CORINTH
(I Cor. 10, 13-22)

With the temptation God will also give you a way out that you may be able to bear it.

Therefore, beloved, flee from the worship of idols. I am speaking as to men of sense; judge for yourselves what I say. The cup of blessing that we bless, is it not the sharing of the blood of Christ? And the bread that we break, is it not the partaking of the body of the Lord?   Because the bread is one, we though many, are one body, all of us who partake of the one bread.

Behold Israel according to the flesh, are not they who eat of the sacrifices partakers of the altar?   What then do I say?   That what is sacrificed to idols is anything or that an idol is anything? No; but I say that what the Gentiles sacrifice "they sacrifice to devils and not to God"; and I would not have you become associates of devils.   You cannot drink the cup of the Lord and the cup of devils; you cannot be partakers of the table of the Lord and of the table of devils.

Or are we provoking the Lord to jealousy?   Are we stronger than he?

SAINT JOHN CHRYSOSTOM

HOMILY 24 ON I CORINTHIANS

May no temptation take hold of you, but such as man can bear: God is faithful, and will not permit you to be tempted beyond your strength; but with the temptation will also give you a way out that you may be able to bear it.[22]

1. Thus, because he (St. Paul) terrified them greatly, relating the ancient examples, and threw them into an agony, saying, *Let him who thinks he stands take heed lest he fall* (I *Cor.* 10, 12); though they had borne many temptations, and had exercised themselves many times therein; for *I was with you,* says he, *in weakness, and in fear, and in much trembling* (I *Cor.* 2, 3): lest they should say, "Why terrify and alarm us?   we are not unexercised in these troubles, for we have been both driven and persecuted, and many and continual dangers have we endured": repressing again their pride, he says, *there has no temptation taken you but such as man can bear,* i.e., small, brief, moderate.   For he uses the expression "man can bear," in respect of what is small; as when he says, *I speak after the manner of men because of the infirmity of your flesh* (*Rom.* 6, 19).   "Think not then great things," says he, "as though you had overcome the storm.   For never have you seen a danger threatening death nor a temptation intending

22. **Cor.** 10, 13.   The Greek text: PG 61, 199-206.   English trans., NPNF (ser. 1), 12, 138-143.

slaughter": which also he said to the Hebrews, *you have not yet resisted unto blood, striving against sin* (*Heb.* 12, 4).

Then, because he terrified them, see how again he raises them up, at the same time recommending moderation; in the words, *God is faithful, who will not permit you to be tempted beyond your strength.* There are therefore temptations which we are not able to bear. And what are these? All, so to speak. For the ability lies in God's gracious influence; a power which we draw down by our own will. Wherefore that you may know and see that not only those which exceed our power, but not even these which are "common to man" is it possible without assistance from God easily to bear, he added, *But will with the temptation also make the way of escape, that you may be able to endure it.*

For, says he, not even those moderate temptations, as I was remarking, may we bear by our own power: but even in them we require aid from him in our warfare that we may pass through them, and until we have passed, bear them. For he gives patience and brings on a speedy release; so that in this way also the temptation becomes bearable. This he covertly intimates, saying, *will also make the way of escape, that you may be able to bear it*: and all things he refers to him.

2. Ver. 14: *Wherefore, my brethren, flee from idolatry.* Again he courts them by the name of kindred, and urges them to be rid of this sin with all speed. For he did not say, simply, depart, but *flee;* and he calls the matter *idolatry,* and no longer bids them quit it merely on account of the injury to their neighbor, but signifies that the very thing of itself is sufficient to bring a great destruction.

Ver. 15: *I speak as to wise men: judge you what I say.* Because he has cried out aloud and heightened the accusation, calling it idolatry; that he might not seem to exasperate them and to make his speech disgusting, in what follows he refers the decision to them, and sets his judges down on their tribunal with an encomium. *For I speak as to wise men,* says he: which is the mark of one very confident of his own rights, that he should make the accused himself the judge of his allegations.

Thus also he more elevates the hearer, when he discourses not as commanding nor as laying down the law, but as advising with them and as actually pleading before them. For with the Jews, as more foolishly and childishly disposed, God did not so discourse, nor did he in every instance acquaint them with the reasons of the commands, but merely enjoined them; but here, because we have the privilege of great liberty, we are even admitted to be counsellors. And he discourses as with friends, and says, *I need no other judges, do you yourselves pass this sentence upon me, I take you for arbiters.*

The Cup of Blessing

3. Ver. 16: *The cup of blessing which we bless, is it not a communion of the blood of Christ?* What do you say, O blessed Paul? When you would appeal to the hearer's reverence, when you are making mention of awful mysteries, do you give the title of *cup of blessing* to that fearful and most tremendous cup? "Yes," says he; "and no mean title is that which was spoken. For when I call it *blessing,* I mean thanksgiving, and when I call it thanksgiving I unfold all the treasure of God's goodness, and call to mind those mighty gifts." Since we too, recounting over the cup the unspeakable mercies of God and all that we have been made partakers of, so draw near to him, and communicate; giving him thanks that he has delivered from error the whole race of mankind; that being afar off, he made them near; that when they had no hope and were without God in the world, he constituted them his own brethren and fellow-heirs. For these and all such things, giving thanks, thus we approach.

"How then are not your doings inconsistent," says he, "O you Corinthians; blessing God for delivering you from idols, yet running again to their tables?" *The cup of blessing which we bless, is it not a communion of the blood of Christ?* Very persuasively spoke he, and full of awe. For what he says is this: "This which is in the cup is that which flowed from his side, and of that do we partake." But he called it a cup of blessing, because holding it in our hands, we so exalt him in our hymn, wondering, astonished at his unspeakable gift, blessing him, among other things, for the pouring out of this self-same draught that we might not abide in error: and not only for the pouring it out, but also for the imparting thereof to us all. "Wherefore if you desire blood," says he, "redden not the altar of idols with the slaughter of brute beasts, but my altar with my blood." Tell me, what can be more tremendous than this? What more tenderly kind?

Blood is a Measure of True Love

This also lovers do. When they see those whom they love desiring what belongs to strangers and despising their own, they give what belongs to themselves, and so persuade them to withdraw themselves from the gifts of those others. Lovers, however, display this liberality in goods, and money, and garments, but in blood none ever did so. Whereas Christ even herein exhibited his care and fervent love for us. And in the old law, because they were in an imperfect state, the blood which they used to offer to idols he himself submitted to receive, that he might separate them from those idols; which very thing again was a proof of his unspeakable affection: but here he transferred the service to that which is far more awful and glorious, changing the very sacrifice itself, and instead of the slaughter of irrational creatures, commanding to offer up himself.

4. *The bread which we break, is it not a communion of the body of Christ?* Wherefore said he not, participation? Because he intended to express something more and to point out how close was the union: in that we communicate not only by participating and partaking, but also by being united. For as that body is united to Christ, so also are we united to him by this bread.

But why adds he also, "which we break?" For although in the Eucharist one may see this done, yet on the cross not so, but the very contrary. For, *A bone of him shall not be broken* (*Exod.* 12, 46). But that which he suffered not on the cross, this he suffers in the oblation for your sake, and submits to be broken, that he may fill all men.

Further, because he said, *a communion of the body*, and that which communicates is another thing from that whereof it communicates; even this which seems to be but a small difference, he took away. For having said, *a communion of the body,* he sought again to express something nearer. Wherefore also he added:

Ver. 17: *For we, who are many, are one bread, one body.*

Unity of Bread and of Man

"For why speak I of communion?" says he, "we are that self-same body." For what is the bread? The body of Christ. And what do they become who partake of it? The body of Christ:

not many bodies, but one body. For as the bread consisting of many grains is made one, so that the grains nowhere appear; they exist indeed, but their difference is not seen by reason of their conjunction; so are we conjoined both with each other and with Christ: there not being one body for you, and another for your neighbor to be nourished by, but the very same for all. Wherefore also he adds, *For we all partake of one bread.* Now if we are all nourished of the same and all become the same, why do we not also show forth the same love, and become also in this respect one?

For this was the old way too in the time of our forefathers: *for the multitude of them that believed, were of one heart and soul (Acts 4, 32).* Not so, however, now, but altogether the reverse. Many and various are the contests between all, and worse than wild beasts are we affected towards each other's members. And Christ indeed made you, so far remote, one with himself: but you do not deign to be united even to your brother with due exactness, but separate yourself, having had the privilege of so great love and life from the Lord. For he gave not simply even his own body; but because the former nature of the flesh which was framed out of earth, had first become deadened by sin and destitute of life; he brought in, as one may say, another sort of dough and leaven, his own flesh, by nature indeed the same, but free from sin and full of life; and gave to all to partake thereof, that being nourished by this and laying aside the old dead material, we might be blended together unto that which is living and eternal, by means of this table.

Communion with Christ's Body

5. Ver. 18: *Behold Israel after the flesh: have not they which eat the sacrifices communion with the altar?* Again, from the Old Covenant he leads them unto this point also. For because they were far beneath the greatness of the things which had been spoken, he persuades them both from former things and from those to which they were accustomed. And he says well, *according to the flesh,* as though they themselves were according to the Spirit. And what he says is of this nature: "even from persons of the grosser sort you may be instructed that they who eat the sacrifices, have communion with the altar." Do you see how he intimates that they who seemed to be perfect have not perfect

knowledge, if they know not even this, that the result of these sacrifices to many oftentimes is a certain communion and friendship with devils, the practice drawing them on by degrees? For if among men the fellowship of salt and the table becomes an occasion and token of friendship, it is possible that this may happen also in the case of devils.

But do you, I pray, consider, how with regard to the Jews he said not, "that they are partakers with God" but, *they have communion with the altar;* for what was placed thereon was burnt: but in respect to the body of Christ, not so. But how? It is *a communion of the Lord's body.* For not with the altar, but with Christ himself, do we have communion.

But having said that they have "communion with the altar," afterwards fearing lest he should seem to discourse as if the idols had any power and could do some injury, see again how he overthrows them, saying,

Ver. 19: *What say I then? That an idol is anything? or that a thing sacrificed to idols is anything?*

Worship of Devils

As if he had said, "Now these things I affirm, and try to withdraw you from the idols, not as though they could do any injury or had any power: for an idol is nothing; but I wish you to despise them." "And if you will have us despise them," says one, "wherefore do you carefully withdraw us from them?" Because they are not offered to your Lord.

Ver. 20: *For that which the Gentiles sacrifice,* says he, *they sacrifice to demons, and not to God.* Do not then run to the contrary things. For neither if you were a king's son, and having the privilege of your father's table, should leave it and choose to partake of the table of the condemned and the prisoners in the dungeon, would your father permit it, but with great vehemence he would withdraw you; not as though the table could harm you, but because it disgraces your nobility and the royal table. For verily these too are servants who have offended; dishonored, condemned, prisoners reserved for intolerable punishment, accountable for ten thousand crimes. How then are you not ashamed to imitate the gluttonous and vulgar crew, in that when these condemned persons set out a table, you run thither and partake of the viands? Here is the cause why I seek to withdraw you. For the intention of the sacrifices, and the person of the receivers, make the things set before you unclean.

And I would not that you should have communion with demons. Perceive also the very word, what force it has to express his feeling? *For it is my wish,* says he, *that you have nothing in common with them.*

6. Next, because he brought in the saying by way of exhortation, lest any of the grosser sort should make light of it as having license, because he said, "I would not," and "judge you"; he positively affirms in what follows and lays down the law, saying,

Ver. 21: *You cannot drink the cup of the Lord, and the cup of demons: you cannot partake of the Lord's table, and of the table of demons.* And he contents himself with the mere terms, for the purpose of keeping them away. Then, speaking also to their sense of shame,

Ver. 22: *Do we provoke the Lord to jealousy?* are we stronger than he? i.e., "Are we tempting him, whether he is able to punish us, and irritating him by going over to the adversaries and taking our stand with his enemies?" And this he said, reminding them of an ancient history and of their fathers' transgression. Wherefore also he makes use of this expression, which Moses likewise of old used against the Jews, accusing them of idolatry in the person of God. *For they,* says he, *moved me to jealousy with that which is not God; they provoked me to anger with their idols* (*Deut.* 32, 21).

"Are we stronger that he?" Do you see how terribly, how awfully he rebukes them, thoroughly shaking their very nerves, and by his way of reducing them to an absurdity, touching them to the quick and bringing down their pride? "Well, but why," someone will say, "did he not set down these things at first, which would be most effectual to withdraw them?" Because it is his custom to prove his point by many particulars, and to place the strongest last, and to prevail by proving more than was necessary. On this account, then, he began from the lesser topics, and so made his way to that which is the sum of all evils: since thus that last point also became more easily admitted, their mind having been smoothed down by the things said before.

Ver. 23, 24: *All things are lawful for me, but all things are not expedient: all things are lawful for me, but all things edify not. Let no man seek his own, but each his neighbor's good."*

Not All Things are Expedient

See his exact wisdom? Because it was likely that they might say, "I am perfect and master of myself, and it does me no harm to partake of what is set before me"; "Even so," says he, "perfect you are and master of yourself; do not however look to this, whether the result involve not injury, nay subversion." For both these he mentioned, saying, "All things are not expedient, all things edify not"; and using the former with reference to one's self, the latter, to one's brother: since the clause, "are not expedient," is a covert intimation of the ruin of the person to whom he speaks; but the clause, "edify not," of the stumbling block to the brother.

Wherefore also he adds, *Let no man seek his own*; which he insists upon everywhere through the whole Epistle and in that to the Romans; when he says, *For even Christ pleased not himself (Rom.* 15, 3): and again, *Even as I please all men in all things, not seeking mine own profit* (I *Cor.* 10, 33). And again in this place; he does not, however, fully work it out here. That is, since in what had gone before he had established it at length, and shown that he nowhere "seeks his own," but both "to the Jews became as a Jew and to them that are without law as without law," and used not his own "liberty" and "right" at random, but to the profit of all, serving all; he here broke off, content with a few words, by these few guiding them to the remembrance of all which had been said.

7. These things therefore knowing, let us also, beloved, consult for the good of the brethren and preserve unity with them. For to this that fearful and tremendous sacrifice leads us, warning us above all things to approach it with one mind and fervent love, and thereby becoming eagles, so to mount up to the very heaven, nay, even beyond the heaven, *For wheresoever the carcass is,* says he, *there also will be the eagles (Matt.* 24, 28), calling his body a carcass by reason of his death. For unless he had fallen, we should not have risen again. But he calls us eagles, implying that he who draws nigh to this body must be on high and have nothing common with the earth, nor wind himself downwards and creep along; but must ever be soaring heavenwards, and look on the Sun of Righteousness, and have the eye of his mind quicksighted. For eagles, not daws, have a right to this table. Those also

shall then meet him descending from heaven, who now worthily have this privilege, even as they who do so unworthily shall suffer the extremest torments.

The Grandeur and Power of God's Body

For if one would not inconsiderately receive a king—(why say I a king? nay, were it but a royal robe, one would not inconsiderably touch it with unclean hands)—though he should be in solitude, though alone, though no man were at hand: and yet the robe is nought but certain threads spun by worms: and if you admire the dye, this too is the blood of a dead fish; nevertheless, one would not choose to venture on it with polluted hands: I say now, if even a man's garment be what one would not venture inconsiderately to touch, what shall we say of the body of him who is God over all, spotless, pure, associate with the divine nature, the body whereby we are, and live; whereby the gates of hell were broken down and sanctuaries of heaven opened? How shall we receive this with so great insolence? Let us not, I pray you, let us not slay ourselves by our irreverence, but with all awfulness and purity draw nigh to It; and when you see It set before you, say to yourself, "Because of this Body am I no longer earth and ashes, no longer a prisoner, but free: because of this I hope for heaven, and to receive the good things therein, immortal life, the portion of angels, converse with Christ; this body, nailed and scourged, was more than death could stand against; this body the very sun saw sacrificed, and turned aside his beams; for this both the veil was rent in that moment, and rocks were burst asunder, and all the earth was shaken. This is even that body, the blood-stained, the pierced, and that out of which gushed the saving fountains, the one of blood, the other of water, for all the world."

Would you also learn its power from another source? Ask of her diseased with an issue of blood, who laid hold not of Itself, but of the garment with which It was clad; nay not of the whole of this, but of the hem: ask of the sea, which bore It on its back: ask even of the devil himself, and say, "Whence have you that incurable stroke? Whence have you no longer any power? Whence are you captive? By whom have you been seized in your flight?" And he will give no other answer than this, "The body that was crucified." By this were his goads broken in pieces; by this was his head crushed; by this were the powers and the principalities made a show of. *For, says he, having put off from himself principalities and powers, he made a show of them openly, triumphing over them in it* (*Col.* 2, 15).

This Body has Overcome the World

Ask also death, and say, "Whence is it that your sting has been taken away? your victory abolished? your sinews cut out? and you become the laughing-stock of girls and children, who was before a terror even to kings and to all righteous men?" And he will ascribe it to this body. For when this was crucified, then were the dead raised up, then was that prison burst, and the gates of brass were broken, and the dead were loosed, and the keepers of hell-gate all cowered in fear. And yet, had he been one of the many, death on the contrary should have become more mighty; but it was not so. For he was not one of the many. Therefore was death dissolved. And as they who take food which they are unable to retain, on account of that vomit up also what was before lodged in them; so also it happened unto death. That body, which he could not digest, he received: and therefore had to cast forth that which he had within him. Indeed, he travailed in pain, while he held him, and was straitened until he vomited him up. Wherefore says the Apostle, *Having loosed the pains of death* (*Acts* 11, 24). For never woman laboring of child was so full of anguish as he was torn and racked in sunder, while he held the body of the Lord. And that which happened to the Babylonian dragon, when, having taken the food it burst asunder in the midst,[23] this also happened unto him. For Christ came not forth again by the mouth of death, but having burst asunder and ripped up in the very midst, the belly of the dragon, thus from his secret chambers (*Ps.* 19, 5) right gloriously he issued forth and flung abroad his beams not to this heaven alone, but to the very throne most high. For even thither did he carry it up.

This body has he given to us both to hold and to eat; a thing appropriate to intense love. For those whom we kiss vehemently,

---

23. Bel and the Dragon, v. 27.

we oftentimes even bite with our teeth. Wherefore also Job, indicating the love of his servants towards him, said, that they oftentimes, out of their great affection towards him, said, *Oh! that we were filled with his flesh!* (*Job* 31, 31). Even so Christ has given to us to be filled with his flesh, drawing us on to greater love.

Fervent Communion

8. Let us draw nigh to him then with fervency and with inflamed love, that we may not have to endure punishment. For in proportion to the greatness of the benefits bestowed on us, so much the more exceedingly are we chastised when he show ourselves unworthy of the bountifulness. This body, even lying in a manger, the Magi reverenced. Indeed, men profane and barbarous, leaving their country and their home, both set out on a long journey, and when they came, with fear and great trembling worshipped him. Let us, then, at least imitate those barbarians, we who are citizens of heaven. For they indeed when they saw him but in a manger, and in a hut, and no such thing was in sight as you behold now, drew nigh with great awe; but you behold him not in the manger but on the altar, not a woman holding him in her arms, but the priest standing by, and the Spirit with exceeding bounty hovering over the gifts set before us. You do not see merely this body itself as they did, but you know also Its power, and the whole economy, and are ignorant of none of the holy things which are brought to pass by It, having been exactly initiated into all.

Let us therefore rouse ourselves up and be filled with horror, and let us show forth a reverence far beyond that of those barbarians; that we may not by random and careless approaches heap fire upon our own heads. But these things I say, not to keep us from approaching, but to keep us from approaching without consideration. For as the approaching at random is dangerous, so non-communicating in those mystical suppers is famine and death. For this Table is the sinews of our soul, the bond of our mind, the foundation of our confidence, our hope, our salvation, our light, our life. When with this sacrifice we depart into the outer world, with much confidence we shall tread the sacred threshold, fenced round on every side with a kind of golden armor. And why speak I of the world to come? Since here this mystery makes earth become to you a heaven. Open only once the gates of heaven and look in; nay, rather not of heaven, but of the heaven of heavens; and then you will behold what I have been speaking of. For what is there most precious of all, this will I show you lying upon the earth. For as in royal palaces, what is most glorious of all is not walls, nor golden roofs, but the person of the king sitting on the throne, so likewise in heaven the body of the King. But this, you are now permitted to see upon earth. For it is not angels, nor archangels, nor heavens and heavens of heavens, that I show you, but the very Lord and owner of these. Perceive how that which is more precious than all things is seen by you on earth; and not seen only, but also touched; and not only touched, but likewise eaten; and after receiving it you go home.

Make your soul clean then, prepare your mind for the reception of these mysteries. For if you were entrusted to carry a king's child with the robes, the purple, and the diadem, you would cast away all things which are upon the earth. But now that is no child of man how royal soever, but the only-begotten Son of God himself, whom you received; do you not thrill with awe, tell me, and cast away all the love of all worldly things, and have no bravery but that wherewith to adorn yourself? Or do you still look towards earth, and love money, and pant after gold? What pardon then can you have? What excuse? Do you not know that all this worldly luxury is loathsome to your Lord? Was it not for this that on his birth he was laid in a manger, and took to himself a mother of low state? Did he not for this say to him that was looking after gain, *But the Son of man has not where to lay his head?* (*Matt.* 8, 20)

And what did the disciples? Did they not observe the same law, being taken to houses of the poor and lodged, one with a tanner, another with a tent-maker, and with the seller of purple? For they inquired not after the splendor of the house, but for the virtues of men's souls.

These therefore let us also emulate, hastening by the beauty of pillars and of marbles, and seeking the mansions which are above; and let us tread under foot all the pride here below with all love of money, and acquire a lofty mind. For if we be sober-minded, not even this whole world is worthy of us, much less porticoes and arcades. Wherefore, I beseech you, let us adorn our souls, let us fit up this house which we are also to have with us when we depart; that we attain even to the eternal blessings, through the grace and mercy of our Lord Jesus Christ, to whom with the Father and the Holy Spirit, be glory, honor and power, now and forever.   Amen.

PART THREE

The Teaching of the Fathers
on the Mass

IRENAEUS OF LYONS
INSCRIPTIONS
CYPRIAN OF CARTHAGE
HILARY OF POITIERS
BASIL OF CAESAREA
AUGUSTINE OF HIPPO
PETER CHRYSOLOGUS
FAUSTUS OF RIEZ
CAESARIUS OF ARLES

The teaching of the Fathers developed parallel to the development of the liturgy from the second to the sixth centuries. Irenaeus
and Cyprian are particularly concerned to safeguard and transmit
the lessons of tradition. In passing the bishop of Lyons strives
to situate the Eucharist in the economy of salvation; it is seen
as the recapitulation of the whole history of sacrifice and
anticipates the *parousia* or second coming. Cyprian relies on
current catechesis to recall that the Eucharist is the body and
blood of Christ; it is the sacrifice of the Lord which saves us
all by inclusion.

The texts of the fourth century Fathers enable us to assess the
importance of the mystery of the Eucharist in the life of the Church,
in the East and West. Two Fathers, both pastors, John Chrysostom
and Augustine, enrich this teaching, the former in his commentary
on the New Testament in particular as we have already seen, and
the latter, in the numerous homilies addressed to the newly baptized.
Chrysostom emphasizes charity in order that communion may be a
true sharing and that the poor may have their share; Augustine
insists on the affinities that exist between the body of Christ and the
Church: the faithful must become the mystery which they receive.

For Hilary and Cyril of Alexandria the Eucharist is above

all the principle of the divine life. It establishes a physical union between Christ and the communicants. It makes the Church share in the very life of God. "The bread is one, we all become one body because we all share in the one bread."

The preaching of the fifth and sixth centuries, which is better known to us through Gallic writers, concerns itself especially with concrete applications, the moral consequences implied by the eucharistic sacrifice for the lives of the faithful.

IRENAEUS OF LYONS
(† 202 A.D.)

The Christian community of Lyons was composed in part of Asiatics from Phrygia. We know the vitality of their Christianity from a letter in the year 177 which recounts the martyrdom of a great number of the brethren. Bishop Pothinus perished in the persecution and was succeeded by the young Irenaeus. A disciple of Polycarp and a witness of the Johannine tradition, he worked all his life to further peace and unity which was threatened by heresy. Two of his literary works survive: the *Apostolic Demonstration,* a sort of catechism, and *Against Heresies,* a refutation of Gnostic errors.

The analysis of Gnostic sects provides Irenaeus with an opportunity to oppose their magical practices with an exposition of the Christian mysteries. The heretics opposed the God of the New Testament to that of the Old. Irenaeus in reply shows the essential unity of God throughout the history of revelation. God is at once the God of Abraham, Isaac and Jacob, and Jesus Christ.

All history converges toward the coming of Christ. This brings to an end the era of preparation and gives consistency to all human aspiration. The sacrifice of the New Covenant perfects and replaces the institutions of the old: the Law, circumcision, and sacrifice. Here Irenaeus outlines a theology of sacrifice in general and of Christian sacrifice in particular.[1] This is given here in translation.

---

1. See A. D'Alès, "La doctrine eucharistique de saint Irénée," **Rech. de sc. relig.** 13 (1923), 24-46; D. Van Den Eynde, "Eucharistia ex duabus rebus constans: S. Irénée, **Adv. Haer.** 4, 18, 5," **Antonianum** 15 (1940), 13-28.

The ecclesial offering of the first-fruits of the earth show firstly that man recognized the living God as the Lord and author of of this created world which nourished the body with bread. At the same time he is the author of the economy of salvation which has been realized by the incarnate Word—his hand—in the creation of the world. Bread, a creature of God, constitutes the new offering of food given by God which is returned to him. The eucharistic action of Christ has consecrated bread and wine into his own body and blood; by the eucharistic act of consecration the Church offers the first-fruits of the new covenant which perfects and sums up all the sacrifices of the past.

The Eucharist which renders efficacious thanks, sanctifies and transforms in a single movement both offerings and offerers; the bread and wine into the body of Christ. As Christ has taken the same body as ourselves, he has saved our flesh and will make it share in his glorified state. He gives us in the Eucharist this same flesh and this same blood which today are in the state of glory as an assurance to us of our own bodily resurrection. Man, body and soul, becomes incorruptible, marked with the seal of resurrection.

The Christian life, through the practice of charity and works of mercy, becomes an interior sacrifice and enriches the gift which it has received. This is the meaning assumed by "our prayers and our oblations which rise without ceasing to the altar." Such is the new cult of the Church, an everyday one, "by which the Christian renders worship to God every day in the temple of God, that is the body of man, in practicing justice for all time." The sacrifice of the Eucharist elevates the whole of existence and restores all of creation to God and the Father.

AGAINST HERESIES [2]

FROM JEWISH SACRIFICES TO THAT OF THE CHURCH

Only the Catholic Church can offer to God the sacrifice which is pleasing to him, announced by the prophets, namely the sacrifice of the Eucharist. It utilizes the products of creation, bread, and wine which, contrary to the allegations of the Gnostics, is good.

---

2. 4, 17-18. Greek text: PG 7, 1019-1029. Eng. trans., ANF I, 482-486.

These elements are consecrated by the Church by the words of Christ as handed down in tradition.

What Sacrifice is Pleasing to God?

1. Moreover, the Prophets indicate in the fullest manner that God stood in no need of their slavish obedience, but that it was in their own interest that he enjoined certain observances in the law. And again, that God needed not their oblation, but [merely demanded it], on account of man himself who offers it, the Lord taught clearly, as I have pointed out. For when he perceived them neglecting righteousness, and abstaining from the love of God, and imagining that God was to be propitiated by sacrifices and the other typical observances, Samuel did even thus speak to them: *God does not desire whole burnt-offerings and sacrifices, he will have his voice to be hearkened to. Behold, a ready obedience is better than sacrifice, and obedience than the fat of rams* (I *Sam.* 15, 22). David also says: *Sacrifice and oblation you did not desire, but mine ears have you perfected; burnt-offerings also for sin you have not required* (*Ps.* 40, 6). He thus teaches them that God desires obedience, which renders them secure, rather than sacrifices and holocausts, which avail them nothing towards righteousness; and [by this declaration] he prophesies the New Covenant at the same time. Still clearer too, does he speak of these things in the fiftieth Psalm: *For if you had desired sacrifice, then would I have given it*: *You will not delight in burnt-offerings. The sacrifice of God is a broken spirit; a broken and contrite heart the Lord will not despise* (*Ps.* 51, 16-17).

Because, therefore God stands in need of nothing, he declares in the preceding Psalm: *I will take no calves out of your house, nor he-goats out of your fold. For mine are all the beasts of the earth, the herds and the oxen on the mountains*: *I know all the fowls of heaven, and the various tribes of the field are mine. If I were hungry, I would not tell you: for the world is mine, and the fullness thereof. Shall I eat the flesh of bulls, or drink the blood of goats?* (*Ps.* 50, 9-13)

Then, lest it might be supposed that he refused these things in his anger, he continues, giving him (man) counsel: *Often unto God the sacrifice of praise, and pay your vows to the Most High; and call upon me in the day of your trouble, and I will deliver you, and you shall glorify me* (*Ps.* 50, 14-15); rejecting, indeed, those things by which sinners imagined they could propitiate God, and showing that he does himself stand in need of nothing; but he exhorts and advises them to those things by which man is justified and draws nigh to God.   This same declaration does Isaiah make: *To what purpose is the multitude of your sacrifices unto me?* says the Lord. *I am full* (*Isa.* 1, 11).   And when he had repudiated holocausts, and sacrifices, and oblations, as likewise the new moons, and the sabbaths, and the festivals, and all the rest of the services accompanying these, he continues, exhorting them to what pertained to salvation: *Wash you, make you clean, take away wickedness from your hearts from before mine eyes: cease from your evil ways, learn to do well, seek judgment, relieve the oppressed, judge the fatherless, plead for the widow; and come, let us reason together, says the Lord* (*Isa.* 1, 16-18).

Humility and Obedience

2. For it was not because he was angry, like a man, as many venture to say, that he rejected their sacrifices; but out of compassion to their blindness, and with the view of suggesting to them the true sacrifice, by offering which shall appease God, that they may receive life from him.   As he elsewhere declares: *The sacrifice to God is an afflicted heart: a sweet savor to God is a heart glorifying him who formed it.*[3]   For if, when angry, he had repudiated these sacrifices of theirs, as if they were persons unworthy to obtain his compassion, he would not certainly have urged these same things upon them as those by which they might be saved.   But inasmuch as God is merciful, he did not cut them off from good counsel.   For after he had said by Jeremiah, *To what purpose bring you me incense from Saba, and cinnamon from a far country?   Your whole burnt-offerings and sacrifices are not acceptable to me* (*Jer.* 6, 20); he proceeds: *Hear the word of the Lord, all Judah.   These things says the Lord, the God of Israel, make straight your ways and your doings, and I will establish you in this place.   Put not your trust in lying words, for they will not at all profit you, saying, The temple of the Lord, the temple of the Lord, it is* [*here*] (*Jer.* 7, 2-3).

---

3. This passage is not now found in Holy Scripture.

3. And again, when he points out that it was not for this that he led them out of Egypt, that they might offer sacrifice to him, but that, forgetting the idolatry of the Egyptians, they should be able to hear the voice of the Lord, which was to them salvation and glory, he declares by this same Jeremiah: *Thus says the Lord; Collect together your burnt-offerings with your sacrifices, and eat flesh. For I spoke not unto your fathers, nor commanded them in the day that I brought them out of Egypt, concerning burnt-offerings or sacrifices: but this word I commanded them, saying, Hear my voice, and I will be your God, and you shall be my people; and walk in all my ways whatsoever I have commanded you, that it may be well with you. But they obeyed not, nor hearkened; but walked in the imaginations of their own evil heart, and went backwards, and not forwards* (Jer. 7, 21-24). And again, when he declares by the same man, *But let him that glories, glory in this, to understand and know that I am the Lord, who doth exercise loving-kindness, and righteousness, and judgment in the earth;* he adds, *For in these things I delight, says the Lord* (Jer. 9, 24), but not in sacrifices, nor in holocausts, nor in oblations. For the people did not receive these precepts as of primary importance, but as secondary, and for the reason already alleged, as Isaiah again says: *You have not* [brought to] *me the sheep of your holocaust, nor in your sacrifices have you glorified me: you have not served me in sacrifices, nor in* [the matter of] *frankincense have you done anything laboriously; neither have you bought for me incense with money, nor have I desired the fat of your sacrifices; but you have stood before me in your sins and in your iniquities* (Isa. 43, 23-24). He says, therefore, *Upon this man will I look, even upon him that is humble, and meek, and who trembles at my words* (Isa. 46, 2). *For the fat and the fat flesh shall not take away from you your unrighteousness* (Jer. 11, 15). *This is the fast which I have chosen, says the Lord. Loose every band of wickedness, dissolve the connections of violent agreements, give rest to those that are shaken, and cancel every unjust document. Deal your bread to the hungry willingly, and lead into your house the roofless stranger. If you have seen the naked, cover him, and you shall not despise those of your own flesh and blood. Then shall your morning light break forth, and your health shall spring forth more speedily; and righteousness shall go before you, and the glory of the Lord shall surround you: and while you*

are yet speaking, I will say, Behold, here I am (*Isa.* 58, 6-9).
And Zacharias also, among the twelve Prophets, pointing out to
the people the will of God, says: *These things does the Lord Omnipotent declare: Execute true judgment, and show mercy and
compassion each one to his brother.   And oppress not the widow,
and the orphan, and the proselyte, and the poor; and let none
imagine evil against you brother in his heart* (*Zach.* 7, 9-10).
And again, he says: *These are the words which you shall utter.
Speak you the truth every man to his neighbor, and execute peaceful judgment in your gates, and let none of you imagine evil in his
heart against his brother, and you shall not love false swearing:
for all these things I hate, says the Lord Almighty* (*Zach.* 8, 16-
17).   Moreover David also says in like manner: *What man is
there who desires life, and would fain see good days?   Keep your
tongue from evil, and your lips that they speak no guile.   Shun
evil, and do good: seek peace, and pursue it* (*Ps.* 34, 13-14).

4. From all these it is evident that God did not seek sacrifices
and holocausts from them, but faith, and obedience, and righteousness, because of their salvation.   As God, when teaching
them his will in Hosea the Prophet, said, *I desire mercy rather
than sacrifice, and the knowledge of God more than burnt-offerings* (*Hos.* 6, 6).   Besides, our Lord also exhorted them to the
same effect, when he said, *But if you had known what [this]
means, I will have mercy, and not sacrifice, you would not have
condemned the guiltless* (*Matt.* 12, 7).   Thus does he bear witness to the Prophets, that they preached the truth; but accuses
these men (his hearers) of being foolish through their own fault.

The Sacrifice of the New Covenant: Jesus Christ

5. Again, giving directions to his disciples to offer to God
the first-fruits of his own created things—not as if he stood in
need of them, but that they might be themselves neither unfruitful
nor ungrateful—he took that created thing, bread, and gave thanks,
and said, *This is My body* (*Matt.* 26, 26).   And the cup likewise,
which is part of that creation to which we belong, he confessed
to be his blood, and taught the new oblation of the New Covenant;
which the Church receiving from the apostles, offers to God
throughout all the world, to him who gives us as the means of
subsistence the first-fruits of his own gifts in the New Testament,
concerning which Malachi, among the twelve Prophets, thus spoke

before-hand: *I have no pleasure in you, says the Lord Omnipotent, and I will not accept sacrifice at your hands. For from the rising of the sun, unto the going down* [of the same], *my name is glorified among the Gentiles, and in every place incense is offered to my name, and a pure sacrifice; for great is my name among the Gentiles, says the Lord Omnipotent* (*Mal.* 1, 10-11);—indicating in the plainest manner, by these words, that the former people [the Jews] shall indeed cease to make offerings to God, but that in every place sacrifice shall be offered to him, and that a pure one; and his name is glorified among the Gentiles.

6. But what other name is there which is glorified among the Gentiles than that of our Lord, by whom the Father is glorified, and man also? And because it is [the name] of his own Son, who was made man by him, he calls it his own. Just as a king, if he himself paints a likeness of his son, is right in calling this likeness his own, for both these reasons, because it is [the likeness] of his son, and because it is his own production; so also does the Father confess the name of Jesus Christ, which is throughout all the world glorified in the Church, to be his own, both because it is that of his Son, and because he who thus describes it gave him for the salvation of men. Since, therefore, the name of the Son belongs to the Father, and since in the omnipotent God the Church makes offerings through Jesus Christ, he says well on both these grounds, *And in every place incense is offered to my name, and a pure sacrifice.* Now John, in the Apocalypse, declares that the "incense" is *the prayer of the saints* (*Rev.* 5, 8).

Chapter 18 — *A Sincere Sacrifice*

1. The oblation of the Church, therefore, which the Lord gave instructions to be offered throughout all the world, is accounted with God a pure sacrifice, and is acceptable to him; not that he stands in need of a sacrifice from us, but that he who offers is himself glorified in what he does offer, if his gift be accepted. For by the gift both honor and affection are shown forth towards the King; and the Lord, wishing us to offer it in all simplicity and innocence, did express himself thus: *Therefore, when you offer your gift upon the altar, and shall remember that your brother has ought against you, leave your gift before the altar, and go your way; first be reconciled to your brother, and then return and offer the gift* (*Matt.* 5, 23-24). We are bound, therefore, to

offer to God the first-fruits of his creation, as Moses also says, *Thou shalt not appear in the presence of the Lord thy God empty* (*Deut.* 16, 16); so that man, being accounted as grateful, by those things in which he has shown his gratitude, may receive that honor which flows from him.

An Offering of Free Men

2. And the class of oblations in general has not been set aside; for there were both oblations there [among the Jews], and there are oblations here [among the Christians]. Sacrifices there were among the people; sacrifices there are, too, in the Church: but the species alone has been changed, inasmuch as the offering is now made, not by slaves, but by freemen. For the Lord is [ever] one and the same; but the character of a servile oblation is peculiar [to itself], as is also that of freemen, in order that, by the very oblations, the indication of liberty may be set forth. For with him there is nothing purposeless, nor without signification, nor without design. And for this reason they (the Jews) had indeed the tithes of their goods consecrated to him, but those who have received liberty set aside all their possessions for the Lord's purposes, bestowing joyfully and freely not the less valuable portions of their property, since they have the hope of better things [hereafter]; as that poor widow acted who cast all her living into the treasury of God (cf. *Luke* 21, 4).

The Sacrifice of the Sinner

3. For at the beginning God had respect to the gifts of Abel, because he offered with single-mindedness and righteousness; but He had no respect unto the offering of Cain, because his heart was divided with envy and malice, which he cherished against his brother, as God says when reproving his hidden [thoughts], *Though you offer rightly, yet, if you do not divide rightly, have you not sinned? Be at rest* (*Gen.* 4, 7); since God is not appeased by sacrifice. For if any one shall endeavor to offer a sacrifice merely to outward appearance, unexceptionally, in due order, and according to appointment, while in his soul he does not assign to his neighbor that fellowship with him which is right and proper, nor is under the fear of God;—he who thus cherishes secret sin does not deceive God by that sacrifice which is offered correctly

as to outward appearance; nor will such an oblation profit him anything, but [only] the giving up of that evil which has been conceived within him, so that sin may not the more, by means of the hypocritical action, render him the destroyer of himself. Wherefore did the Lord also declare: *Woe unto you, scribes and Pharisees, hypocrites, for you are like whited sepulchres. For the sepulchre appears beautiful outside, but within it is full of dead men's bones, and all uncleanness; even so you outwardly appear righteous unto men, but within you are full of wickedness and hypocrisy (Matt. 23, 27-28)*. For while they were thought to offer correctly so far as outward appearance went, they had in themselves jealousy like to Cain; therefore they slew the Just One, slighting the counsel of the Word, as did also Cain.

For [God] said to him, *Be at rest;* but he did not assent. Now what else is it to "be at rest" than to forego intended violence? And saying similar things to these men, he declares: *You blind Pharisee, cleanse that which is within the cup, that the outside may be clean also (Matt. 23, 26)*. And they did not listen to him. For Jeremiah says, *Behold neither your eyes nor your heart are good; but* [they are turned] *to your covetousness, and to shed innocent blood, and for injustice, and for man-slaying, that you may do it (Jer. 22, 17)*. And again Isaiah says, *You have taken counsel, but not for me; and made covenants,* [but] *not by my Spirit (Isa. 30, 1)*. In order, therefore, that their inner wish and thought, being brought to light, may show that God is without blame, and works no evil—that God who reveals what is hidden [in the heart], but who works not evil—when Cain was by no means as rest, he says to him: *To you shall be his desire, and you shall rule over him (Gen. 4, 7)*. Thus did he in like manner speak to Pilate: *You should have no power at all against me, unless it were given you from above (John 19, 11)*, God always giving up the righteous one [in this life to suffering], that he, having been tested by what he suffered may [at last] be accepted; but that the evil-doer, being judged by the actions he has performed, may be rejected.

A Pure Sacrifice

Sacrifices, therefore, do not sanctify a man, for God stands in no need of sacrifice; but it is the conscience of the offerer that sanctifies when it is pure, and thus moves God to accept [the offering] as from a friend. *But the sinner, says he, who kills a calf [in sacrifice] to me, is as if he slew a dog (Isa.* 66, 3).

4. Inasmuch, then, as the Church offers with single-mindedness, her gift is justly reckoned a pure sacrifice with God.   As Paul also says to the Philippians, *I am full, having received from Epaphroditus the things that were sent from you, the odor of a sweet smell, a sacrifice acceptable, pleasing to God (Phil.* 4, 18).

For it behooves us to make an oblation to God, and in all things to be found grateful to God our Maker, in a pure mind, and in faith without hypocrisy, in well-grounded hope, in fervent love, offering the first-fruits of his own created things.   And the Church alone offers this pure oblation to the Creator, offering to him, with giving of thanks, [the things taken] from his creation.

Heresies Offer Insults

But the Jews do not offer thus: for their hands are full of blood; for they have not received the Word, through whom it is offered to God.   Nor, again, do any of the assemblies of the heretics [offer this].   For some, by maintaining that the Father is different from the Creator, do, when they offer to him what belongs to this creation of ours, set him forth as being covetous of another's property, and desirous of what is not his own.   Those, again, who maintain that the things around us originated from apostasy, ignorance, and passion, do, while offering unto him the fruits of ignorance, passion, and apostasy, sin against their Father, rather subjecting him to insult than giving him thanks.   But how can they be consistent with themselves, [when they say] that the bread over which thanks have been given is the body of their Lord, and the cup his blood, if they do not call himself the Son of the Creator of the world, that is, his Word, through whom the tree fructifies, and the fountains gush forth, and the earth gives *first the blade, then the ear, then the full corn in the ear (Mark* 4, 28).

5. Then, again, how can they say that the flesh, which is nourished with the body of the Lord and with His blood, goes

to corruption, and does not partake of life? Let them, therefore, either alter their opinion, or cease from offering the things just mentioned. But our opinion is in accordance with the Eucharist, and the Eucharist in turn establishes our opinion. For we offer to him his own, announcing consistently the fellowship and union of the flesh and Spirit. For as the bread, which is produced from the earth, when it receives the invocation of God, is no longer common bread, but the Eucharist, consisting of two realities, earthly and heavenly; so also our bodies, when they receive the Eucharist, are no longer corruptible, having the hope of the resurrection to eternity.

We Need to Offer Sacrifice

6. Now we make offering to him, not as though he stood in need of it, but rendering thanks for his gifts, and thus sanctifying what has been created. For even as God does not need our possessions, so do we need to offer something to God; as Solomon says: *He that has pity upon the poor, lends unto the Lord (Prov. 19, 17).*

For God, who stands in need of nothing, takes our good works to himself for this purpose, that he may grant us a recompense of his own good things, as our Lord says: *Come you blessed of my Father, receive the kingdom prepared for you. For I was hungry, and you gave me to eat; I was thirsty, and you gave me to drink; I was a stranger, and you took me in; naked, and you clothed me; sick, and you visited me; in prison, and you came to me (Matt. 25, 34).* As, therefore, he does not stand in need of these [services], yet does desire that we should render them for our own benefit, lest we be unfruitful; so did the Word give to the people that very precept as to the making of oblations, although he stood in no need of them, that they might learn to serve God: thus is it, therefore, also his will that we, too, should offer a gift at the altar, frequently and without intermission. The altar, then, is in heaven [4] (for towards that place are our prayers and oblations directed); the temple likewise [is

---

4. [The **Sursum Corda** seems here in mind. The object of Eucharistic adoration is the Creator, our "great High Priest, passed into the heavens," and in bodily substance there enthroned, according to our author.]

there], as John says in the Apocalypse, *And the temple of God was opened*: the tabernacle also: *For, behold,* he says, *the tabernacle of God, in which he will dwell with men* (*Rev.* 11, 19; 21, 3).

CHRIST REDEEMS US BY HIS FLESH WHICH HE GIVES IN THE EUCHARIST [5]

Saint Irenaeus simultaneously combats two Gnostic errors: one which attributes creation to a demiurge other than the Father, the other which denies the resurrection of the flesh. Both are refuted by means of the Eucharist. Bread and wine are creatures of God. Would he have approved of them if he were not their author? These gifts when consecrated confer incorruptibility on our flesh.

God Came among His Own

1. Vain also are those who claim that God came to those things which did not belong to him, as if covetous of another's property; in order that he might deliver up that man who had been created by another, to that God who had neither made nor formed anything, but who also was deprived from the beginning of his own proper formation of men. The advent, therefore, of him whom these men represent as coming to the things of others, was not righteous; nor did he truly redeem us by his own blood, if he did not really become man, restoring to his own handiwork what was said [of it] in the beginning, that man was made after the image and likeness of God; not snatching away by stratagem the property of another, but taking possession of his own in a righteous and gracious manner. As far as concerned the apostasy, indeed, he redeems us righteously from it by his own blood; but as regards us who have been redeemed, [he does this] graciously. For we have given nothing to him previously, nor does he desire anything from us, as if he stood in need of it; but we do stand in need of fellowship with him. And for this reason it was that he graciously poured himself out, that he might gather us into the bosom of the Father.

---

5. **Adv. Haer.** 5, 2 (PG 7, 1123-28). Eng. trans. ANF 1, 528.

The Flesh Will Be Saved

2. But vain in every respect are they who despise the entire dispensation of God, and disallow the salvation of the flesh, and treat with contempt its regeneration, maintaining that it is not capable of incorruption.   But if this indeed do not attain salvation, then neither did the Lord redeem us with his blood, nor is the cup of the Eucharist the communion of his blood, nor the bread which we break the communion of his body (I *Cor.* 10, 16).   For blood can only come from veins and flesh, and whatsoever else makes up the substance of man, such as the Word of God was actually made.

By his own blood he redeemed us, as also his Apostle declares, *In whom we have redemption through his blood, even the remission of sins (Col.* 1, 14).   And as we are his members, we are also nourished by means of the creation (and he himself grants the creation to us, for he causes his sun to rise, and sends rain when he will) (*Matt.* 5, 45).   He has acknowledged the cup (which is a part of the creation) as his own blood, from which he bedews our blood; and the bread (also a part of the creation) he has established as his own body, from which he gives increase to our bodies.

Eucharist and Resurrection

3. When, therefore, the mingled cup and the manufactured bread receives the Word of God, and the Eucharist of the blood and the body of Christ is made, from which things the substance of our flesh is increased and supported, how can they affirm that the flesh is incapable of receiving the gift of God, which is life eternal, which [flesh] is nourished from the body and blood of the Lord, and is a member of him?—even as the blessed Paul declares in his Epistle to the Ephesians, that *we are members of his body, of his flesh, and of his bones (Eph.* 5, 30).   He does not speak these words of some spiritual and invisible man, *for a spirit has not bones nor flesh (Luke* 24, 39), but [he refers to] that dispensation [by which the Lord became] an actual man, consisting of flesh, and nerves, and bones,—that [flesh] which is nourished by the cup which is his blood, and receives increase from the bread which is his body.

And just as a cutting from the vine planted in the ground fructifies in its season, or as a corn of wheat falling into the earth and becoming decomposed, rises with manifold increase by the Spirit of God, who contains all things, and then, through the wisdom of God, serves for the use of men, and having received the Word of God, becomes the Eucharist, which is the body and blood of Christ; so also our bodies, being nourished by it, and deposited in the earth, and suffering decomposition there, shall rise at their appointed time, the Word of God granting them resurrection to the glory of God, even the Father, who freely *gives to this mortal immortality, and to this corruptible incorruption* (I *Cor.* 15, 53), because *the strength of God is made perfect in weakness* (II *Cor.* 12, 9). In order that we may never become puffed up, as if we had life from ourselves, and exalted against God, our minds becoming ungrateful; let us learn by experience that we possess eternal duration from the excelling power of this Being, not from our own nature, so that we may neither undervalue that glory which surrounds God as he is, nor be ignorant of our own nature, but that we may know what God can effect, and what benefits man receives, and thus never wander from the true comprehension of things as they are, that is, both with regard to God and with regard to man. And might it not be the case, perhaps, as I have already observed, that for this purpose God permitted our resolution into the common dust of mortality, that we, being instructed by every mode, may be accurate in all things for the future, being ignorant neither of God nor of ourselves?

INSCRIPTIONS

The Inscriptions have preserved for us moving testimonies of the faith in the Eucharist of the early Christians.

"These inscriptions," says Mommsen, "pertain not to literature but to life." Biblical and liturgical echoes are frequent. The faithful repeat what Irenaeus has just developed and what is the teaching of the entire Church: the body and blood of Christ received in the Eucharist is a pledge of the resurrection of the body and of life everlasting.

Abercius and Pectorius say this explicitly. Other Inscriptions are content to inscribe a loaf, or a fish, symbols of the Eucharist, Christ being "the Fish of the living" as one Inscription puts it.

INSCRIPTION OF ABERCIUS *

"The citizen of a chosen city, this [monument] I made [while] living, that there I might have in time a resting-place for my body. My name is Abercius, the disciple of a holy shepherd,[6] who feeds flocks of sheep on mountains and in plains, who has great eyes that see everywhere. It was he who taught me the book worthy of belief. For he (the shepherd) sent me to Rome to contemplate majesty, and to see a queen golden-robed and golden-sandalled; there also I saw a people bearing a shining mark.[7] And I saw the land of Syria and all its cities—Nisibis [I] saw when I passed over Euphrates. But everywhere I had brethren. I had Paul.... Faith everywhere led me forward, and everywhere provide as my food a fish of exceeding great size and perfect, which a holy virgin (Mary) drew with her hand from a fountain ... and this (faith) ever gives to her friends to eat, it having wine of great virtue, and giving it mingled with bread."

INSCRIPTION OF PECTORIUS OF AUTUN [8]

O divine offspring of the heavenly Ichthus [9] (fish), receive with a heart full of respect the life immortal among mortals.

Friend, refresh your soul with the divine waters, the ever-flowing waters of wisdom which give wealth.

Receive from the Savior of saints the nourishment sweet as honey:

Eat for your hunger, drink for your thirst;
Take the Fish in the palms of your hands.
Master and Savior nourish us with the Fish.

---

* Abercius was bishop of Hierapolis, in Phrygia in Asia Minor, under Marcus Aurelius. His epitaph is a little earlier than 200. The fragment found by Ramsey was given to Leo XIII and is now in the Lateran museum. Cf. "Aberkios," RAC 1, 12-17.

6. Christ was already represented under the form of a shepherd.

7. The seal of baptism.

8. An epitaph found in Autun, probably a 4th or 5th century copy of a 2nd century original, contemporary with Irenaeus of Lyons.

9. Ichthus, a Greek word for "fish," an acrostic for "Jesus Christ, Son of God Savior." See C. Vogel, "Le repas sacré au poisson chez les Chrétiens," Rev. de Sc. Relig. (1966) 1-26.

May my mother rest in peace, I pray you, light of the dead.
Aschandius my father
with my dear mother and my brothers
with all the gratitude of my soul
I beg you,
in the peace of the Fish
Remember your Pectorius.

CYPRIAN OF CARTHAGE
(✝ 258)

The bishop of Carthage is above all a pastor; his concern
is with directing the flock entrusted to him. His writings help
to fulfill this pastoral charge. Apart from a certain number of
works he has left us an important correspondence which is a
valuable source of information on the Christian life in the third
century.

Letter 63, sometimes published separately as a sort of treatise,
was written to Caecilius. It was provoked by the abuse of a
sect called the Aquarii which, for ascetical reasons, used water instead of wine for Mass. The bishop opposed the tradition of the
gospels and the apostles to this innovation. His fundamental
principle is: Do what Christ has done.

The division of the letter is clear:
What Jesus Christ has done must be repeated (1-2).
Even the Old Testament, in its figures (Noah, Melchisedech) and
its teaching of the prophets, announced that Jesus would use wine
and not water (3-8).
The account of the Supper shows how the prophecies have been
fulfilled in the institution of the Eucharist (9-10).
Cyprian then explains the symbolism of the two elements—the
water is a figure of the people, the wine, of the blood of Christ
(11-15).
He concludes that one of the rules of faith is to follow the lessons
and example of Christ and he refutes the objections of the Aquarii
(16-19).

We can extract from the letter of Cyprian the broad lines of
a treatise on the Eucharist:

The Eucharist is a true sacrifice. Cyprian uses expressions
like offer, oblation, sacrifice, sanctify. "It has been given to us
at the last Supper by Christ himself, who is then "the author and

teacher of this sacrifice." "It contains the sacrifice of Christ, who first offered himself in sacrifice to God his Father." It is for him that the Mass derives all its efficacy. It contains the mystery of the dead and risen Christ.

On Calvary Christ "carried all of us in himself." His sacrifice includes us all. The water blended with the wine symbolizes this indissoluble union. It is the same as the manifold grains of wheat which unite to form but the one bread: "so in Christ, who is the heavenly bread, we may know is one body, to which our number is joined and united."

This symbolism of the grains uniting to form the one body of Christ and the people of God was dear to Cyprian and passed to the whole of Latin literature down to the Middle Ages.

The Eucharist not merely makes the Church—it is the Church. Behind the symbolism is found the reality which it represents. Reality and symbolism are aspects of the same mystery. They must not be seen as opposites, since the symbol will become what it symbolizes. The teaching of Cyprian will be taken up and developed by Augustine of Hippo.

LETTER 63 — CYPRIAN [10] TO BROTHER CECIL,[11] GREETING

A Disturbing Innovation: Consecration without Wine

1. Although I know, dearly beloved brother, that very many bishops, placed by the divine condescension in charge of the Churches of the Lord in the whole world, keep the order of evangelical truth and of the tradition of the Lord and do not depart by human and novel institution from that which Christ, the Master, both taught and did, yet since certain ones, either through ignorance or through simplicity, in consecrating the Chalice of the Lord and in ministering to the people, do not do that which Jesus Christ, our Lord and God, the Author and Teacher of this sacrifice, did and taught, I consider it a matter both of obligation and of necessity to write to you a letter concerning this that, if anyone is still held captive in this error, when he has the light of truth, he may return to the root and origin of the tradition of the Lord.

---

10. 253 A.D. For text cf. PL 4, 372-389. Eng. trans. FC 51, 202.
11. Cf. Letter 4, n. 2.

Do not think, dearly beloved brother, that we thus boldly presume, of our own human will or that of another, to write to you since we consider always with humble and modest sentiments our own mediocrity.   But when something is clearly prescribed by God's inspiration and command, it is necessary for the faithful servant to obey the Lord, excused by all because he who is compelled to fear an offense for the Lord unless he does what he is commanded is assuming nothing arrogantly to himself.

2. But know that we have been warned in offering the chalice that the tradition of the Lord must be observed and that nothing should be done otherwise by us than what the Lord first did for us, that the chalice which is offered in his commemoration should be offered mixed with wine.   For when Christ says: *I am the true vine* (*John* 15, 1), the blood of Christ is, indeed, not water, but wine.   Nor can his blood, by which we are redeemed and vivified, which is foretold by the testimony and pledge of all the Scriptures, be seen to be in the chalice when wine, wherein the blood of Christ is shown, is wanting to the chalice.

The Evidence of the Old and New Testament

3. For we find, also, in Genesis concerning the sacrament that Noe anticipated this same thing and projected the figure of the passion of the Lord there because he drank wine, because he was inebriated, because he was made naked in his home, because he was reclining with his thighs naked and exposed, because that nakedness of the father was noticed by his second son and reported outside, but covered by the other two, the oldest and the youngest, and other things which it is not necessary to follow up since it is sufficient to comprehend this alone: that Noe, showing forth a type of future truth, drank not water, but wine, and so expressed the figure of the passion of the Lord (cf. *Gen.* 9, 20-27).

4. Likewise, in the priest Melchisedech, we see the sacrament of the sacrifice of the Lord prefigured according to what the divine Scripture testifies and says: *And Melchisedech, the king of Salem, brought out bread and wine, for he was a priest of the most high God and he blessed Abraham* (cf. *Gen.* 14, 18-19).   But that Melchisedech portrayed a type of Christ, the Holy Spirit declares in the Psalms, saying in the person of the Father to the Son: *Before the day star . . . I have begotten you . . . .*

You are a priest forever according to the order of Melchisedech (*Ps.* 110, 3-4). This order, indeed, is this coming from that sacrifice and thence descending because Melchisedech was *a priest of the most high God,* because he offered bread, because he blessed Abraham. For who is more a priest of the most high God than our Lord Jesus Christ, who offered sacrifice to God the Father and offered the very same thing which Melchisedech had offered, bread and wine, that is, actually, his body and blood.

And with respect to Abraham, that prior blessing extended to our people. For if Abraham believed God and it was reputed to him for justice, whoever, assuredly believes in God and lives by faith is found a just man and is shown blessed already in the faithful Abraham and justified as the blessed Apostle Paul proves, saying: *Abraham believed God, and it was credited to him as justice. You know, therefore, that they who are of faith, are the sons of Abraham. But the Scriptures, foreseeing that God would justify the Gentiles by faith, announced to Abraham beforehand that all the nations would be blessed in him. Therefore, those who are of faith are blessed with faithful Abraham* (cf. *Gal.* 3, 6-9). Whence in the Gospel we find that *sons are raised to Abraham* from stones, that is, collected from the Gentiles (cf. *Matt.* 3, 9). And when the Lord praised Zachaeus, he answered and said: *Today salvation has come to this house, since he, too, is a son of Abraham* (*Luke* 19, 9).

That, therefore, in Genesis through the priest Melchisedech the blessing should be ceremoniously celebrated in respect to Abraham, the image of the sacrifice is primary, constituted actually in the bread and wine. Accomplishing and fulfilling this action, the Lord offered bread and a chalice mixed with wine and he, who is the plenitude, fulfilled the truth of the prefigured image.

5. But also the Holy Spirit through Solomon shows forth the type of the sacrifice of the Lord, making mention of the Immolated Victim and of the bread and wine and also of the altar and of the apostles. *Wisdom,* he says, *has built a house and she has set up seven columns. She has slain her victims, mixed her wine in a chalice, and has spread her table.* And she has sent her servants, inviting with the highest commendation to the chalice, saying: *Let whoever is simple turn in to me; and to those who lack understanding, she said: Come and eat of my food, and drink the wine which I have mixed for you* (cf. *Prov.* 9, 1-15). He declares the

wine is mixed, that is, he announces in a prophetic voice that the chalice of the Lord is mixed with water and wine, that it may appear that what had been foretold before was accomplished in the passion of the Lord.

6. In the blessing of Juda, also, this same thing is signified when the figure of Christ is also expressed there that he should have to be praised and adored by his brethren, that he should press down the backs of enemies departing and fleeing, with the hands with which he bore the cross and conquered death, and that he himself is the Lion of the tribe of Juda and reclines sleeping in his passion and arises and is himself the hope of the Gentiles. To these things, the divine Scripture adds and says: *He shall wash his garment in wine and his robe in the blood of the grape* (cf. *Gen.* 49, 11). But when the blood of the grape is mentioned, what else is shown forth but the wine of the chalice, the blood of the Lord.

7. And does not, also, the Holy Spirit, speaking in Isaiah, testify this same thing concerning the passion of the Lord, saying: *Why are your vestments red and your garments as from treading the winepress full and well-trodden?* (cf. *Isa.* 63, 2) For can water make vestments red or is it water which is trodden by the feet in the winepress or forced out by the press? The mention of wine is placed there, indeed, that in the wine the blood of the Lord may be known and that which was afterwards manifested in the chalice of the Lord might be foretold by the Prophets who announced it. The treading and pressing of the winepress are also spoken of since wine cannot be prepared for drinking in any other way unless the cluster of grapes is first trodden and pressed. Thus, we could not drink the blood of Christ unless Christ had first been trodden upon and pressed and unless he had first drunk the chalice and should then give it to drink to the believers.

Water Alone is the Matter of Baptism, not of the Eucharist

8. But as often as water alone is named in the Holy Scriptures, baptism is preached as we see signified in Isaiah. *Remember not the events of the past,* he says, *the things of long ago consider not; see, I am doing new things which now will spring forth and you will know them. In the desert I make a way, in the wasteland, rivers . . . for my chosen people to drink, my people whom I won*

that they might announce my virtues (Isa. 43, 18-21). God announced there through the Prophet that among the Gentiles, in places which before had been without water, rivers should afterwards abound and should provide water for the elect of God, that is, those made the sons of God through the regeneration of baptism.

Likewise, again, it is foretold and predicted before that the Jews, if they should thirst and seek Christ, would drink among us, that is, they would obtain the grace of baptism. *If they have thirsted,* he said, *in the deserts, he will give them water; he will bring forth water out of the rock for them, and the rock will be split and the water will gush out, and my people will drink (Isa.* 48, 21). This is fulfilled in the Gospel when Christ, who is the Rock, is pierced by the blow of the lance in his passion. And he, indeed, warning us again of what was before predicted by the Prophet, cries out and says: *If anyone thirst, let him come and drink. He who believes in me,* as the Scripture says, *from within him there shall flow rivers of living water (John* 7, 37-38).

And that it might be the more manifest that the Lord is speaking there not of the chalice, but of baptism, Scripture adds, saying: *He said this, however, of the Spirit whom they who believed in him were to receive (John* 7, 39). But through baptism the Holy Spirit is received and thus, to the baptized and to those who have received the Holy Spirit, it is granted to drink the chalice of the Lord. But let it disturb no one, that, when the divine Scripture is speaking of baptism, it says that we are thirsty and we drink since the Lord also in the Gospel says: *Blessed are they who thirst and hunger for justice* (cf. *Matt.* 5, 6), because what is received with an avid and thirsty desire is drunk more fully and profitably. Likewise, in another place, the Lord speaks to the Samaritan woman, saying: *Everyone who drinks of this water will thirst again. He, however, who drinks of the water that I will give shall never thirst (John* 4, 13-14). And by this, indeed, is signified the baptism of the saving water, which once it is received, assuredly, is not repeated; as for the rest, the chalice of the Lord is always both thirsted for and drunk in the Church.

9. There is no need for very many arguments, dearly beloved brother, to prove that baptism is signified always by the appellation of water and, thus, we ought to know since the Lord, when he

came, manifested the truth of baptism and of the chalice; he taught that faithful water, the water of everlasting life, is given in baptism to the believers; he taught, in truth, by the example of his teaching power that the chalice is mingled with the union of wine and water.   For taking the chalice on the day of his passion, he blessed it and gave it to his disciples, saying: *All of you drink of this; for this is the blood of the covenant, which is being shed for many unto the forgiveness of sins. I say to you, I will not drink henceforth of this fruit of the vine, until that day when I shall drink it new with you in the kingdom of my Father* (*Matt.* 26, 27-29). In this part, we find that the chalice which the Lord offered was mixed and that he called blood what had been wine.

Whence it appears that the blood of Christ is not offered if wine is lacking in the chalice and that the sacrifice of the Lord is not celebrated with lawful sanctification unless the oblation and our sacrifice correspond to the passion.   But in what way shall we drink the new wine of the creature of the vine with Christ in the kingdom of the Father if we do not offer the wine of Christ in the sacrifice of God the Fahter and do not mingle the chalice of the Lord according to the teaching of the Lord?

It is the Wine, not the Water, that Becomes the Blood of Christ

10. The blessed Apostle Paul, moreover, elected by God and sent and appointed as a preacher of evangelical truth, writes these same things in his Epistle, saying: *The Lord Jesus, on the night in which he was betrayed, took bread and gave thanks and broke,* and said, *This is my body which is for you; do this in remembrance of me. In like manner also he took the cup, after he had supped,* saying, *This cup is the new covenant in my blood; do this as often as you drink it, in remembrance of me. For as often as you shall eat this bread and drink the cup, you proclaim the death of the Lord, until he comes* (I *Cor.* 11, 23-26).

But if this is taught by the Lord and the same is confirmed and handed down by his Apostle, that as often as we drink in commemoration of the Lord, we should do this which the Lord did, we find that what was commanded is not observed by us unless we do the same things which the Lord did and, mixing the chalice in like manner, we do not withdraw from the divine teaching. But that we must not depart at all from the evangelical teachings and that the disciples ought also to observe and do those same things which the Master taught and did, the blessed Apostle teaches more resolutely and strongly in another place, saying: *I marvel that you are so quickly deserting him who called you to grace . . . to another gospel; which is not another, except in this respect that there are some who trouble you, and wish to pervert the gospel of Christ. But even if we or an angel from heaven should preach a gospel to you other than that which we have preached to you, let him be anathema! As we have said before, so now I say again: If anyone preach a gospel to you other than that which you have received, let him be anathema!* (*Gal.* 1, 6-9)

11. Since, therefore, neither the Apostle himself nor an angel from heaven can announce otherwise or teach anything else than that which Christ once taught and his apostles preached, I marvel, indeed, whence this practice has come, contrary alike to both evangelical and apostolic discipline, that water, which alone cannot represent the blood of Christ, is offered in some places in the chalice of the Lord. The Holy Spirit is not quiet about the sacrament of this matter in the Psalms, when he makes mention of the chalice of the Lord and says: *Your chalice which inebriates, how excellent it is* (cf. *Ps.* 23, 5). But the chalice which inebriates is assuredly mixed with wine. For water cannot inebriate anyone.

But thus the chalice of the Lord inebriates as Noe drinking wine in Genesis also was inebriated. But because the inebriation of the chalice and of the blood of the Lord is not such as the inebriation coming from worldly wine, when the Holy Spirit says in the Psalms: *Your chalice which inebriates,* he adds, *how excellent it is!* Because, actually, the chalice of the Lord so inebriates that it makes sober, that it raises minds to spiritual wisdom, that from this taste of the world each one comes to the knowledge of God and, as the mind is relaxed by that common wine and the soul is relaxed and all sadness is cast away, so, when the blood of the Lord and the life-giving cup have been drunk, the memory of the old man is cast aside and there is induced forgetfulness of former worldly conversation and the sorrowful and sad heart which was formerly pressed down with distressing sins is now relaxed by the joy of the divine mercy. This, then, at last, can delight the one who drinks in the Church of the Lord if what is drunk keeps to the truth of the Lord.

The Significance of the Water in the Eucharist

12. How perverse it is, in truth, and how contrary that, although the Lord made wine from water at the marriage, we should make water from wine, when the Sacrament of this matter ought to warn and instruct us that in the Sacrifices of the Lord we should rather offer wine. For, since among the Jews spiritual grace was wanting, the wine failed also; for the vineyard of the Lord of hosts is the House of Israel.

But Christ, who teaches and shows that the people of the Gentiles were coming into that place which the Jews had lost and that we were arriving afterwards through the merit of faith, made wine from water, that is, He showed that the people of the Gentiles rather would resort together and come to the nuptials of Christ and of his Church when the Jews were leaving. For the divine Scripture declares in the Apocalypse that the waters signify the peoples, saying: *The waters that you saw on which that harlot sits, are peoples and crowds and nations of the heathen and tongues* (Rev. 17, 15). We perceive that this is actually, also, contained in the sacrament of the chalice.

13. For, because Christ, who bore our sins, also bore us all, we see that people are signified in the water, but in the wine the blood of Christ is shown. But when water is mixed with wine in the chalice, the people are united to Christ, and the multitude of the believers is bound and joined to him in whom they believe. This association and mingling of water and wine are so mixed in the chalice of the Lord that the mixture cannot be mutually separated. Whence nothing can separate the Church, that is, the multitude established faithfully and firmly in the Church, persevering in that which it has believed, from Christ as long as it clings and remains in undivided love.

But thus, in the consecrating of the chalice of the Lord, water alone cannot be offered, nor can wine alone. For, if anyone offers wine alone, the blood of Christ begins to be without us. If, in truth, the water is alone, the people begin to be without Christ. But when both are mixed and, in the union, are joined to each other and mingled together, then the spiritual and heavenly sacrament is completed. Thus, in truth, the chalice of the Lord is not water alone, or wine alone, unless both are mixed together, just as flour alone or water alone cannot be the body of the Lord unless both have been united and joined and made solid in the structure of one bread. By this sacrament itself, our people are shown to be united; just as many grains collected in one and united and mixed form one bread, so in Christ, who is the heavenly bread, we may know is one body, to which our number is joined and united.

Follow Christ's Command to the Letter

14. There is no reason, dearly beloved brother, for anyone to think that the custom of certain ones should be followed, if any in the past have thought that water alone should be offered in the chalice of the Lord; for we must seek whom they themselves have followed. For if, in the sacrifice which Christ offered, no one is to be followed but Christ himself, certainly we ought to obey and to do what Christ did and what he commanded to be done since he himself says in the Gospel: *If you have done what I command you, no longer do I call you servants, but friends* (*John* 15, 14-15). And that Christ alone ought to be obeyed, his Father even states from heaven, saying: *This is my dearly beloved Son, in whom I am well pleased; hear him* (*Matt.* 17, 5).

Wherefore, if Christ alone is to be heard, we ought not to attend to what anyone else before us thought ought to be done, but what Christ, who is before all, did first. Neither ought we to follow the custom of men, but the truth of God since through Isaiah, the Prophet, God speaks and says: *But in vain do they* 13). And again in his Gospel, the Lord repeats this same thing, *worship me, teaching the precepts and doctrines of men* (*Isa.* 29, saying: *You made void the commandment of God to choose your tradition* (*Mark* 7, 13). But in another place, he states: *Whoever does away with one of these least commandments, and so teaches men, shall be called least in the kingdom of heaven* (*Matt.* 5, 19).

But if it is not allowed to break the least of the commandments of the Lord, how much more important is it not to infringe upon matters which are so great, so tremendous, so closely connected to the very sacrament of the passion of the Lord and of our redemption, or in any way for human tradition to change what has been divinely instituted? For, if Christ Jesus, our Lord and God, is himself the High Priest of God the Father, and first offered himself as a sacrifice to his Father and commanded this to be done in commemoration of himself, certainly the priest who imitates that which Christ did and then offers the true and full sacrifice in the Church of God the Father, if he thus begins to offer according to what he sees Christ himself offered, performs truly in the place of Christ.

15. Otherwise, all of the discipline of religion and of truth is subverted unless that which is prescribed spiritually is kept faithfully, unless in the Morning Sacrifice that which each one fears is that he should be redolent of the blood of Christ through the savor of the wine. Thus, therefore, the brotherhood begins also to be kept back from the passion of Christ in persecutions while it learns in the oblations to be ashamed about his blood and bloodshed. But, in turn, the Lord in the Gospel says: *Whoever is ashamed of me . . . of him will the Son of Man be ashamed* (*Mark* 8, 38). And the Apostle also speaks, saying: *If I were trying to please men, I should not be a servant of Christ* (*Gal.* 1, 10). For how can we who blush to drink the blood of Christ shed our blood for Christ?

16. Or is anyone enticed by this contemplation that, although water alone seems to be offered in the morning, yet, when we come to dinner, we offer a mixed chalice? But when we dine, we cannot call the people to our banquet that we may celebrate the truth of the sacrament with all of the brotherhood present. But, in fact, the Lord offered the mixed chalice not in the morning but after dinner. Ought we then to celebrate the sacrifice of the Lord after dinner so that by repeated sacrifices we may offer the mixed chalice? It was fitting for Christ to offer the sacrifice about evening of the day that the very hour might show the setting and evening of the world as it is written in Exodus: *And the whole multitude of the children of Israel shall slaughter it in the evening* (*Exod.* 12, 6). And again in the Psalms: *The lifting up of my hands as evening sacrifice* (*Ps.* 141, 2). But we celebrate the resurrection of the Lord in the morning.

17. And since we make mention of his passion in all sacrifices, for the passion of the Lord is, indeed, the sacrifice which we offer, we ought to do nothing other than what he did. For Scripture says that, as often as we offer the chalice in the commemoration of the Lord and of his passion (I *Cor.* 11, 26), we should do that which it is certain the Lord did. And, dearly beloved brother, let him look to it, if anyone of our predecessors either through ignorance or through simplicity did not observe

this and did not keep that which the Lord taught us to do by his example and by his teaching. Pardon from the mercy of the Lord may be given to his simplicity. It cannot, in truth, be forgiven in us, who now are admonished and instructed by the Lord to offer the chalice of the Lord mixed with wine, according to what the Lord offered, and to direct letters to our colleagues concerning this matter also, that everywhere the evangelical law and the tradition of the Lord should be kept and that there should be no departure from that which Christ both taught and did.

18. For what else is it further to disdain those things and to persevere in the former error than to run into the rebuke of the Lord, who threatens in the Psalm and says: *Why do you declare my justices, and profess my covenant with your mouth for you have hated discipline and cast my words behind you? If you saw a thief, you kept pace wtih him, and with adulterers you threw in your lot* (*Ps.* 50, 16-18). For to declare the justices and the covenant of the Lord and not to do the same thing which the Lord did, what else is that but to cast aside his words and to despise the discipline of the Lord and to commit, not earthly, but spiritual robberies and adulteries? For he who steals from evangelical truth the words and deeds of our Lord both corrupts and adulterates the divine teaching. as it is written in Jeremiah: *What has the straw to do with the wheat?* he says, ... *Therefore behold I am against the prophets,* says the Lord, *who steals my words everyone from his neighbor ... and lead my people astray by their lies and by their errors* (cf. *Jer.* 23, 28, 30, 32). Likewise in another place in the same man: *She played the harlot with wood and stone. And with all this, she did not return to me* (*Jer.* 3, 9-10).

We ought to observe religiously and fearfully and solicitously to beware that this robbery and adultery should not even now fall upon us. For if we are bishops of God and of Christ, I do not find anyone we ought to follow more than God and Christ since he himself in his Gospel emphatically says: *I am the light of the world. He who follows me will not walk in darkness, but will have the light of life* (*John* 8, 12). Lest we walk, therefore, in darkness, we ought to follow Christ and to observe his precepts since he himself in another place, sending his apostles, said: *All power in heaven and on earth has been given to me. Go, therefore, and make disciples of all nations, baptizing them in the name of the Father, and of the Son, and of the Holy Spirit, teaching them to observe all that I have commanded you (Matt. 28, 18-20).*

Wherefore, if we wish to walk in the light of Christ, let us not depart from his precepts and admonitions, giving thanks, that, while he instructs us for the future as to what we should do, he forgives us for the past because we have sinned through simplicity. And since already his second coming is drawing near to us, more and more his kind and great condescension enlightens our hearts with the light of truth.

19. It is, therefore, fitting to our religion and to fear of God, both for the peace and for the office of our bishopric, dearly beloved brother, to keep the truth of the tradition of the Lord in mixing and in offering the Chalice of the Lord and to correct what seems to have been an earlier error among certain people, according to the admonition of the Lord, that, when he begins to come in his brightness and heavenly majesty, he may find that we are holding firmly to what he advised us, observing what he taught, doing what he did. I trust that you, dearly beloved brother, are always well.

HILARY OF POITIERS
(315-367)

Belonging to a pagan family, Hilary was converted to the faith through reading the Scriptures. Although married he was conse-created bishop of the community of Poitiers. He was an intrepid defender of the faith of Nicaea and was sent into exile for his stand. During his exile in Asia Minor he was introduced to Eastern theology. He wrote there a treatise, *De Trinitate,* which is more exactly an exposition of the Christian faith.

By way of proving that there exists between the Father and the Son a substantial union and not just the moral one admitted by the heretics, he gives us an excursus on the Eucharist which establishes a physical, and not just a moral union between Christ and his communicants.

The following excerpt is a translation of the celebrated passage which affirms the real union which exists between Christ and those who go to Communion. Christ is united to them in two ways: first by assuming their nature, and then by coming to them in Communion.   The first is the foundation for the second.   In coming to us Christ enables us to live the divine life which by becoming incarnate he came to bring to all mankind.   This enables the Christian to participate in the mystery and the life of God.   The Middle Ages would make frequent use of these forceful statements.

FROM THE HOLY EUCHARIST TO THE HOLY TRINITY

The Eucharist Confers a Real Communion

But the Lord, who leaves nothing vague in the consciousness of the faithful, has informed us about that very result that is produced by the power of nature, when he says: *That they may be one, as we are one: I in them and you in me; that they may be perfected in unity* (*John* 17, 22-23).   I now ask those who speak of a unity of will between the Father and the Son, whether Christ is in us by the truth of his nature or by the harmony of the will?   If the Word has indeed become flesh, and we indeed receive the Word as flesh in the Lord's supper, how are we not to believe that he dwells in us by his nature, he who, when he was born as man, has assumed the nature of our flesh that is bound inseparably with himself, and has mingled the nature of his flesh to his eternal nature in the mystery of the flesh that was to be communicated to us?

All of us are one in this manner because the Father is in Christ and Christ is in us.   Therefore, whoever will deny that the Father is not in Christ by his nature let him first deny that he [13] is not in Christ by his nature, or that Christ is not present within him, because the Father in Christ and Christ in us cause us to be one in them.   If, therefore, Christ has truly taken the flesh of our body, and that man who was born from Mary is truly Christ, and we truly receive the flesh of his body in the sacramental mystery (and we are one, therefore, because the Father is in him and he is in us), how can you assert that there

---

12. Latin text: **De Trinitate,** VIII, 13-17.   P.L., 10, 245-249.   Eng. trans. FC., 25, 284.

13. That is, the one who denies the unity of nature between the Father and the Son.

is a unity of will, since the sacrament confers its own nature on us, which is the sign of perfect unity? [14]

True Flesh and Blood

We should not talk about the things of God in a human or worldly sense, nor should the perversity of a strange and impious knowledge be extorted from the soundness of the heavenly words by a violent and imprudent manner of teaching. Let us read what has been written and hold fast to what we have read, and then we shall fulfill the duty of perfect faith. We speak in an absurd and godless manner about the divinity of Christ's nature in us— the subject which we are discussing—unless we have learned it from him. He himself declares: *For my flesh is food indeed, and my blood is drink indeed. He who eats my flesh and drinks my blood abides in me and I in him (John 6, 56-57).* It is no longer permitted us to raise doubts about the true nature of the body and the blood, for, according to the statement of the Lord himself as well as our faith, this is indeed flesh and blood. And these things that we receive bring it about that we are in Christ and Christ is in us. Is not this the truth? Those who deny that Jesus Christ is the true God are welcome to regard these words as false. He himself, therefore, is in us through his flesh, and we are in him, while that which we are with him is in God.

How are We in Him?

How deeply we are in him through the sacrament of the flesh and blood that has been communicated to us is evident from his own testimony, when he declares: *And this world no longer sees me. But you shall see me, for I live and you shall live, since I am in the Father, and you in me, and I in you (John 14, 19-20).* If he wished us to understand merely a spiritual unity, why did he explain, as it were, the steps and the order of the unity that was to be brought about, unless it were that, while he was in the Father

---

14. Through the reception of the Body and Blood of Christ in the Eucharist we share in His nature and, through Him, with that of His heavenly Father.

by the nature of the Godhead, we, on the other hand, should be in him by his corporeal birth, and again that we should believe that he would dwell in us by the mystery of the sacraments, and thus the perfect unity would be taught by means of the mediator, since he himself remains in the Father while we remain in him, and while he remains in the Father he remains in us, and in this manner we would arrive at the unity of the Father, since we would also be in the nature of him [the Son], who is in the nature of him [the Father] by birth, while he himself [the Son] ever remains in us by his nature.

He himself thus testifies how natural is this unity in us: *He who eats my flesh, and drinks my blood, abides in me and I in him* (*John* 6, 57). No one will be in him unless he himself has been in him, while he has assumed and taken upon himself the flesh of him only who has received his own. Previously, he had already given an explanation of the perfect unity when he declared: *As the living Father has sent me and as I live through the Father, so he who shall eat my flesh shall live through me* (*John* 6, 59). Consequently, he lives through the Father, and, as he lives through the Father, we live in the same manner through his flesh. Every illustration is adapted to the nature of our understanding in order that we may grasp the matter under discussion by means of the example that is set before us. Accordingly, this is the cause of our life, that we, who are carnal, have Christ dwelling in us through his flesh, and through him we shall live in that state in which he lives through the Father. Hence, if we live through him by his nature according to the flesh, that is, have received the nature of his flesh, why should he not possess the Father in himself by his nature according to the Spirit, since he himself lives through the Father? But he lives through the Father while his birth has not brought him an alien and a distinct nature, while that which he is, is from him and yet is not removed from him by any hampering dissimilarity of nature, while through his birth he possesses the Father in himself in the power proper to its nature.

Accordingly, we have mentioned these facts because the heretics, who have misrepresented the unity between the Father and the Son as one merely of will, have used the example of our unity with God just as if we were united to the Son, and through the Son to the Father, only by our obedience and agreement in the true religion, and the reality of a mutual participation in the nature has not been conferred upon us through the sacrament of the body and blood, although we are to proclaim the mystery of the true and natural unity both because of the glory which the Son has given to us as well as because of the Son who remains in us, while at the same time we are united to him in a corporeal and inseparable manner.

BASIL OF CAESAREA
(† 379)

The illustrious bishop of Caesarea counsels frequent, even daily, Communion. His letter gives us information on the practices of his day in Cappadocia.

LETTER 93.[15] TO THE PATRICIAN CAESARIA, ABOUT COMMUNION

Frequent Communion at Caesarea

Now, to receive Communion daily, thus to partake of the holy body and blood of Christ, is an excellent and advantageous practice; for Christ himself says clearly: *He who eats my flesh and drinks my blood has life everlasting* (*John* 6, 55). Who doubts that to share continually in the life is nothing else than to have a manifold life? We ourselves, of course, receive Communion four times a week, on Sundays, Wednesdays, Fridays, and Saturdays; also on other days, if there is a commemoration of some saint.

Communion without a priest in time of persecution

As to the question concerning a person being compelled to receive Communion by his own hand in times of persecution, when there is no priest or deacon present, it is superfluous to show that the act is in no way offensive, since long-continued custom has confirmed this practice because of the circumstances themselves.

In fact, all the monks in the desert, where there is no priest, reserve Communion in teir house and receive it from their own hands. In Alexandria and in Egypt, each person, even the laity, has Communion in his own home, and, when he wishes, he

---

15. For Greek text cf. PG 32, 484-85. Eng. trans. FC 13, 208.

receives with his own hand. For, when the priest has once and for all completed the sacrifice and has given Communion, he who has once received it as a whole, when he partakes of it daily, ought reasonably to believe that he is partaking and receiving from him who has given it.

Even in the church the priest gives the particle, and the recipient holds it completely in his power and so brings it into his mouth with his own hand. Accordingly, it is virtually the same whether he receives one particle from the priest or many particles at one time.

AUGUSTINE OF HIPPO

For forty years, first as priest and then as bishop, Augustine never ceased preparing catechumens for baptism and explaining the Eucharist to the newly-baptized and the faithful of his city. It would be interesting to compare his teaching with that which he himself received in Milan from the lips of Ambrose at the time when he was preparing to receive baptism and the Eucharist.

No more than the other Fathers Augustine has not constructed a systematic theology of the Eucharist. He had no occasion to defend the faith against heretics, and so much the better. Only the ministry of the Word provided him with an occasion to develop this doctrine in his commentaries on biblical texts which treated of the Eucharist, and in his explanations to the newly-baptized of the "holy mysteries" which they were receiving. Elsewhere he makes many an allusion to the liturgy of the Mass, to the meaning of the rites and prayers (Sermons 227 and Denys 2). For the newly-baptized, baptism and Eucharist were an enrollment in one and the same sacramental experience, making him participate in the dead and risen Christ. Augustine takes up with pleasure the image of the wheat, from the casting of the grain into the ground until the harvest and the baking of the bread, to explain the spiritual history of the baptized.

A text whose authenticity is more doubtful compares the Mass to the sacrifice of the Old Covenant which announced "a unique sacrifice to come." It affirms the identity of the sacrament of the altar with the reality of the Cross: "what you will discover in the bread is hanging on the cross, what is in the cup has trickled from his side." Augustine returns elsewhere, in the *City of*

God, to describing the offering of the redeemed city which is offered with the universal sacrifice of the high-priest who is at once "mediator, priest and sacrifice."

"Christ once immolated in person is immolated for all time sacramentally," Augustine writes to Boniface (*ep.* 98). The Mass for him is the real and repeated offering of the body of Christ in its entirety, head and members; it is real participation in the body and blood of Christ to form the one body of Christ.

Augustine loved to develop the relationship between the eucharistic body and the mystical body. Christ's body in the Eucharist becomes the mysitcal body of the Church. It perfects what baptism has begun, the Head effecting the unity of the whole body: "You have received that which you are; become that which you have received," says St. Augustine. And he goes on: "If, then, you are the body of Christ and his members, it is your sacrament that reposes on the Lord's table; it is your sacrament that you have received. To that which you are, you respond 'Amen,' and this response makes you belong. You hear the words 'The body of Christ' and you respond 'Amen.' Become a member of the body of Christ that your 'Amen' may be true."

The Pauline text—*you all are one body*—recurs frequently. Between Christ and his Church, then, there is a mystical identification. Far from denying the reality of Christ's sacramental presence as has been too often thoughtlessly said, Augustine sees the mystical body as the guarantee of his real presence.

The Bishop of Hippo is not content with doctrinal considerations: he draws concrete, practical conclusions. He constantly insists on unity, the concord and charity which the members of the same body and same soul ought to have in their daily lives. The Donatist schism made this Christian unity more imperative.

The Eucharist does not produce magical effects. It is not a facility, but a potency; it does not do away with Christian effort but encourages it. The mystery implicit in the Eucharist is realized painfully throughout the whole of life by daily effort and daily dying to oneself. This effort can even sometimes demand martyrdom.

For Augustine the Mass constitutes the very mystery of the Church and the heart of the Christian faith. It resumes all the truths of the Creed, as Sermon 272 tells us.

SERMON 227 [16] — TO NEOPHYTES, ON THE SACRED MYSTERIES

Unity in the Same Body

I am not unmindful of the promise by which I pledged myself to deliver a sermon to instruct you, who have just been baptized, on the sacrament of the Lord's table, which you now look upon and of which you partook last night. You ought to know what you have received, what you are going to receive, and what you ought to receive daily.

That bread which you see on the altar, consecrated by the word of God, is the Body of Christ. That chalice, or rather, what the chalice holds, consecrated by the word of God, is the Blood of Christ. Through those accidents the Lord wished to entrust to us his body and the blood which he poured out for the remission of sins. If you have received worthily, you are what you have received, for the Apostle says: *The bread is one; we though many, are one body* (I *Cor.* 10, 17). Thus he explained the sacrament of the Lord's table: *The bread is one; we though many, are one body.* So by bread you are instructed as to how you ought to cherish unity.

Was that bread made of one grain of wheat? Were there not, rather, many grains? However, before they became bread these grains were separate; they were joined together in water after a certain amount of crushing. For, unless the grain is ground and moistened with water, it cannot arrive at that form which is called bread.

So, too, you were previously ground, as it were, by the humiliation of your fasting and by the sacrament of exorcism. Then came the baptism of water; you were moistend, as it were, so as to arrive at the form of bread.[17] But, without fire, bread does not yet exist. What, then, does the fire signify? The chrism. For the sacrament of the Holy Spirit is the oil of our fire.

---

16. Latin text: PL 38, 1099-1101. Eng. tr. FC 38, 195. This sermon bears a very close resemblance in many details to Sermon 6 (Den.), translated and discussed by D. J. Kavanagh, O.S.A., in **Fathers of the Church** 11, 321-326.

17. See Kavanagh, **loc. cit.**, for a similar discussion and an excellent commentary.

What Means: Lift up Your Hearts?

Notice this when the Acts of the Apostles are read. (Soon the reading of the book is going to begin; today the reader is beginning that book which is called the Acts of the Apostles.) [18] He who wishes to advance has the source of advancement. When you come to church, put aside empty talk; concentrate your attention on the Scriptures. We are your books. Attend, then, and see that the Holy Spirit will come on Pentecost. And thus he will come: he will show himself in tongues of fire. For he enkindles charity by which we ardently desire God and spurn the world, by which our chaff is consumed and our heart purified as gold. Therefore, the fire, that is, the Holy Spirit, comes after the water; then you become bread, that is, the body of Christ. Hence, in a certain manner, unity is signified.

You now have the sacraments in their order. At first, after the prayer, you are admonished to *lift up your heart*. This befits the members of Christ. For, if you have become members of Christ, where is your Head? Members have a head. If the Head had not preceded, the members would not follow. Where has your Head gone? What did you recite in the Creed? *"On the third day he rose again from the dead; he ascended into heaven; he sits at the right hand of the Father."* Therefore, our Head is in heaven. Hence, when the *"Lift up your heart"* is said, you answer: *"We have [them lifted up] to the Lord."* [19] Then, because this lifting up of your hearts to God is a gift of God and lest you should attribute to your own strength, your own merits, and your own labors the fact that you have your hearts thus lifted up to the Lord, after the answer, "We have our hearts lifted up to the Lord," the bishop or priest who is officiating also says: *"Let us give thanks to the Lord our God,* because we have our hearts raised up to him. Let us give thanks to him, because if he did not give [the grace], we would have our hearts fixed on the earth." And you bear witness to this, saying: "It is right and just for us to give thanks to him who caused us to raise our hearts up to our Head."

---

18. In St. Augustine's time, the lector read the text from Scripture and the bishop then commented on it.

19. From the Preface of the Mass.

A Visible and Invisible Communion

Then, after the consecration of the Holy Sacrifice of God, because he wished us also to be his sacrifice, a fact which was made clear when the Holy Sacrifice was first instituted, and because that sacrifice is a sign of what we are, behold, when the sacrifice is finished, we say the Lord's Prayer which you have received and recited. After this, the *"Peace be with you"* is said, and the Christians embrace one another with the holy kiss. This is a sign of peace; as the lips indicate, let peace be made in your conscience, that is, when your lips draw near to those of your brother, do not let your heart withdraw from his.

Hence, these are great and powerful sacraments. Do you wish to know how they are commended? The Apostle says: *Whoever eats the body of Christ or drinks the cup of the Lord unworthily, will be guilty of the body and blood of the Lord* (I *Cor.* 11, 27). What does it mean to receive unworthily? To receive in mockery, to receive in contempt. Let the sacrament not appear of trifling value to you because you can see it. What you see passes; but the invisible, that which is not seen, does not pass; it remains. Behold, it is received; it is eaten; it is consumed. Is the body of Christ consumed? Is the Church of Christ consumed? Are the members of Christ consumed? God forbid! Here they are cleansed; there they will be crowned. Therefore, what is signified will last eternally, even though it seems to pass.

Receive, then, so that you may ponder, so that you may possess unity in your heart, so that you may always lift up your heart. Let your hope be, not on earth, but in heaven; let your faith be firm and acceptable to God. Because you now believe what you do not see, you are going to see where you will rejoice eternally.

SERMON 272: TO THE NEWLY BAPTIZED, ON THE
BLESSED SACRAMENT [20]

Faith and Understanding

What you see on the altar of God you saw last night also. But you have not heard yet what it is, what it means, how great the

---

20. Sermon 272: Latin text, PL 38, 1246-48. English trans., T. Halton.

mystery is. What do you see then? Bread and a chalice. That is what your eyes tell you. But your faith demands that you know further that the bread is the body of Christ, the chalice the blood of Christ. This is a brief description but will it suffice for faith? No, faith demands more. For the Prophet says, *If you do not believe you will not understand* (*Isa.* 7, 9). You can now say to me: You demand that we believe; explain so that we may understand.

But this is a reflection which can come to your soul: we know where our Lord Jesus Christ received his flesh—from the Virgin Mary. As an infant he was suckled and nourished; he grew up, and became a young man. He suffered persecution at the hands of the Jews; he hung from the cross. He was taken down from the cross and buried; on the third day he rose again and on the appointed day he ascended into heaven. That is where he raised his body and from there he will come to judge the living and the dead. He is there now sitting at the right hand of the Father. How then can bread be his body or how can the contents of the chalice be his blood?

We are the Body of Christ

Brethren, these things are called sacraments because in them the appearance is one thing but the reality is another. What appears to the senses is one thing, a material object, but what is grasped by the mind is a spiritual grace. If you wish then to grasp the body of Christ hear the words of the Apostle to the faithful: *You are the body of Christ and his members* (I *Cor.* 12, 27). If then you are the body of Christ and his members, it is your sacrament that reposes on the altar of the Lord. It is your sacrament which you receive. You answer "Amen" to what you yourself are and in answering you are enrolled. You answer "Amen" to the words "The body of Christ." Be, then, a member of the body of Christ to verify your "Amen."

How, then, is the body in the bread? What we say here is not just our own opinion, but let us hear again and again the same Apostle when, in speaking of this sacrament, he says, *Being one bread we are one body* (I *Cor.* 10, 17). Understand and rejoice: Unity, Truth, Piety, Charity. *One bread*—what is this "one bread?" Recall that bread is not made from one grain but from many. When you were exorcised you were ground, so to speak; when baptized, scattered; when you received the fire of the Holy Spirit, you were baked. Be what you see, and receive what you are.

The Apostle said this of the bread. What we are to understand about the chalice, though not expressed, is sufficiently clear. So, bread, that it might have a unified appearance is formed from scattering many grains in the water to form one paste, thus providing a symbol of the first Christians of whom the Scripture says: *There was to them one soul and one heart in God* (*Acts* 4, 32). It is the same with the wine. Recall, brethren, how wine is made. Many grapes hang from the vine cluster, but when squeezed only one liquid is formed.

A Sacrament of Peace

This is the model which Christ the Lord has given to us. He wants us to adhere to him. He has instituted on his altar the sacrament of our peace and unity. He who receives the sacrament of unity but fails to preserve the bond of peace receives instead of a profitable sacrament a witness of self-condemnation.

Turn, then, to the Lord our God and omnipotent Father with a pure heart, and within the limits of our weak nature let us give profuse and sincere thanks. Invoke his unique mercy with all our heart that he may deign to hear our prayers graciously, that he may expel the Adversary by his power from our thoughts and actions, that he may increase our faith, direct our minds, inspire us with holy thoughts, and conduct us to happiness through Christ Jesus his Son. Amen.

SERMON 329: ON THE FEAST OF A MARTYR [21]

The death of a martyr is a precious thing, thanks to the death of Christ

1. How glorious are the deaths of the holy martyrs! They always make the Church flourish. They enlighten us on the suitability of the words of our chant: *Precious in the eyes of the Lord is the death of his faithful ones* (*Ps.* 116, 15). It is really precious

---

21. Latin text: PL 38, 1454-56. English trans., T. Halton.

to our eyes and to the eyes of him for whose sake those deaths have been endured. For they depend for their worth on his precious death. How many deaths he purchased by his own, for if he had not died like the grain sown in the ground the wheat would not have multiplied.

You have heard his word at the moment of the approach of his passion, that is to say at the moment when he approached our redemption: *If the grain of wheat does not fall in the earth and die it remains alone. But if it dies it brings forth much fruit (John 12, 24, 25).*

On the cross he has accomplished a great deal: He has opened the treasure containing our ransom. When his side was pierced with the lance there trickled from it the ransom price of the whole world. The faithful and the martyrs have been purchased by his blood, but the faith of the martyrs is a faith which has proved itself: it is sealed in their own blood. They have paid back what they received, and have fulfilled the words of the evangelist John: *As Christ has laid down his life for us we ought to lay down our lives for the brethren (I John 3, 16).* And again we read: *When you sit down to dine with a ruler keep in mind who is before you (Prov. 23, 1, 2).*

The ruler's table is that on which the Lord himself is the food on the table. Nobody gives himself to his guests as food: but Christ the Lord does so. He is the host, the food and the drink. The martyrs have understood what they have eaten and drunk so that they might render a similar return.

Martyrdom is a Grace

2. How would they be able to make a return if he had not given them the wherewithal from his prior earnings? In the psalm verse which we have chanted, *Precious is the death of his faithful ones,* what is the significance of these words for us? A man contemplates how much he has received from God, how great are the gifts of grace from his creator, how he has come in pursuit of Him when he was lost, and on finding him how He granted him pardon, how He has aided his weakness in his struggles and has not failed him in his difficulties, how He has crowned him after victory, and given Himself as the price. All this he has taken into consideration and has cried out, saying, *How shall*

I make a return to the Lord for all the good he has given back to me. He did not want to be ungrateful. He wanted to make a return, but he had not the wherewithal.

He did not say, "What return will I make for what he has given to me," but rather *for all the good he has given back to me.* The Lord has not just "given"; he has "given back" or "repaid." If he has given back it is something which we have first given him. We have given him iniquities, but he has returned us his favors. We have given him evil for good, but he has returned us good for evil.

The Prophet, then, is wondering what return he can make. His mind is upset, for he has found no way of paying his debt: *How shall I make a return to the Lord for all the good he has done for me?* And, as if he had found the wherewithal for his return, *The cup of salvation I will take up,* he exclaims, *and I will call upon the name of the Lord (Ps.* 116, 4). What does this mean? He was certainly thinking of making some return, and see, now he is seeking to take something: *I will take up the cup of salvation,* he says.

What is this cup? This is the chalice of the passion, bitter but salutary. The sick man would be reluctant to take the medicine if the doctor did not taste it first. It is of this chalice that Christ speaks when He says, *Father, if it is possible, let this cup pass away from me (Matt.* 26, 39).

The sons of Zebedee had demanded through their mother the choice seats, that they might sit one on the right and the other on the left. The Lord answered them, *Can you drink of the cup of which I am about to drink? (Matt.* 20, 22) You seek the heights: the mountain is reached through the valley. You want the throne of glory? First of all drink the chalice of humiliation. Of this same chalice the martyrs have said, *the cup of salvation I will take up and I will call upon the name of the Lord.*

Are you not afraid of failure? No, he answers. Why? *Because I will call upon the name of the Lord.* How would the martyrs be victorious if he were not first victorious in them who said, *Take courage, I have overcome the world (John* 16, 33). Their heavenly king has directed their spirit and their tongue; through them He has vanquished the demon on the earth, and has crowned the martyrs in heaven. Happy are they to have drunk of this chalice! Their sufferings are over, their glory has begun.

Reflect, brothers: apply your heart and spirit to what your

eyes cannot see, and see that *the death of His faithful ones is precious in the eyes of the Lord.*

SERMON ON THE SACRAMENT OF THE ALTAR, ADDRESSED TO THE NEOPHYTES [22] (SERMO DENYS 3)

The Sacrifice of the New Covenant

1. The obligation to preach and the concern to form Christ in you who are entrusted to us as children compel us to instruct your tender youth. Born again of water and the Holy Spirit, you now see the food and drink on the altar in a new light. You perceive with a new piety the meaning of this great, divine sacrament, this noble, marvellous medicine, this pure, simple sacrifice, unknown in all the earthly cities of Jerusalem or to that Tabernacle which Moses constructed or to the Temple built by Solomon (those were but shadows of the things to come). Our sacrifice as was foretold by the prophet is immolated *from the rising of the sun to its setting* and a victim of praise is offered to God according to the grace of the New Testament.

No longer a bloody victim from the flocks is sought, no longer a sheep or goat is led to the sacred altars, but the sacrifice of our day is the Body and Blood of the High Priest Himself. The Psalms already foretold as much about him: *You are a priest forever according to the order of Melchisedech (Ps. 110, 4).* We read and find in the book of Genesis that Melchisedech, priest of the most high God, brought bread and wine when he blessed Abraham our father *(Gen. 14, 18).*

Christ is Our Sacrifice

2. Christ, our Lord, has offered in suffering for us the flesh which he received from us at his birth. He has become prince of priests forever and has left the disposition of sacrifice which you see, namely his own flesh and blood. The water and blood which issued from his body when struck by the lance has remitted our sins. Mindful of this grace that achieves your salvation which he, being God, operates in you, approach Communion with fear

---

22. PL 46, 826-28. Its authenticity is controverted but is accepted by Morin (cf. PLS 2, 406). English trans., T. Halton.

and trembling. Recognize in the bread what hangs on the Cross; recognize in the chalice the water and blood trickling from his side.

The old sacrifices of the people of God prefigured in a variety of ways this unique sacrifice to come. Christ is the sheep by reason of innocence and simplicity of soul; He is the goat through his resemblance to our sinful flesh. And whatever else the sacrifices of the Old Testament have foretold in many divine ways pertain to this one divine revelation of the New Testament.

The Real Presence

3. Take, then, and eat the body of Christ, since you yourselves have become members of the body of Christ. Take and drink the blood of Christ. Do not be disunited; eat your bond. Do not cheapen yourselves; drink the precious blood. Just as this is converted into you when you consume it, so you are converted into the body of Christ when you live in obedience and piety.

For he, when his own passion was approaching, in celebrating the Pasch with his disciples, took bread, blessed it and broke it and said: *This is my body which is being given for you* (*Luke* 22, 19). Likewise he blessed the chalice and gave it to them, saying, *This is my blood of the new covenant which is being shed for many unto the remission of sins* (*Matt.* 26, 28). You read or heard this in the Gospel, but did not know that this Eucharist was the Son of God. But now, clean of heart and in a pure conscience with body purified by clean water, *Approach him and be enlightened, that your faces be not red with shame* (*Ps.* 34, 5).

For if you worthily receive the mystery of the New Covenant through which you hope for an eternal inheritance, keeping the new commandment that you love one another, you will have life in you: *the bread that I will give is my flesh for the life of the world* (*John* 6, 52). And: *unless you eat my flesh and drink my blood you shall not have life in you* (*John* 6, 54).

The Effects of the Eucharist

4. Having life in him you shall be in one body with him. The body of Christ has not given us this mystery to cause division among us.

The Apostle tells us that this is taught in Scripture: *the two shall become one flesh. This is a great mystery—I mean in reference to Christ and his Church* (*Eph.* 5, 31, 32). And in another place he says about the Eucharist itself: *Because the bread is one, we though many are one body* (I *Cor.* 10, 17). You begin to receive what you have begun to be, provided you do not receive unworthily, eating and drinking judgment to yourselves: *whoever eats this bread or drinks the cup of the Lord unworthily will be guilty of the body and the blood of the Lord. But let a man prove himself and so let him eat of that bread and drink of the cup; for he who eats and drinks unworthily . . . eats and drinks judgment for himself* (I *Cor.* 11, 27-29).

Conditions for Worthy Reception

5. You receive worthily if you guard against the leaven of evil doctrine so that you are *unleavened bread of sincerity and truth* (I *Cor.* 5, 8), if you guard that *leaven of charity which a woman took and hid in three measures of flour until all of it was leavened* (*Matt.* 13, 33). This woman is the wisdom of God become flesh by the virgin who disseminated his gospel throughout the world with the three sons of Noah rescued from the Flood as the three measures of flour *until all of it was leavened.* This all (which is *Holos* in Greek) you will become if you guard the bond of peace: the "all" will be both catholic and Catholic.[23]

EXPLANATION OF THE MASS TO THE NEWLY BAPTIZED [24]
(SERMON DENYS 6)

What does Eucharist Mean?

1. What you see, dearly beloved, on the Lord's table is bread and wine, but the bread and wine becomes the body and blood of the Word at the intervention of the Word. For the Lord who *in the beginning was the Word, and the Word was with God and the Word was God* (*John* 1, 1), out of mercy which caused him

---

23. The pun on the Greek **holos,** all, universal, catholic, is hard to translate in English.

24. PL 46, 834. Its authenticity is disputed by Adam and Geiselmann but accepted by Lambot (cf. PLS 2, 407). English trans., T. Halton.

not to despise what he had created in his own image, this *Word become flesh and dwelt among us* (*John* 1, 14), as you know. Because the Word himself has assumed manhood, i.e., the body and soul of a man, he has become man while remaining God. For this reason and also because he has left us in this sacrament his own body and blood, he has made us the same as himself. For we have also become his body and through his mercy we are what we have received.

Recall what this creation of bread once was: how the earth begot it, the rain nourished it, and ripened it; then human labor brought it through various stages—transporting it to the threshing floor, threshing and winnowing it, storing it, bringing it out, grinding, kneading and baking it until at long last bread is produced.

Think too of your own progress: you were brought into existence from non-existence; you were brought to the Lord's threshing floor by the toil of oxen, i.e., by those preaching the Gospel; you were threshed. When you were on probation as catechumens you were in storage in the granary. You enrolled your names, thereby beginning to be ground by fastings and exorcisms. Afterwards you were brought to the water as in the kneading process, and thus became unified. You were baked by the heat of the Holy Spirit and you became the bread of the Lord.

Symbol of Unity

2. See what you have received. Just as you see that what was made is a unity let you also be one by retaining one faith, one hope, undivided charity. When the heretics receive the Eucharist they admit testimony against themselves, because they are pursuing division whereas this bread is a pointer to unity.

Likewise the wine existed in many grapes but is now reduced to unity. It is one in the sweetness of the chalice after the bitter process of squeezing in the winepress. Similarly, you, after your fastings, labors, humility and contrition, have already come in the name of the Lord to his chalice: you are there on the Lord's table, you are actually present in the chalice. You form this mystery with us: we are united in one, we drink together because we live together.

You are going to hear what you heard yesterday. But today

you will get an explanation of what you heard, and of the responses you made or perhaps failed to make. But you were told yesterday what you should answer today.

Description of the Mass

3. After the salutation which you know, i.e., *Dominus vobiscum* or the Lord be with you, you heard *sursum corda,* lift up your hearts. The entire life of true Christians is a *sursum corda.* I said "true" Christians, not just nominal ones. The whole life of a true Christian is an elevation of heart. What do we mean by "an elevation of heart"? It is hope, not in yourself but in God, for you are below, God is above. If you hope in yourself your heart remains below, not above. So, when you hear the priest's *Sursum corda* you answer, *Habemus ad Dominum,* we have lifted them up to the Lord. Strive to answer truthfully, because your answer is within the sacred mysteries. So let it be as you say, and not have your conscience contradicting the words you mouth.

And since it is on God's strength and not by your own that you have lifted your heart up to God, the priest in turn says, *Let us give thanks to the Lord our God.*

Why *give thanks?* Because we have our heart lifted up, and unless he had lifted it up we would have laid prostrate on the ground. And hence it is that the things are accomplished in the holy prayers which you are going to hear so that at the intervention of the word it becomes the body and blood of Christ. For if you take away the word it remains mere bread and wine; add the word and it becomes something very different.

How "something very different?" The body and blood of Christ. Take away, then, the word and it is bread and wine: add the word and it will become the sacrament. To this you say, *Amen.* To say "Amen" is to subscribe your assent. Amen in Latin is *verum,* true.

The Lord's Prayer is then recited. You have already learned and memorized it. Why is it recited before receiving Christ's body and blood? Because of human frailty—a bad thought, perhaps, a slip of the tongue, a sinful glance, listening to an off-color story—if through worldly temptation and human weakness you have succumbed to some such sin, it is remitted by the Lord's Prayer at the words: *Forgive us our trespasses.* We can then ap-

proach the altar in the safe knowledge that we are not eating
and drinking judgment for ourselves.

After this the *Pax vobiscum,* Peace be to you, is said. The
kiss of peace is most significant. Let it be an act of real love.
Do not be a Judas, for he kissed Christ with his lips while betraying Him in his heart. Perhaps somebody entertains hostility
toward you, and you cannot convince him or win him around:
you are forced to be tolerant. Do not harbor evil for evil
in your heart. Return love for hate and your kiss of peace
will be genuine. What I have said is brief but of the greatest
importance. Do not underestimate my words because of their
brevity, but cherish them because of their weight. For we must
not overburden you with words in order to ensure that you will
retain what you hear.

MAI SERMON 129: ON THE EUCHARIST [25]

Ever Living Bread

1. In what terms have you heard the Lord invite you? Who
invites? Who is invited? What has he prepared? The Lord
has invited his servants and has prepared himself for their
nourishment. Who would dare to eat his own master? And
nonetheless he says: *He who eats me lives by me (John* 6, 57).

To eat Christ is to eat life. Nor does he die that we may
eat, but he gives life to the dead. When he is eaten he refreshes
the exhausted but is not himself exhausted. Let us not hesitate
then, brethren, to eat this bread; have no fear that having eaten
it we may exhaust it and find nothing further to eat. Let us eat
Christ; he lives in being eaten for he rose in death. For we
do not reduce his body by eating it. That is what happens in the
sacrament and the faithful know how they eat the flesh of Christ:
each one receives a particle and each particle is known as the
Eucharist itself.

Christ is eaten in particles, but he remains one and entire. He
is eaten in particles in the sacrament and he remains one and
entire in your heart. He was totally with the Father when he

---

25. Published by Cardinal Mai, n. 29 in his edition of Augustine, reproduced in PLS 2, 518-519. English trans., T. Halton.

came to the Virgin; he filled her womb without departing from him. He became flesh that men might eat him, and he remains entire with the Father that he may nourish the angels.

Know, then, brethren,—and both the initiated and the non-initiated should know it—that when Christ was made man, *Man ate the bread of angels* (*Ps.* 78, 25). Whence, how, in what way, by what merits could man have eaten the bread of angels if the Creator of angels had not become man? Let us eat, then, secure in the knowledge that what is eaten is not destroyed and let us eat lest we be destroyed.

What does it mean, to eat Christ? It does not simply mean to eat him sacramentally. For a number receive unworthily and about these the apostle says, *He who eats and drinks unworthily . . . eats and drinks judgment to himself* (I *Cor.* 11, 29).

How to Eat Christ's Body

2. But how ought we to eat Christ? As he himself said: *He who eats my flesh and drinks my blood abides in me and I in him* (*John* 6, 56). If, then, he abides in me and I in him, he truly eats and drinks me. The one who does not abide in me, nor I in him, even though he receives the sacrament, only acquires a great reproach. He who abides in me is elsewhere described as *he who keeps my commandments, abides in me and I in him* (*John* 3, 24).

Take care, brethren, lest in absenting yourselves from the body of the Lord you risk the danger of dying from starvation. For he himself has said, *He who does not eat my flesh and drink my blood will not have life in him* (*John* 6, 53). If you absent yourself from eating his body and drinking his blood, you risk death; but if you eat and drink it unworthily you risk eating and drinking judgment to yoursleves.

The path of life is straight and narrow. Live in justice and the path will be made easy. Do not promise yourselves life, those of you who live in sin, for when man promises himself what God does not promise he is only deceiving himself. A prejudiced witness, you promise yourself what truth denies you. Truth testifies: if you live in sin you will die in eternity. And do you dare tell yourself: I will both live in sin here and in eternity with Christ. How can truth lie and you tell the truth? *Every man is a liar* (*Ps.* 116, 11).

Therefore you cannot live a good life if He does not help you by His presence and His gifts. Pray, therefore and eat. Pray and you will be liberated from those straits. For He will fill you in your good works and in your life with virtue. Examine your conscience. Your mouth will be filled with God's praise and the joy of God. Freed from the narrow straits you will say, *You have made room for my goings under me and my footsteps did not fail* (*Ps.* 18, 36).

SERMON ON THE DAY OF EASTER [26]

A New Bread

1. You are reborn into a new life; therefore you are called neophytes. You especially who for the first time now witness this, hear the explanation which we promised you of why these things are so. Hear also, you the initiated who have long since been admitted to the mysteries. The recollection is good lest we become careless and forgetful.

What you see on the table of the Lord, as far as appearances go, you are in the habit of seeing on your own tables; the appearance is the same, but not the substance. For you too are the same person that you were; your appearances are the same. And yet you *are* new. The same as ever in bodily appearance, you are new in sanctifying grace. This, too, is new. Up to now, as you see, it is bread and wine. The consecration arrives and this bread will become the body of Christ, and this wine will become the blood of Christ. This is done through the name of Christ and through the grace of Christ, so that it retains the appearance of bread but its substance is no longer the same. For up to now if it were eaten it would fill the belly but now when it is eaten it nourishes the mind.

When you were being baptized, or rather before you were baptized, on Saturday, we spoke of the sacrament of baptism to you, in which you were to be baptized. And we said to you (I hope that you haven't forgotten) that this was or is the virtue

---

26. This is sermon Morin Guelferbytanus 7 (PLS 2, 554-556; Solano 2, 227-231). English trans., T. Halton.

of baptism that it is a burial with Christ, as the apostle says: *For we were buried with him by means of baptism into death, in order that, just as Christ has arisen from the dead, so we also may walk in newness of life* (Rom. 6, 4).

Likewise we must now commend to you and tell you what it is that you receive or are about to receive. We base it not on sentiment, nor on presumption, nor on human arguments, but on the authority of the apostle. Hear briefly the words of the apostle, or rather the words of Christ through the apostle, speaking of the authority of the Apostle. Hear briefly the words of the Apostle, or rather the words of Christ through the Apostle, speaking of it quickly but weigh the words rather than count them. They are few in number but they are extremely weighty.

One bread, he said. All the loaves placed here are *one bread.* All the loaves placed today on all the altars of Christ throughout the world are *one bread.* But what does *one bread* mean? He has told us very briefly: *Though many we are one body.* This bread is the body of Christ about which the Apostle speaks addressing the Church: *you are the body of Christ and his members* (I *Cor.* 12, 27). You are what you receive by the grace which redeemed you; you subscribe to it when you answer, *Amen.* The elements which you see constitute the sacrament of unity.

The Eucharist, Sacrament of Unity

2. Now that the Apostle has briefly indicated to you the nature of this bread, consider more carefully the manner in which bread is made. How is it done? First, there is the threshing. Then it is ground, kneaded, baked; in the kneading it is refined, in baking it becomes solid. Where is your process of sifting? In fastings, in vigils, in exorcisms. Kneading is not done without water: you were baptized. Baking is troublesome but essential. How are you baked? In the fire of temptations which are an intimate part of life. But how is it essential? *The furnace proves the potter's vessels; so the trial of tribulation proves the just* (*Ecclus.* 27, 5).

Just as individual grains unite in the kneading to form one bread, so the harmonious charity unites all into the one body of Christ. The grapes are to the blood of Christ what the grains of what are to his body. For the wine is formed by being pressed, and many individual drops unite in a single flow and become wine. Thus the mystery of unity is present in both the bread and the wine.

Man's Elevation is Effected by Grace

3. The word you heard at the Lord's table, *Dominus vobiscum,* The Lord be with you, we also are in the habit of saying from the apse, and we say it as often as we pray, because it is a good thing for the Lord to be always with us, since we are nothing without him.

Another word that resounds in your ears: see how you answer it at the altar of God. For we say by way of request and exhortation: *Sursum corda,* lift up your hearts. Do not stay prostrate, for the heart corrupts on the ground: raise it up to the heavens. Now whither do we lift up our hearts? What is your answer? Whither are they lifted up? *We have lifted them up to the Lord.* Let each lift up his own heart, good or evil though it be. When is it evil? It is evil in men of whom it is written, *You have cast them down when they were raised up* (*Ps.* 73, 18).

Lift up your hearts: if it is not lifted up to the Lord, that is pride, not justice. So when we say, *Lift up your hearts,* because the heart can also be lifted up in pride, you respond, *We have lifted them up to the Lord, our God.* This is to be lifted up properly, not be puffed up. And, since it is proper to lift up the heart to the Lord, have we done it? Could we have done it by our own strength? Have we raised up what is earthly, that is what we are, to the heavens? By no means. God did it. He gave us the ability. He sent us his helping hand. He extended his grace. He raised up what was on the ground. And so when we say. *Lift up your hearts* and respond, *We have lifted them up to the Lord* let us not take the credit for ourselves for lifting them up. We should add. *Let us give thanks to the Lord our God.*

These mysteries are brief but important. What we say is brief but from the heart. You say these words to yourselves quickly, without a book, without reading, and without lengthy discussion. Recall what you are and the attitude which you should maintain so that you may attain to the blessings which God has promised you.

PETER CHRYSOLOGUS
(† 450)

Somewhat neglected by posterity, Peter Chrysologus, bishop of Ravenna, is a pastor in every sense of the word. We know very little of his life. His work, consisting of sermons and homilies, witness to his pastoral sense and psychological acumen. His favorite theme in his preaching was: Live the Mass.

Sermon 95, dealing with the incident of Jesus dining with the publican, relates the interview with the woman sinner. "He was invited to dine and He gave Himself as food to be eaten." In the sinner the bishop sees the Church, composed of sinners but which is saved by His work of mercy and gesture of love. Every action brings the Master a little nearer in person.

Sermons 108 and 109 explain the meaning of the word of the Apostle: Offer your body as a living host. "Man is himself the host and priest when he does not seek outside himself for the sacrifice which he will immolate to God, when man 'with Him, and in Him, and for Him,' carries his offering to God, remaining the host and without ceasing to be at the same time priest."

We have here a model of what a homily should be—at once refined, doctrinal, practical, and brief.

SERMON 95 [27] — THE CONVERSION OF MAGDALEN ALLEGORICALLY INTERPRETED (LUKE 7, 36-50)

All the deeds which Christ is reported to have performed while he was in his body on earth are based on historical truth in such a way that they are always found to be replete with heavenly symbols. In our two preceding sermons we have already treated what was on the surface of the Gospel text. Therefore, pray that through the light of the Holy Spirit we may, as we promised, lay open its deeper meanings. A sermon is unworthy if it uses nothing more than human exposition to penetrate what God has done.

---

27. See the recent, Dom Alejandro Olivar, Los Sermones de San Pedro Crisologo (Monteserrat, 1962). For text cf. PL 52, 467-69. Translation, with modifications, is from FC 17, 147.

Dining with the Pharisee

The text says: *Now one of the Pharisees asked him to dine with him.* Brethren, the Pharisee is the Catholic Jew, for he believes in the resurrection, and disagrees with the Sadducee who denies it. That is why this Pharisee invited Christ, that is, the Author of the resurrection, to dine with him. For, he who dines with Christ cannot die. Indeed he lives forever.

"He asked the Lord to dine with him." You ask, O Pharisee, to dine with him. Believe, be a Christian, that you may feed upon him. *I am the bread,* he says, *that has come down from heaven (John* 6, 51). God always gives greater gifts than he is asked for. He was being asked to give the hope of eating with him, and he gave himself as food to be eaten. Moreover, he granted all this in such a way that he did not refuse that for which he was asked. Does he not promise this of his own accord to his disciples? *You have continued with me will eat and drink at my table in my kingdom (Luke* 22, 28, 30). O Christian, what can he, who here gave himself to you to be eaten, refuse to you in the future? He who prepared such great provisions to sustain you on your journey, what has he not prepared for you in that everlasting abode? *You will eat at my table in my kingdom.* You have heard about the banquet of God; do not be anxious about the quality of this banquet. He who deserves to be present at a king's table will eat whatever the king possesses through his power and control of his kingdom. Similarly, he who comes to the banquet of the Creator will have among his enjoyments whatever is contained in creation. But, let us return to what we intended to say.

So he went into the house of the Pharisee. Into what house? Assuredly, it was into the synagogue that he went and reclined at table. Brethren, Christ reclined at table in the synagogue during the time when he reposed in the grave, but he transmitted his body to the table of the Church, that this flesh from heaven might be a help to salvation for the nations who would eat it. *Unless you eat the flesh of the Son of Man, and drink of his blood, you shall not have life in you (John* 6, 53). Those who have been initiated into the heavenly mysteries [28] know how the flesh of Christ is eaten, and how his blood is drunk.

---

28. **Sacramenta,** referring to the **disciplina arcani.** In many cases the catechumens were not told about the Eucharist.

The Sinner in the Town

And behold, it says, *a woman in the town who was a sinner.*
Who is this woman? Beyond any doubt, she is the Church. *A
sinner in the city.* In what city? In that one of which the Prophet
had said: *How is the faithful city, Sion, become a harlot? (Isa.
1, 21)* And elsewhere: *I have seen iniquity and contradiction
in the city, and in the midst thereof are iniquity, labor and injustice. And usury and deceit have not departed from its streets
(Ps. 55, 10, 11).* Therefore, in a city surrounded by walls of
perfidy; fortified by towers of pride, criss-crossed by streets of
iniquities, locked up by gates of quarrels, blackened by the smoke
of deceit, hardened by flintstones of usury, aggravated by vexations
of business, and disgraced by houses of ill repute, that is, by temples
of the idols. It was in this city that this woman, that is, the Church,
was bearing up under the depressing guilt which sprang from the
heavy silt of so many past sins.

But then she heard that Christ had come to the house of the
Pharisee—that is, to the synagogue. She heard that there—that is,
at the Jewish Pasch—he had announced the mysteries of his
passion, disclosed the sacrament of his body and blood, and
revealed the secret of our redemption. She ignored the Scribes
like contemptible doorkeepers. *Woe to you lawyers! you who
have taken away the key of knowledge (Luke 11, 52).* She
broke open the doors of quarrels, and despised the very assembly
of the chief Pharisees. Ardent, panting, perspiring, she made
her way to the large inner chamber of the legal banquet. There
she learned that Christ, betrayed amid sweet cups and a banquet
of love, had died through the fraud of the Jews, according to the
Prophet's statement: *For if my enemy had reviled me, I would
verily have borne with it. And if he that hated me had spoken
evil things against me, I would perhaps have hidden myself from
him. But thou, a man of one mind, my guide, and familiar, who
did take sweetmeats together with me: in the house of God
we walked with consent (Ps. 55, 12-14).*

The Sinner's Perfume

Upon learning that he was at table in the Pharisee's house—
that is, that in the synagogue he had been sentenced altogether
unjustly through every conceivable pretext, had suffered, been

crucified, and buried. Nevertheless, the Chruch does not let
that great injury inflicted on him deter her from fervor of
faith. Instead, she carries her ointment, she bears the oil of
Christian anointing. She did not deserve to see the bodily face
of Christ. Therefore, she stands behind him, not in place
but in time. She clings to his footsteps that she may follow
him. And soon she pours out tears of love more than of
repentance, that she may deserve to see him when he returns,
whom she did not deserve to see when he was going away. Therefore, with welling love she sheds her tears upon the feet of the
Lord. With her hands of good works she holds the feet of those
who preach his kingdom. She washes them with tears of charity,
kisses them with praising lips, and pours out the whole ointment
of mercy, until he will turn to her—(what means this word,
turn? It means, come back)—until he will come back to her
and say to Simon, say to the Pharisees, say to those who deny,
say to the Jewish people: *I came into your house; you gave me
no water for my feet.*

And when will he speak these words? When he will come
in the majesty of his Father, and separate the just from the unjust
like a shepherd who separates the sheep from the goats, and will
say: *I was hungry and you did not give me to eat; I was thirsty
and you gave me no drink; I was a stranger and you did not
take me in (Matt. 25, 42).* This is tantamount to saying: you
did not give me water for my feet. But this woman while she was
bathing the feet of my disciples, anointing them, and kissing them,
did to the servants [29] what you did not do for the Master, she
did for the feet what you refused to the Head, she expended upon
the lowliest members what you refused to your Creator. Then
he will say to the Church: *Your sins, many as they are, are forgiven you because you have loved much.* For the remission of
sins will take place when all the matters conducive to sin will
be gone, when corruptibility will put on incorruptibility, when
mortality will gain immortality, when the flesh of sin will become
flesh altogether holy, when earthly slavery will be exchanged
for heavenly domination, and the human army elevated into the
divine kingdom.

Pray, brethren, that we, too, assembled in the cause of the
Church, may merit to arrive at the benefits we have enumerated,

---

29. The "least fo the servants" referred to in **Matt.** 25, 42.

which Christ himself has promised. To him, along with the
Holy Spirit, is there honor and glory forever. Amen.

SERMON 108 [30] — MAN AS BOTH A PRIEST AND A SACRIFICE
TO GOD (ROM. 12, 1)

This is an unusual kind of piety, which requests both that it
may pray and give a present. For, today, the blessed Apostle
is not asking for human gifts, but conferring divine ones, when he
prays: *I exhort you, by the mercy of God*. When a physician
persuades the sick to take some bitter remedies, he does so by
coaxing requests. He does not use a compelling command. He
knows that weakness, not choice, is the reason why the sick man
spits out the healthful medicines, whenever he rejects those which
will aid him. Also, a father induces his son to live according
to the rigor of discipline not by force, but by love. He knows
how harsh discipline is to a youthful disposition.

The Mercy of God

If one sick in body is thus enticed by requests toward getting
cured, and if a boyish disposition is with difficulty thus coaxed
to prudence, is it strange that the Apostle, always a physician
and a father, prays with these words, in order to entice human
souls which bodily diseases have wounded to accept divine
remedies? *I exhort you by the mercy of God*.

He is introducing a new kind of exhortation. Why does
he not exhort through God's might, or majesty, or glory, rather
than by his mercy? Because it was through that mercy alone
that Paul escaped from the criminal state of a persecutor, and
obtained the dignity of his great apostolate. He himself tells
us this: *For I formerly was a blasphemer, a persecutor and
a bitter adversary; but I obtained the mercy of God* (I *Tim*. 1,
13). A little further on he continues: *This saying is true
and worthy of entire acceptance, that Jesus Christ came into the
world to save sinners, of whom I am the chief. But I obtained
mercy to be an example to those who shall believe in him for
the attainment of life everlasting* (I *Tim*. 1, 15-16).

I exhort you, by the mercy of God. Paul asks—rather, God

---

30. Text: PL 52, 499-501; Translation, FC 17, 166.

himself is asking through Paul, because God prefers to be loved than feared. God is asking because he wants to be not so much a Lord as a Father. God is asking through his mercy, that he may not punish in his severity. Hear God asking: *I have spread forth my hands all the day* (*Isa.* 65, 2). Is not he who spreads forth his hands asking by his very demeanor? *I have spread forth my hands.* To whom? To a people. And to what people? To an unbelieving people, yes, more, to a contradicting one. *I have spread forth my hands.* He opens his arms, he enlarges his heart, he proffers his breast, he invites us to his bosom, he lays open his lap, that he may show himself a Father by all this affectionate entreaty.

Also hear God asking in another way: *O my people, what have I done to you, or in what have I molested you?* (*Mich.* 6, 3) Does he not say the following: If my divinity is something unknown, at least let me be known in the flesh. Look! You see in me your own body, your members, your heart, your bones, your blood. If you fear what is divine, why do you not love what is characteristically human? If you flee from me as the Lord, why do you not run to me as your Father? But perhaps the greatness of my passion, which you brought on, confounds you. Do not be afraid. This cross is not mine, but it is the sting of death. These nails do not inflict pain upon me, but they deepen your love of me. These wounds do not draw forth my groans; rather, they draw you into my heart. The extending of my blood entices you into my bosom; it does not increase my pain. As far as I am concerned, my blood does not flow in vain, but is paid down as a ransom price for you. Therefore, come, return and at least thus have experience of me as a Father whom you see returning good things for evils, love for injuries, such great charities for such great wounds.

Living Sacrifices

Let us now hear the contents of the Apostle's exhortation. *I exhort you to present your bodies.* By requesting this, the Apostle has raised all men to priestly rank. *To present your bodies as a living sacrifice.* O unheard of function of the Christian priesthood, inasmuch as man is both the victim and the priest for himself! Because man need not go beyond himself in seeking what he is to immolate to God! Because man, ready to offer sacrifice to God, brings with himself, and in himself, what is for himself! Because the same being who remains as the victim, remains also as a priest! Because the victim is immolated and still lives! Because the priest who will make atonement is unable to kill! Wonderful indeed is this sacrifice where the body is offered without [the slaying of] a body, and the blood without bloodshed.

I exhort you, says the Apostle, *by the mercy of God, to present your bodies as a living sacrifice.* Brethren, Christ's sacrifice is the pattern from which this one comes to us. While remaining alive, he immolated his body for the life of the world. And he truly made his body a living sacrifice, since he still lives although he was slain. In the case of such a victim, death suffers defeat. The victim remains, the victim lives on, death gets the punishment. Consequently, the martyrs get a birth at the time of their death. They get a new beginning through their end, and a new life through their execution. They who were thought to be extinguished on earth shine brilliantly in heaven.

Become a Sacrifice

I exhort you, brethren, he says, *by the mercy of God, to present your bodies as a sacrifice, living, holy.* That is what the Prophet sang: *Sacrifice and oblation you would not, but a body you have perfected for me.* [31] Be, O man, be both a sacrifice to God and a priest. Do not lose what the divine authority gave and conceded to you. Put on the robe of sanctity, gird yourself with the belt of chastity. Let Christ be the covering of your head. Let the cross remain as the helmet of your forehead. Cover your breast with the sign of heavenly knowledge. Keep the incense of prayer ever burning as your perfume. Take up the sword of the spirit. Set up your heart as an altar. Free from anxiety, move your body forward in this way to make it a victim for God.

God seeks faith from you, not death. He thirsts for self-dedication, not blood. He is placated by good will, not by slaughter. God gave proof of this when he asked holy Abraham for his son as a victim (cf. *Gen.* 22, 1-18). For what other than

---

31. **Ps.** 39, 7, as quoted in **Heb.** 10, 5.

his own body was Abraham immolating in his son? What other than faith was God seeking in the father, since he ordered the son to be offered, but did not allow him to be killed?

Therefore, O man, strengthened by such an example, offer your body. Do not merely slay it, but also cut it up into numerous members, that is, the virtues. For your skills at practicing vice die as often as you offer these members, the virtues, to God. Offer up faith, that faithlessness may suffer punishment. Offer a fast, that gluttony may cease. Offer up chastity, that lust may die. Put on piety, that impiety may be put off. Invite mercy, that avarice may be blotted out. That folly may be brought to naught, it is always fitting to offer up holiness as a sacrificial gift. Thus your body will become your sacrificial victim, if it has been wounded by no javelin of sin. Your body lives, O man, it lives as often as you have offered to God a life of virtues through the death of your vices. The man who deserves to be slain by a life-giving sword cannot die. May our God himself, who is the Way, the Truth, and the Life, deliver us from death and lead us to life.

SERMON 109 [32] — THE WHOLE MAN, BODY AND SOUL,
AS A REASONABLE SACRIFICE TO GOD (ON ROM. 12, 1)

The Sacrifice of the Whole Man

Our preceding sermon touched merely the opening words of the Apostle's passage. Today let us hear what the Lord inspires us to say about the words which follow. He began thus: *I beseech you,* the text says, *by the mercy of God to present your bodies as a living sacrifice.* By these words does the Apostle mean that bodies alone are worthy to be victims offered to God? And does he either fail to mention, or pass over, or abandon souls as something disapproved for this purpose? Is not the soul from heaven and the body from earth? Is not the body ruled, while the soul rules? Does not the soul reign, and the body serve? Does not the body live, and the soul vivify? Does not the soul remain, and the body decay? Does not the body suffer age, while the soul cannot? Finally, is not death itself, which has power

---

32. For text, cf. PL 52, 501-503; trans., FC 17, 171.

over the body alone, unable to occur while the soul is present? Then what is the reason why the soul gets no mention, and only the body is thus summoned to be a victm of God?

Brethren, in this passage the Apostle honors the body without diminishing the importance of the soul. Sins master the body, crimes bind it fast, and transgressions depress it. Vices corrupt it, and passions weigh it down. Therefore, the Apostle desires to release the body. He is eager to set it free, he is striving to elevate it, and he is hastening to purify it by expiation. He wants the body to ascend to the sources of the soul, rather than to have the soul descend to the nature of the body. He desires the body to accompany the soul to heaven, rather than to have the soul follow the body to the earth. Hear Scripture describe the type and magnitude of the vexations with which the body burdens the soul: *For the corruptible body is a load upon the soul, the earthly habitation presses down the mind that muses upon many things* (*Wisd.* 9, 15)). Clearly, therefore, the Apostle desires not a degradation of the soul but an elevation of the body. He wishes both the body and the soul, that is, the whole man, to become a holy victim, a sacrifice pleasing to God. The Psalmist declares that the soul, too, is a sacrificial offering to God when he says: *A sacrifice to God is an afflicted spirit* (*Ps.* 51, 19).

A Just Sacrifice

To present your bodies as a sacrifice, living, holy, pleasing to God. Because man is pleasing by the fact, not that he lives, but that he lives well. He becomes a sacrificial victim not merely by offering himself to God, but by offering himself to God in a holy manner. A spotted victim makes God angry just as much as an unblemished victim placates him. Hear God saying: *Do not offer to me anything lame, or half-blind, or polluted because it is intended for death, but something mature without blemish* (*Lev.* 22, 18). Hence it is that the Apostle seeks a "living" sacrifice for God. Therefore, brethren, if we as the incense of that propitiation . . . . [33]

Cain is proof of this. As an ungrateful priest, he so shared his few possessions with God, from whom he had received

---

33. There is a lacuna in the text here.

everything, that he offered the worst of them upon the altar. He kept back for himself what was best, and thereby gave offense. The upshot was that when he evilly arranged this division with his Master, he separated himself and his descendants both from life and from the human race (cf. *Gen.* 4, 1-17).

Therefore, let us follow Abel to his reward, and let us not accompany Cain to his punishment. Abel, bringing a lamb to be sacrificed to God, was accepted as a lamb. Cain, bringing his stubble, found it to be tinder for himself, fuel through which he himself was to be set afire.

What is a Reasonable Service?

To present your bodies as a sacrifice, living, holy, pleasing to God, your reasonable service. A service which is not reasonable makes God angry to the same extent that one which is reasonable appeases him. A service is reasonable when it is not disturbed by presumption, or disordered by rashness, or profaned by transgressions, or colored by pretense. To show service to a king, all the soldiers in a military outpost stand in fear. Human power demands a punctilious service. The obeying servant watches in fear to discover the whim of his master who commands. For, alert devotion brings a reward of just remuneration, while presumptuous service does not escape the penalty of its rashness. Who rashly undertakes to serve in a king's palace if he is not invited? Who without a title has dared to profess himself a soldier? Who without the fillets indicating a dignity rashly assumes title to it? If these are matters of anxiety and caution among men, if they are based on reason, if they prosper through orderly arrangements and if they are preserved because of reverence, then how much more in our relations with God is devotion something to be cautious about! How much more should we be reverent in our service, and solicitous in our worship, that we may offer a reasonable service to God?

Examples of Service that was not Reasonable

Your reasonable service, the Apostle says. A service which is warm because it is reasonable is true fervor, but one which is not restrained by reason is fanaticism. Consequently, the Jewish nation, when it sought a god for itself in an unreasonable way,[34] lost God to whom it had been giving a reasonable service. The sons of Aaron,[35] unmindful of making their service reasonable, and presuming to add earthly fire to that ordained by God, changed the flame used on the sanctifying sacrifices into a flame of vengeance against themselves.   When Saul,[36] swollen with pride at the height of his kingly authority, thought that what was permitted to the priesthood was permitted also to himself, he became a rash violator of the altar, and lost the kingly authority he had received.   The Jew, while he cultivated the Law without the reasonableness of the Law, put the Author of the Law to death. The Gentile, unmindful of reasonableness while serving monstrous gods and whole clans of gods, did not deserve to come to the service of God who is one and true.   Arius thinks that he does a service to the Father by blaspheming the Son.   And while he is attributing a beginning to the Son, the pitiful man is putting an end to the Father.   Photinus,[37] while denying that the Son is co-eternal with the Father, concludes that the Father was not always Father.   So it is that all sorts of heresies where they insult the divinity, and lie about the Trinity through their terminology, render a blasphemous service.

In contrast, brethren, let us make our bodies fit to be a living sacrifice to God.   Let us take care that our service be reasonable, that our faith be true, our conscience pure, our minds well balanced, our hope firm, our heart clean, our flesh chaste, our senses holy, our spirit pious, our reason prudent, our charity undiluted, our mercy generous, our life holy, our appearance modest.   To the perfect service of Christ, let humility always accompany our steps.

FAUSTUS OF RIEZ
(† c. 495)

Faustus [38] was at first a monk in the celebrated island of Lerins where he must have known Honoratus, the founder of the

34. I.e., by adoring the golden calf. Cf. **Exod.** 32, 1-35.

35. Nadab and Abihu. Cf. **Lev.** 10, 1-7.

36. **I Kings** 15, 1-35, especially v. 23.

37. On the heresy of Photinus, cf. Epiphan. **Adv. haer.**, 3, 1 (MG 42, 373).

38. See G. Weigel, **Faustus of Riez. An Historical Introduction** (Philadelphia, 1938).

monastery. He succeeded him as abbot, later becoming bishop of the Provençal town of Riez (lower Alps). He was one of the most brilliant spirits in Gaul in the fifth century. He was involved in the theological discussions of his time. He has left us a collection of sermons which give us an insight into preaching in Provence in the course of the fifth century.

A collection of sermons attributed to one Eusebius certainly depends on Faustus. It contains a sermon on "The Body and Blood of Christ" which was certainly inspired by him. This homily depends on three sources: that of Cyprian, Ambrose and the Greek. It is inspiring both from a doctrinal point of view and as a reflection of fifth century preaching.

Two points are of special importance—the teaching on the transformation of the elements and on the sacrifice of the Mass.

The author speaks of the change of the bread and wine "into the substance of Christ." This must not be judged by the senses but by faith. Faithful to the tradition of Ambrose of Milan Faustus affirms: the power of the divine word which has created the world realizes the conversion of the created elements into the body and blood of Christ. We are witnessing a formulation whose publication has become famous and which was constantly reworked throughout the Middle Ages.

The same homily teaches the meaning of the sacrifice of the Mass, its commemorative character, its efficacy stemming from the sacrifice of the Cross, its nature which made it the offering of the redemption. "Since the redemption was in continuous and tireless motion for the redemption of men, the offering of the redemption should likewise be perpetual, and the perennial victim be abiding in memory and be always present in our hearts. This is the true, unique and perfect host which we must judge by faith, not by appearances, by interior sentiment rather than by the external senses."

Thus we celebrate on the altar, veiled in mystery, the offering of Calvary. The Church presents to God continuously the victim which was offered once for all. "The offering of the victim of Calvary, the Mass in its central act, the consecration, is the work of the invisible priest who operates by the efficacious words of institution, the miraculous conversion of the elements into his body and blood."

This teaching, originating in Gaul, in formulas so remarkably

precise, will profoundly influence the theology elaborated in the
Latin Middle Ages.

A HOMILY ON THE BODY AND BLOOD OF CHRIST [39]

Christ in the Eucharist Carries on the Blessings of the Redemption

1. The greatness of heavenly blessings transcends the limits
of the human mind. Accordingly divine providence has so
ordained that devout faith can grasp what our reason, weighed
down with material cares, cannot grasp and that a healthy faith
supports the intellect. Since, on account of Adam's sin, we
are liable to birth and death, God looks down from on high
on the magnitude of our transgressions and shapes the gift of
redemption to conform with the nature of our captivity. He
did this so that he might offer death to which he was not subject
for the death which was our due, for we had no more the
resources of life than had he the limitation of death. He assumed,
therefore, our mortal nature, so that life joined to immortality
might die for the dead. And since the body he assumed was
to be taken away from our sight and returned to the stars, it was
necessary that he should consecrate for us on this day the sacrament of his body and blood so that it might be legitimately
worshipped continuously in this sacrament which he had offered
once for our redemption. Since the redemption was in continuous
and tireless motion for the redemption of men, the offering of the
redemption should likewise be perpetual and the perennial victim
be abiding in memory and be always present in our hearts.

This is the true, unique and perfect host which we must judge
by faith, not by appearances, by interior sentiment rather than
by the external senses. It is this which the divine authority
guarantees to us: *My flesh is food indeed, and my blood is drink
indeed (John 6, 56).*

---

39. Text: PL 30, 271-76 in the Supplement to the works of St. Jerome.
In fact the homily forms part of the Gallican collection (n. 16) of the 2nd
half of the 5th cent., the work of an author of Provence. English trans.,
T. Halton.

The Eucharist, Source of Our Regeneration

2. Away, then, with all equivocation of the infidels, since the author of the gift is also the one who guarantees its truth. For a visible priest in virtue of a secret power converts by his own words visible elements into his body and blood saying: *Take and eat: this is my body,* and continuing the consecration: *Drink of this: this is my blood (Matt.* 26, 26, 28). Accordingly just as at the Lord's behest the lofty heavens, the depths of the sea and the expanses of the earth were suddenly created from nothing, so by the same divine omnipotence in the spiritual words of the sacrament his power is revealed and reality obeys it.

Ask yourself, then, you who have been regenerated in Christ, how great and how celebrated are the achievements of the divine blessing, and do not judge it extraordinary or impossible that what is earthly and mortal should be changed into the very substance of Christ.

3. Long estranged from life and a stranger to divine mercy and the way of salvation, you were nothing but an exile because of the death in your soul. But suddenly introduced to the laws of God and renewed by the mysteries of salvation you passed, not visibly, but by faith, into the body of the Church.

By a hidden purification you deserved to be transformed from a son of perdition into an adopted son of God. Retaining all your physical dimensions you have visibly become greater than your former self without any quantitative increase, and while retaining your original personality you have become a very different person by the workings of faith. Nothing has been added to your stature externally, but you have undergone a complete interior transformation, as man has become the son of Christ and Christ has taken form in the soul of man. Just as without bodily perception you have been rid of your baseness and invested with a new dignity, just as Christ has healed your wounds, cleansed your stains, and washed your uncleanness, without any help from your eyes or your senses, so when you approach the holy altar to be nourished by the food from heaven, contemplate, adore and marvel at the sacred body and blood of your God, grasp it with your mind, take it to heart, and above all absorb it in your interior being.

The Manna of the Old Covenant, a Figure of the Eucharist

4. But if the manna of the Old Law of which we read, *He rained manna upon them for food and gave them heavenly bread* (*Ps.* 78, 24), gave to the taste of each one who took it the pleasure which he desired, being one thing when taken and another when received, for its taste was formed invisibly on the senses of each recipient, if then this manna came down from heaven and surpassed its natural properties and specific appearances in the variety of its tastes, if the dispensation of the giver endowed his creature with such diversity that taste provided what was lacking to sight, because the novelty and worth of this food depended on the desire of the recipient and the heavenly gift refreshed each one with a variety of tastes by the bounty of him who rained down this bread upon them: since this is so, let faith accomplish now what hunger did then, and let God now accomplish through faith what food did then for bodily taste, as we read, *A man shall approach and the heart is deep and God shall be exalted* (*Ps.* 64, 6). And so what delight was caused in that instance to the taste is achieved in the present instance by the Blessing in the senses. Let the power of the consecration itself help you to understand and perceive the sacrifice of the true body of the Lord, and let him who was then prefigured for you in the manna be manifested to you now in grace.

5. That Christ himself was prefigured by the manna is shown clearly by the words of the Prophet, saying: *He rained manna upon them for food and gave them the bread of angels* (*Ps.* 78, 24).

And what is the bread of angels except Christ, who fills us with the nourishment of his love and the brightness of his glory? And he gives us this bread, as the Prophet says: *On the sixth day let it be twice as much as they bring in on other days* (*Exod.* 16, 5). While at first the manna was given by the Law from Sunday and was refused only on the sabbath, so it was prescribed that the Church, which had consecrated Sunday, the day of the resurrection, to Christ, should be the place for his reception, and that he should be denied to the synagogue in which the cult of the sabbath persisted. Thus the sabbath day is deprived of the heavenly bread.

Concerning this bread the Old Testament writes: *he that gathered much had nothing over and he that gathered little had no lack* (*Exod.* 16, 18), in that the reception of the Eucharist is not a matter of quantity but of efficacy. For the body of the Lord distributed by the priest is as present in a small particle as in the totality of the species. When the Church of the faithful receives it, the whole is received by the assembly and likewise the whole in individuals. This meaning is derived from the words of the Apostle: *He who had much had nothing over, and he who had little had not less* (II *Cor.* 8, 15).

This cannot be said of ordinary bread. Place ordinary bread before hungry men and it would not reach each individual in its entirety. Each would only receive his portion in pieces and fragments. But when the true bread is received, individuals receive just as much as the whole assembly; one, or two, or any number receives the whole without diminution, because this blessed sacrament can be distributed, but it cannot be exhausted in being distributed.

The Eucharist is Prefigured by the Sacrifices of Melchisedech and the Blessing of Jacob

6. We see the form of this sacrifice already described in the texts of the Jews: for we read of Melchisedech in Genesis: *Melchisedech the king brought out bread and wine and blessed Abraham. For he was a priest of the most high God* (*Gen.* 14, 18). And while future circumcision by the prepuce, that is by the pagan, is blessed, the glory of the Church is foretold, and the gentile people acquired from the unfaithful synagogue is preferred. The genealogy or origin of this Melchisedech has revealed the notion of that time; and the offering of bread and wine prefigured the sacrifice of Christ about which the Prophet foretells: *You are a priest for ever according to the order of Melchisedech* (*Ps.* 110, 4).

7. For Moses also, speaking of this mystery, designates bread, wine and blood under one denomination; and in the blessing of the Patriarch, he indicates at greater length the announcement of the passion of our Lord, saying, *He washes his garment in wine,*

his robe in the blood of grapes. [40]   Notice how clearly the created object, wine, is taken to mean the blood of Christ.   And recognize what you should furthermore seek from the twofold species: *Unless you eat,* it says, *the flesh of the son of man, and drink his blood, you shall not have life in you (John 6, 53).*

This is a clear and decisive refutation of the Pelagians who, carried away by impiety, dare to say that baptism should be conferred on infants not for this life but for the next one.   For under these divine words in which the Gospel says, *You will not have life in you,* must be the clear meaning that every soul which has not received the gift of baptism is deprived not merely of future glory but of the present life.

Meaning of the Water Mingled with Wine in the Chalice

8. That this wine of our Lord's blood must be mingled with water is clearly shown not merely by tradition but also by very nature of the passion itself.   Blood and water flowed from his sacred side when he was pierced with the lance, as had been foretold by the Prophet long before: *He smote the rock so that water gushed out (Ps.* 78, 20).   And the apostle: *They drank from the rock which followed them (I Cor.* 10, 4).   You see that Christ's mercy follows the one who drinks Christ's grace.   In Solomon we read it predicted of Christ himself: *Wisdom has built herself a house (Prov.* 9, 1), that is, he assumed a human body in which the fullness of divinity dwells: *she has set up her seven pillars (Prov.* 9, 1), because it is filled with the blessing of a sevenfold grace: *she has slaughtered her beasts, she has mixed her wine, she has also set her table (Prov.* 9, 2).   And in the following: *Come, eat of my bread and drink of the wine I have mixed for you (Prov.* 9, 2).   That is what we read of the wine mingled with water.

9. Let us now seek the reason why the Lord has wished the two elements to be mingled.   When at the wedding feast of the Jews the wine, that is to say, faith was lacking (*John* 2, 3) because the fruit of the vineyard failed, concerning which it is written,

---

40. **Gen.** 49, 11.   This deals with the blessing given to Juda at the point of death by Jacob.

when I looked for the crop from grapes it brought forth thorns
(*Isa.* 5, 4) (and so a crown of thorns was placed on the Redeemer's
head), when the Lord at the time of the marriage, that is when
the spouse joined himself to his Church in the joy of Easter,
he turned water into wine, plainly prefiguring the multitude of
races that would come from the grace of his blood.   That the
waters signify peoples is clear from the sacred text as we read,
The waters that you saw . . . are peoples and nations and tongues
(*Rev.* 17, 15).   And so we notice that peoples are prefigured
in the word "waters" and that the blood of our Lord's passion
is indicated in the wine.   And so, when water and wine are mingled
in the sacraments, the faithful are incorporated and joined with
Christ, and united with him by a bond of perfect charity so
that we can say with the Apostle, *Who shall separate us from the
love of Christ?   Shall tribuation, or distress, or persecutions?*
(*Rom.* 8, 35) and so forth.

The Bread, Symbol of Unity in Christ of Christians

10. Further, we should see an evident sign of the unity of
God's people in the very fact that we know that the bread is
composed of numerous grains of wheat.   Just as the grain which
is perfected to its white color only by the care of the thresher,
and the single substance of bread is got by mixing water in the
dough and baking it, so the various races and diverse nations assembled in one faith become the one body of Christ, and the
Christian people emerge, like countless grains of wheat, winnowed
and sifted from the infidel nations by faith.   Then it is assembled
in unity, separated from the cockle of infidels, and, instructed
by the teaching of the two Testaments, as the wheat is subjected
to the twin operation of the millstones, it emerges gleaming, and
is transformed into its original state of pristine splendor, and by
the water of baptism and the fire of the Holy Spirit it is baked
to form the body of that eternal bread.

11. Just, then, as the grains cannot be separated from the
combination of the one piece of bread, and just as waters mingled
with wine cannot return to their former state, so the wise faithful
who know that they have been redeemed by the blood and passion
of Christ ought to be like members inseparable from their head,
so united by their docile faith and ardent piety that they cannot
be separated from him voluntarily or even under compulsion

by any earthly ambition and that they remain inseparable even in death.

And let no one doubt that mere creatures can, at God's omnipotent behest, pass into the nature of the body of the Lord when he sees man himself become the body of Christ through the workings of divine mercy.

The Eucharist, a Miracle Comparable to Creation

12. Just as a convert to the Christian faith is still in the bondage of the old debt before the words of baptism, but once these have been pronounced he is stripped of all the dross of sin, so when created things are placed on the holy altars to be blessed by heavenly words before they are consecrated by the invocation of his name, they merely contain the substance of bread and wine but are changed into the body and blood of Christ after the words are pronounced.

What wonder is it if he who by a word can create can also convert created objects by a mere word?   Indeed it seems to be a lesser miracle to change for the better an already created object.   What, pray, can be difficult to him who could without difficulty form man from the slime of the earth, who could clothe him in his own divine image, easily recall him from hell, restore him from perdition, raise him from the dust, elevate him from earth to heaven, make him into an angel, endow his human body with his own radiance, sublimate his shadow to share in his kingdom.   Thus he who assumed our human body in all its frailty would assume us and invest us with his own immortality.   For which glorious resurrection may he deign to prepare us by works of piety, who lives and reigns for ever and ever.   Amen.

CAESARIUS OF ARLES [41]
(470-542)

The most illustrious bishop of Gaul in the sixth century and the inheritor of the whole Latin tradition of Hilary, Ambrose, Augustine and Fulgentius of Ruspe, Caesarius was born in the neighborhood of Chalon-sur-Saône.   He was a monk of the abbey

---

41. Cf. C. Vogel, Césare d'Arles (Paris 1965).

of Lerins. The abbot, Porcaire, sent him to Arles for health reasons, where the bishop received him among his own clergy, conferred on him the diaconate, then the priesthood in 499, and finally made him head of a suburban monastery.

In 503 Caesarius succeeded to the See of Arles and thereafter dedicated himself to the administration of his diocese. It was by no means a sinecure at a time of barbarian invasions when regimes succeeded one another in "Gallic Rome." He convoked and presided over a number of Councils from Orange to Marseilles.

He was above all an indefatigable preacher, drawing heavily from the contributions of his predecessors, especially St. Augustine. For the use of his priests he composed sermons—"wielding his scissors"—filching good thoughts from anywhere he could find them without worrying about copyright.

Concerned above all about the concrete needs of his public, which was composed of rather unsophisticated souls, Caesarius preached on virtues and vices, sufferings and glory, repentance and temperance.

Charity was particularly dear to his heart as the sermon published below shows. It constitutes the whole of the Christian life and should both precede and prolong the eucharistic act, thus giving it its real meaning. Repentance ought to precede the Eucharist.

SERMON 227: ON THE CONSECRATION OF THE ALTAR [42]

Repentance to Precede the Eucharist

1. As often, dearly beloved brethren, as we celebrate a feast of an altar or a temple, what is done in temples made with hands is completely fulfilled in the spiritual edifice of our bodies if we attend faithfully and diligently and live in holiness and justice. For he did not lie who said, *for holy is the temple of God and this temple you are* (I *Cor.* 3, 17). And again, *Or do you not know that your members are the temple of the Holy Spirit?* (I *Cor.* 6, 19) Without any merit on our part we have deserved to be-

---

42. For text see PL 39, 2166-68; also **Sancti Caesarii Arelatensis Sermones,** ed. D. G. Morin (Corpus Christianorum 104, 2), 897-900. Eng. tr. T. Halton.

come a temple of God by the grace of God.   Therefore let us strive with his help to the best of our ability that the Lord may not find anything offensive to his venerable eyes in his temple, I mean in ourselves.   Let the abode of our heart be free of vices and filled with virtues.   Let it be closed to the devil and opened to the gate of the kingdom of heaven by the keys of our good works.   For just as the gate is closed to us by bad works as by earthly crossbars and locks, so it is undoubtedly opened by good works.

2. And so, dearly beloved brethren, let us each examine his conscience, and when he sees that he has been wounded by some sin, let him first strive to cleanse his conscience by prayer, fasting, or almsgiving, and so dare to approach the Eucharist.   If he recognizes his guilt and is reluctant to approach the holy altar, he will quickly be pardoned by the divine mercy, *for whoever exalts himself shall be humbled and whoever humbles himself shall be exalted* (*Matt.* 23, 12).   If then, as I have said, a man, conscious of his sins, humbly decides to stay away from the altar until he reforms his life he will not be afraid of being completely excluded from the eternal banquet of heaven.

3. I ask you then, brethren, to pay careful attention.   If no one dares approach an influential man's table in tattered, soiled garments, how much more should one refrain in reverence and humility from the banquet of the eternal king, that is, from the altar of the Lord, if one is smitten with poisonous envy, or anger, or is full of rage and fury?   For it is written, *go first and be reconciled to your brother, and then come and offer your gift* (*Matt.* 5, 24).   And again, *Friend, how did you come in here without a wedding garment?*   And when he kept silent the man said to the attendants, *Bind his hands and feet and cast him forth into the darkness outside, where there will be weeping, and gnashing of teeth* (*Matt.* 22, 12, 13).   The same sentence awaits the man who dares present himself at the wedding feast, that is at the Lord's table, if he is guilty of drunkenness, or adultery, or retains hatred in his heart.

Dearly beloved, let the Lord keep us from such recklessness and grant that either we should never want to commit such wickedness, or if indeed we have fallen let us eagerly strive without delay to rid ourselves by penance and peace of soul, and let us hasten to purify ourselves by generous almsgiving, lest perchance we should come covered with the wounds of sin before the tribunal of the eternal judge, and be driven away for ever from that eternal Church and from that heavenly Jerusalem.

Exterior Darkness

4. Consider, brethren, I beg you, if today somebody is thrown out from the congregation of this Church for some crime, how great will be his grief and tribulation of soul? And if it is an intolerable grief to be cast out of this Church when the person excluded can eat and drink and converse with others and has a hope of being allowed to come back into the Church, how great do you think will be the grief if somebody is excluded from the assembly of angels and of all the saints, for it will not be sufficient punishment for him to be excluded but besides he is cast out into exterior darkness to be burned in everlasting fire.

He who deserves to be excluded from that heavenly Jerusalem will not just be punished by being forbidden to eat and drink; he will also endure the flames of hell, *where there will be weeping, and gnashing of teeth,* and wailing, lamentation and repentance without avail; where there is the worm that dies not, and the fire which is not extinguished; where death is sought and is not found. Why is death sought in hell and not found? Because those who were offered life in this world and refused it will seek for death in hell and will be unable to find it there. Night will be there without day, bitterness without sweetness, darkness without light; neither wealth, nor parents, nor spouses nor children can help there, where a sinner will find nothing except what he transmits from this life by living chastely and justly in abundance of almsgiving.

Manner of Receiving Holy Communion

5. Reflecting then on these matters, dearly beloved, let us strive to approach this altar with God's help with such chastity, sobriety and peace of soul that we may not be judged fit for exclusion from the altar of eternity. The one that approaches the earthly altar with purity of body, cleanness of heart, and a sincere and free conscience will make an easy transition to the altar of heaven.

Finally, dear brethren, what I suggest is neither difficult nor troublesome. I see you do frequently what I am saying. All the men who desire to receive Communion wash their hands, and all the women use clean linen cloths when they receive the body of Christ. What I am asking is not difficult, dear brothers; let the men wash their consciences with almsgiving just as they wash their hands with water. Likewise let the women have a chaste body and a spotless heart when they receive the body of Christ just as they use a clean linen cloth, and let them receive the sacrament of Christ with a good conscience.

Brethren, I ask you, does anyone wish to put his clothes in a closet that is full of dirty clothes? Now if clean clothes are not put in a closet full of dirty ones, how can you have the effrontery to receive the eucharistic Christ in a soul which is defiled with the filth of sin?

And, now that we have started using these examples from everyday life, may I suggest another one with which you are very familiar? I don't think that anyone puts a burning coal or anything inflammable into the closet in which he keeps his best clothes. Why, brethren? Because he is afraid that his best clothes will be burnt. I ask you, brothers, why a man who is reluctant to place anything inflammable in the clothes press is not equally afraid to kindle the flames of anger in his own soul? But we see clearly and plainly why this is so: we do not put anything inflammable in the closet because we love our clothes, but we do not extinguish the flames of anger because we do not love, in fact we hate, our souls, according to Scriptures: *he who loves iniquity hates his soul* (*Ps.* 11, 5).

6. And so, dearly beloved brethren, reflecting attentively on these examples, let us strive, with God's help, to take the best possible care of our inner closets, that is our conscience, so that when the day of the judgment comes we may appear in that eternal and blessed Church where evil can never dwell, and which the good will never leave, and we will not be cast out into exterior darkness with the old clothes, but robed in the stole of immortality, and adorned with the gems of chastity and justice, and clad in the radiance of almsgiving, we may deserve to hear the words: *Come, blessed of my Father, receive the kingdom* (*Matt.* 25, 34), and, *Good and faithful servant, enter into the joy of the Lord* (*Matt.* 25, 21). May the Lord lead you under his protection to this joy, he who lives and rules for ever and ever. Amen.

BIBLIOGRAPHY

LITURGICAL AND PATRISTIC TEXTS

F. E. Brightman and C. E. Hammond, *Liturgies Eastern and Western* (Oxford 1896, vol. 1 repr. 1965).

I. Biffi, ed. *Enciclopedia eucaristica* (Milan 1964).

F. X. Funk, *Didascalia et Constitutiones apostolorum* 1 (Paderborn 1905).

J. Goar, *Euchologium seu Rituale Graecorum* (Paris 1647, repr. 1960).

A. Hamman, *Early Christian Prayers* (tr. W. Mitchell, Chicago 1961).

A. Heilmann, ed. *Texte der Kirchenväter*, vol. 4, (Munich 1964).

Hippolyte de Rome: *La tradition apostolique* (SC II, éd. B. Botte, Paris 1946).

J. Quasten, *Monumenta eucharistica et liturgica vetustissima* (Bonn 1935, 2nd ed. *Floril. patrist.*, 7).

E. Renaudot, *Liturgiarum orientalium collectio*, 2 vol. (Frankfurt, 1847).

J. Solano, *Textos eucaristicos primitivos* (Madrid 1952-1954).

B. Thompson, *Liturgies of the Western Church* (New York 1961).

PATRISTIC STUDIES

K. Adam, *Die Eucharistielehre des hl. Augustinus* (Paderborn, 1908).

————, in *Theologische Quartalschrift*, 112 (1931), 490-536.

A. d'Alès, "La doctrine eucharistique de saint Irénée," *Rech, de sc. relig.* 13 (1923) 24-46.

A. Astori, *L'eucaristia nei primi tre secoli della Chiesa* (Milan 1935).

G. Bareille, art. "Eucharistie," *Dict. de théol. cathol.* 5. 1121-1183.

P. Batiffol, *Etudes d'histoire et de théologie positive*, vol. 2: *L'Eucharistie* (Paris 1930).

E. Beck, "Die Eucharistie bei Ephräm," *Orient. christianus* 38 (1954), 41-67.

J. Beran, "De ordine missae secundum Tertulliani *Apologeticum*," *Miscellanea liturgica*, L. C. Mohlberg, vol. 2, 7-32.

J. Betz, *Die Eucharistie in der Zeit der griechischen Väter* vol. 1 (Fribourg, 1955), vol. 2, pt. 1 (Fribourg, 1961).

W. Bieder, "Das Abendmahl im christlichen Lebenszusammenhang bei Ignatius von Antiochien," *Evangelische Theologie* 16 (1956) 75-97.

R. S. Bour, "Eucharistie," *Dict. de théol. cat.* 5, 1183-1210.

E. Boularand, "L'eucharistie d'après le Ps. Denys l'Aréopagite," *Bull. de litt. eccl.* 58 (1957) 193-217.

B. Capelle, *Travaux liturgiques*: 11. *Histoire de la Messe* (Paris, 1962)

P. Th. Camelot, "Réalisme et symbolisme dans la doctrine eucharistique de saint Augustin", *Rev. des sc. phil. et théol.* 31 (1947), 294-410.

H. Chadwick, "Eucharist and Christology in the Nestorian Controversy," *Journ. of Theol. Stud.* 2 (1951) 145-164.

E. Dekkers, *Tertullian en de geschiedenes der Liturgie* (Bruges, 1947).

P. Dinesen, "Die Epiklese in Rahmen altkirchlicher Liturgien," *Studia Theologica* 16 (1962) 42-107.

L. Duchesne, *Christian Worship*. Its Origin and Evolution (London 1949).

C. Fitzgerald, *De sacrificio coelesti secundum sanctum Ambrosium* (Mundelein, 1944).

J. Gaillard, "Dimanche," *Dict. Spir.* 3. 948-982.

J. R. Geisselmann, *Die Abendmahllehre an der Wende der christlichen Spätanike zum Frühmittelalter* (Munster 1933).

A. Hamman, "Eucharistie," *Dict. Spir.* 1553-1586, 1593-1597.

R. P. Hanson, "The liberty of the bishop to improvise in the Eucharist," *Vigiliae Christianae* 15 (1961) 173-176.

M. Goguel, *L'Eucharistie des origines à Justin martyr* (Paris 1910)

T. G. Jalland, "Justin Martyr and the President of the Eucharist" *Studia Patristica*, 5. 83-85.

J. A. Jungmann, *Missarum Sollemnia* 3 vols. (Paris, 1956-1958).

———, *The Early Liturgy* (London, 1963).

A. Kavanagh, "Thoughts on the Roman Anaphora" *Worship* 40 (1966) 2-16.

A. Kavanagh, "Thoughts on the Roman Anaphora," *Worship* 40 (Mundelein, 1950).

W. Lampen, "Doctrina S. Joannis Chrysostomi de Christo se offerentes," *Antonianum* 18 (1943) 3-16.

G. Lecordier, *La doctrine de l'eucharistie chez saint Augustin* (Paris, 1930).

L. Ligier, "Autour du sacrifice eucharistique. Anaphores orientales et anamèse juive de Kippur," *Nouv. Rev. Théol.* 82 (1960) 40-55.

St. Lisiecki, *Quid sanctus Ambrosius de sanctissima eucharistia docuerit* (Breslau, 1910).

J. Maier, *Die Eucharistielehre der drei grossen Kappadozier* (Fribourg, 1915).

H. du Manoir, *Dogme et spiritualité chez saint Cyrille d'Alexandrie* (Paris, 1944).

A. Naegle, *Die Eucharistielehre des hl. Johannes Chrysostomus, des Doctor Eucharistiae* (Fribourg, 1900).

Otilio del Nigno Jesús, "Doctrina eucaristica de san Justino, filosofo y martiri," *Revista española de teologia* 4 (1944) 3-58.

O. Perler, "Logos und Eucharistie nach Justinus 1 Apol. c. 66" *Divus Thomas* 18 (1940) 296-316.

A. Piolanti, *L'Eucaristia* (Rome, 1957), esp. 115-171.

J. Quasten, "The Liturgical Mysticism of Theodore of Mopsuestia," *Theological Studies* 15 (1954) 431-439.

E. C. Ratcliff, "The Sanctus and the Pattern of the Early Anaphora," *Journ. of Eccl. Hist.* 1 (1950) 29-36, 125-134.

F. J. Reine, *The Eucharistic Doctrine and Liturgy of the Mystagogical Catecheses of Theodore of Mopsuestia* (Washington, 1942).

Ch. Ruch, art., "Messe," DTC 10. 864-964, and A. Gaudel, *ibid.* 964-993.

M. B. de Soos, "Le mystère liturgique d'après saint Léon le Grand," *Liturgiegeschichtliche Quellen und Forschungen* 34 (1958).

G. C. Smit, "Epiclèse et théologie des sacrement," *Mélanges Science Relig.* 15 (1958) 95-136.

A. Stuiber, "Eulogia," *Reallex. für Antike und Christentum* 46 (1965) 900-928.

J. M. R. Tillard, *The Eucharist, Pasch of God's People* (Alba House, N. Y., 1967).

I. Volpi, *Communione e salvezza in S. Agostino* (Rome, 1954).

G. Wainwright, "The Baptismal Eucharist before Nicaea," *Studia Liturgica* 4 (1965) 9-36.

M. S. Weglewicz, *Doctrina sancti Hieronymi de sanctissima eucharistia* (Rome 1931).

A. W. Ziegler, "Das Brot von unseren Feldern. Ein Beitrag zur Eucharistielehre des hl. Irenäus," in *Pro mundi vita. Festschrift zum Eucharistischen Kongresz* (Munich, 1960), 21-43.

COMPARATIVE TABLE

ST. PAUL	ST. JUSTIN AT ROME c. 150	ST. JOHN CHRYSOSTOM

I. Liturgy of

	Reading of Prophets and Apostles Homily Common Prayers	Bible readings Alternating Chants Homily Gospel Litany Prayer

II. Liturgy of

Breaking of Bread (Fraction)
Repast
Consecration of wine and eucharistic prayer
	Kiss of peace
	Bringing of bread & wine
	Consecration (Eucharist)
	Gloria
	Anamnesis
	Amen
	
	Distribution of Communion to faithful
		Prayer of the faithful
		Kiss of peace
		Offertory
		Anaphora:
		    Introduction
		    Gloria
		    Anamnesis
		    Epiclesis
		    Fraction
		
		Communion:
		    Ps. 34 chant
		    Distribution
		    Thanksgiving
		
		Dismissal

OF THE MASS

ST. AUGUSTINE	CHARLEMAGNE	MODERN TIMES	TODAY
		The Word (Recent introductions)	(What has disappeared in our Mass)
1st Prayer Biblical readings Homily Prayer of the Catechumens	*Introit* and *Gloria Patri* *Kyrie* *Gloria* *Prayer* Epistle Chants Gospel	Prayers at foot of altar (by Pius V 1570)	Psalm chant for 1st entry Reading from O.T.

The Eucharist

ST. AUGUSTINE	CHARLEMAGNE	MODERN TIMES	TODAY
2nd Prayer Sursum corda	Offering of faithful Prep. of wine and bread	Offertory prayers (1474)	Solemn 2nd entry of offering

Canon
 	
Pater noster
Kiss of peace
Communion
3rd Prayer
	Canon (same as
	today)
	Pater noster
	Fraction
	Mingling of
	Species
	Pax vobis:
	Kiss of peace
	Communion:
	  of clergy
	  of faithful
	Psalm chant
	Postcommunion
	Ita missa
	est
		Agnus
		Dei (7th cent.)
		
		Prayers
		before
		Communion
		(14th cent.)
		
		Placeat
		
		Last Gospel
		(15th cent.)
		
		Prayers
		at foot
		of altar
		{Leo XIII
		1884)
			Litany
			Prayer
			(Restored in
			1964)
			
			3rd Procession
			for Communion
			(psalm
			chant)

CHRONOLOGICAL TABLE

	LITURGIES		FATHERS	
			East	*West*
50	Acts and St. Paul			
150				Justin
200	*Apostolic Tradition*			Irenaeus
250				Cyprian (✝ 258)
300	*Syria*	*Egypt*		
350	*Apostol. Constit.* Lits. of Basil and J. Chrysostom	*Euchologium of Serapion*	Ephrem (✝ 373) Basil (✝ 379) Cyril of Jer. (✝ 387)	Hilary (✝ 367) Ambrose (✝ 397)
400			John Chrysostom (✝ 407) Cyril of Alexandria (✝ 444)	Augustine (✝ 430)
450				Peter Chrysologus (✝ 450)
500				Faustus of Riez (✝ c. 495) Caesarius of Arles (✝ 543)
550				

INDEX

Aaron 61, 83, 231
Abel 60, 177, 230
Abercius 183-184
Abraham 188, 211, 228
Active participation 16
Agapé 16
Almsgiving 30, 241, 243
Altar 29, 30, 114, 211
Ambrose, St. 25, 45, 202, 232, 239
Amen 17, 18, 20, 22, 203, 207, 215, 219
Anamnesis 29, 35, 36, 38, 45, 48, 63, 73, 76
Anaphora 22, 23, 27, 31, 48, 70-77
Angels 61-62
Apostolic Constitutions 20, 22, 23, 31, 40, 48-69
Apostolic Tradition 19, 23, 31, 35-37, 48
Aquarians 25, 185, 186, 194, 197
Augustine, St. 20, 21, 24, 26, 27, 29, 30, 83, 115-124, 169, 186, 202-220, 239

Baptism 21, 25, 49, 51, 52, 82, 102, 189, 190, 204, 218, 219, 239
Basil the Great, St. 20, 23, 32, 69, 70-74, 169, 201-202
Bishop 19, 27, 43, 51, 52, 53, 57, 66, 68
Blessing, final 23, 38, 47, 68-69
Blood of Christ 113, 136, 150, 153, 156-182, 187, 189, 191, 192, 193, 195, 203, 204, 219, 237
Body of Christ 27, 29, 30, 123, 135, 162, 163, 197, 203, 204, 207, 212
Bread 171, 181, 186, 202, 204, 207-208, 214, 219, 236, 238
Bread, breaking of 15, 23, 157, 182
Bread of life 82, 106-153, 216

Caesarius of Arles 32, 169, 239-243

Calvary 186, 232
Canon 23, 24
Catacombs 26
Catechumens 20, 21, 39, 48, 49, 50, 202, 214, 222
Catholic 46, 213
Celebrant 21, 22, 23, 27
Charity 219, 238, 240
Church 223-224, 242 See Body of Christ
Circumcision 85, 170
Clement of Rome 48
Communion 23, 26, 27, 48, 67, 86, 102, 103, 157, 158, 198, 201, 206, 216-218, 242
Communion, frequent 201-202
Consecration 16, 90, 91, 215, 218, 233 See Institution narrative
Corinth, Eucharist at 83, 153-166
Covenant 92, 175, 202, 211
Creation 28, 239
Creed 203, 205
Cross 202
Cyprian 24, 25, 29, 30, 169, 185-197
Cyril of Alexandria 29, 83, 125-153, 169
Cyril of Jerusalem 25, 26, 27

Deacon 17, 22, 49, 50, 53, 56, 57, 66, 67, 68, 73, 74
Devil 159
Dialog 16
Didache 16, 46
Diptychs 77
Diversification of liturgies 19, 23

Effects of Communion 212, 214
Emmaus 15
Energumens 50, 51, 65
Ephraem, St. 89-93
Epiclesis 35, 37, 46, 48, 64, 76
Eucharist 16, 18, 20, 26, 171, 212, 213
Euchologium of Serapion 20, 23,

31, 37-47
Exodus 19, 20
Exorcism 204

Faith 119, 206, 228, 237
Father 226
Faustus of Riez 25, 32, 169, 231-239
Fervent Communion 164
First-fruits 28, 29, 130, 131, 171, 175
Fish 183, 184
Flesh and blood 123, 199, 207

Gnosticism 28, 170, 181
Good Friday 22
Gregory of Nazianzus 21, 49, 69

Heretics 96, 142, 144, 170, 179, 181, 201, 231, 237
Hilary of Poitiers 29, 32, 169, 198-201, 239
Hippolytus 35   See Apostolic Tradition
Holy Thursday 15, 69
Holy Saturday 69
Holy Spirit   See Epiclesis
Homily 18, 20, 21, 37, 48, 49, 221, 248
Honey 19, 149, 152
Host 221
Humility 173

Ignatius of Antioch 16, 46
Improvisation 35
Incarnation 108, 117, 141, 151, 198, 213
Incorruptibility 182
Inscriptions 169, 183-185
Institution narrative 19, 22, 24, 35, 36, 45, 48, 72, 82, 88-106, 234
Intoxication, spiritual 124, 192
Irenaeus 24, 25, 28, 32, 169-183

Jerome 22

John Chrysostom 20, 21, 23, 24, 27, 29, 30, 50, 69, 74-77, 93-106, 107-115, 154-166, 169, 248
Judas 91, 94, 120, 122, 123, 216
Justin Martyr 16, 17-19, 22, 24, 25, 28, 248

Kiss of peace 16, 17, 18, 22, 27, 48, 56, 206, 216
Kyrie eleison 22

Laity 201
Lawrence, St. 123, 124
Leaven 87, 140, 213
Litany prayer 40, 48f., 53-56, 64-66
Liturgy of the Eucharist 18, 22, 81
Liturgy of St. James 23
Liturgy of the Word 18, 19, 20, 21, 26
Liturgy, Alexandrian 23, 45
Liturgy, Syrian 23, 69-77
Liturgy, Western 23-24
Loaves of proposition 25, 131, 132
Lord's prayer 23, 27, 206, 215
Love   See Charity

Manichaeans 108
Manna 25, 110, 125, 126, 127, 135, 149, 235
Martyr 16, 26, 30, 208-211
Mary 30   See Incarnation
Mass of faithful 26, 53, 215
Melchisedech 25, 61, 187, 188, 211, 236
Methodius of Olympus 25
Milk 19
Miracles 136
Mysteries 114, 134, 148, 170, 202, 218, 220

Natural law 62

Offertory 16, 19, 22, 30, 57
Offertory procession 22
Origen 19, 21

Paradise 20
Particles 202, 216, 236
Pasch 25, 81, 83, 94, 223
Paschal lamb 25, 84
Passion 194, 195, 209, 210
Peace 208   See Kiss of peace
Pectorius 184-185
Penitent 48, 52-53, 65
Peter, St. 98-102, 121, 152
Peter Chrysologus, St. 32, 169, 221-231
Pharisee 222
Prayer of faithful 22
Preface 18, 35, 36, 44, 48, 58-62, 70-71, 74-75, 205
President of assembly 16, 17, 19, 50
Processional entry 20
Psalms 20, 26

Reading, scriptural 17, 18, 20, 49, 205
Real presence 203, 212
Recapitulation 169
Redemption 128, 181, 223, 226, 232, 233
Reservation, eucharistic 201
Resurrection 111, 129, 130, 171, 180, 181, 182, 183, 195, 222

Sabbath 87, 88, 235
Sacrifice 170, 171-180, 185, 206, 211, 226, 227-231
Sanctus 19, 22, 27, 48, 62, 71
Saul 231
Service 230-231

Sick 41, 42, 225
Side of Christ 25, 202, 209, 211, 212
Sonship, divine 144-146
Sunday 17, 28, 38
Supper, Last 15, 89, 104, 185
Sursum corda 22, 180, 205, 215, 220
Synagogue 15

Temptation 154-155
Tertullian 19, 27
Testament 94, 95, 136   See Covenant
Thanksgiving 68   See Eucharist
Theodore of Mopsuestia 26, 27, 29
Trinity 197, 198, 200
Transubstantiation 232, 238
Typology 25, 130, 131, 185, 187, 189, 211, 212, 235-237

Unity 29, 119, 157-158, 161, 170, 186, 194, 198, 200, 203, 204, 205, 206, 207, 212, 214, 219, 238
Unleavened bread 87
Unworthy Communion 104-106, 141, 162, 206, 213, 217

Washing of hands 26, 48, 57
Water 189-191, 193   See baptism, wine and water
Wine and water 185, 186, 189, 193, 195, 237
Works, good 241

Xystus, St. 124

SCRIPTURAL INDEX

Genesis
1, 26: 59
2, 8: 60
3, 19: 138
4, 7: 177, 178
14, 18-19: 187
49, 11: 189, 237

Exodus
3, 15: 95
12, 1-12: 83-84
12, 6: 195
12, 15: 87
12, 16: 87
12, 19: 87
12, 43-44: 85
12, 46: 157
16, 5: 235
16, 18: 236
20, 10: 88

Leviticus
24, 5-7: 131

Numbers
15, 17-21: 130

Deuteronomy
16, 16: 177
18, 15: 107

1 Samuel
15, 22: 172

Job
31, 31: 112, 164
38, 8: 59

Psalms
11, 6: 243
18, 36: 218
23, 5: 192
34, 5: 212

34, 8: 26
34, 13-14: 175
36, 9: 143
40, 6: 172
50, 9-13: 172
50, 14-15: 172-173
50, 16-18: 196
51, 10: 50
51, 16-17: 172
51, 19: 229
55, 12-14: 223
64, 6: 235
78, 20: 237
78, 24, 25: 126, 217, 235
104, 2: 58
106, 2: 103
107, 34: 61
110, 3-4: 188, 236
110, 4: 211
116, 4: 210
116, 11: 217
116, 15: 208
119, 103: 149
121, 8: 50
130, 3-4: 53
141, 2: 195
141, 9: 55

Proverbs
1, 9: 142
4, 15: 146
8, 9: 133
9, 1-5: 188, 237
19, 17: 180
20, 9: 52
23, 1, 2: 209

Wisdom
9, 15: 229

Ecclesiasticus
27, 5: 219

Isaia
1, 11: 173
1, 16: 52
1, 16-18: 173
1, 21: 223
5, 4: 238
5, 20, 149
7, 9: 120, 135, 207
29, 13: 194
30, 1: 178
32, 6: 143
40, 22: 58
43, 18-21: 189-190
43, 23-24: 174
45, 19: 148
46, 2: 174
48, 21: 190
53, 5: 128
55, 8-9: 134
57, 15: 55
58, 6-9: 174-175
63, 2: 189
65, 2: 226
66, 3: 179

Jeremiah
3, 9-10: 196
5, 22: 59
6, 20: 173
7, 2-3: 173
7, 21-24: 174
9, 24: 174
9, 25: 85
11, 15: 174
22, 17: 178
23, 28: 196

Ezekiel
33, 8: 105
33, 11: 53

Hosea
6, 6: 175

Micah
6, 3: 226

Zachariah
7, 9-10: 175
8, 16-17: 175

Malachi
1, 10-11: 176

Matthew
3, 11: 131
5, 19: 194
5, 23-24: 176, 241
8, 20: 165
12, 7: 175
13, 33: 140, 213
16, 22: 99
16, 23: 120
17, 5: 194
22, 12, 13: 241
23, 12: 241
23, 26: 178
23, 27-28: 178
24, 28: 161
25, 21: 243
25, 34: 180, 243
25, 42: 224
26, 18: 104
26, 26-29: 89, 93, 96, 136, 175, 191, 212, 234
26, 30: 97
26, 31: 97
26, 32: 98
26, 33: 98, 101
26, 34, 35: 100
26, 39: 210
28, 18-20: 196

Mark
4, 28: 179
7, 13: 194
8, 38: 195
10, 18: 122
14, 22-24: 88

Luke
1, 35: 142
7, 14: 137
7, 47: 102
11, 52: 223
15, 7: 52
19, 9: 188
22, 15: 95
22, 19-20: 88, 92, 212
22, 25: 93
22, 28, 30: 222
22, 31, 32: 99
24, 39: 182

John
1, 1: 213
1, 14: 138
3, 10: 134
3, 24: 217
4, 13-14: 190
5, 35: 132
6, 41-42: 107
6, 48-50: 125
6, 51-59: 106, 136, 199, 200, 201, 212, 216, 217, 222, 237
7, 37-38: 190
7, 39: 190
8, 12: 196
8, 52: 109
12, 24-25: 209
13, 1: 81
14, 6: 153
14, 9: 146
14, 19-20: 199
15, 1: 187
15, 14-15: 194
15, 22: 128, 148
16, 33: 210
17, 4: 63
17, 11: 129
17, 19: 129
19, 11: 178
21, 22: 101

Acts
1, 7: 101
1, 15: 101
2, 42: 15
4, 32: 158, 208
10, 41: 96
11, 24: 163

Romans
5, 1: 86
6, 4: 219
6, 10: 127
6, 19: 154
8, 8-10: 119, 153
8, 13: 87
8, 35: 238
12, 1: 228
15, 3: 161

I Corinthians
2, 3: 154
2, 9: 147
2, 14: 133
3, 17: 240
4, 7: 120
5, 6: 140
5, 7-8: 81, 84, 213
6, 19: 240
8, 1: 118
8, 6: 58, 151
9, 24: 86
10, 3-4: 83, 237
10, 13-22: 153-154
10, 16: 156, 182
10, 17: 207, 213, 219
10, 18: 158
10, 19-20: 159
10, 33: 161
11, 23-25: 83, 89, 191
11, 26: 15
11, 27: 206, 213
11, 29: 114, 141, 217
12, 27: 207, 219
15, 53: 183

II Corinthians
2, 15: 132
3, 17: 152
5, 6: 87
8, 15: 236
12, 9: 183

Galatians
1, 6-9: 192
1, 10: 195
3, 6-9: 188
6, 4: 99

Ephesians
5, 30: 112, 182
5, 31-32: 213
6, 15: 86

Philippians
3, 1: 127
3, 3: 85

3, 13-14: 86
3, 19: 107

Colossians
1, 14: 182
1, 15: 58
2, 9: 152
2, 11, 12: 85
2, 14: 52
2, 15: 163

I Timothy
1, 13-16: 225
5, 15: 120

Hebrews
2, 14: 128
2, 17: 128
4, 13: 150
10, 1: 147

10, 5-7: 128, 227
10, 28-29: 115
12, 1: 86
12, 4: 155

I Peter
2, 9: 65
2, 24: 129

I John
1, 1-2: 143
3, 16: 209
5, 6: 153
5, 20: 143

Revelation
5, 8: 176
11, 19: 181
17, 15: 193, 238
21, 3: 181